ESTONIAN
VOCABULARY

ENGLISH-ESTONIAN

The most useful words
To expand your lexicon and sharpen
your language skills

9000 words

Estonian vocabulary for English speakers - 9000 words

By Andrey Taranov

T&P Books vocabularies are intended for helping you learn, memorize and review foreign words. The dictionary is divided into themes, covering all major spheres of everyday activities, business, science, culture, etc.

The process of learning words using T&P Books' theme-based dictionaries gives you the following advantages:

- Correctly grouped source information predetermines success at subsequent stages of word memorization
- Availability of words derived from the same root allowing memorization of word units (rather than separate words)
- Small units of words facilitate the process of establishing associative links needed for consolidation of vocabulary
- Level of language knowledge can be estimated by the number of learned words

T&P Books Publishing
www.tpbooks.com

ISBN: 978-1-78071-687-9

This book is also available in E-book formats.
Please visit www.tpbooks.com or the major online bookstores.

ESTONIAN VOCABULARY
for English speakers

T&P Books vocabularies are intended to help you learn, memorize, and review foreign words. The vocabulary contains over 9000 commonly used words arranged thematically.

- Vocabulary contains the most commonly used words
- Recommended as an addition to any language course
- Meets the needs of beginners and advanced learners of foreign languages
- Convenient for daily use, revision sessions, and self-testing activities
- Allows you to assess your vocabulary

Special features of the vocabulary

- Words are organized according to their meaning, not alphabetically
- Words are presented in three columns to facilitate the reviewing and self-testing processes
- Words in groups are divided into small blocks to facilitate the learning process
- The vocabulary offers a convenient and simple transcription of each foreign word

The vocabulary has 256 topics including:

Basic Concepts, Numbers, Colors, Months, Seasons, Units of Measurement, Clothing & Accessories, Food & Nutrition, Restaurant, Family Members, Relatives, Character, Feelings, Emotions, Diseases, City, Town, Sightseeing, Shopping, Money, House, Home, Office, Working in the Office, Import & Export, Marketing, Job Search, Sports, Education, Computer, Internet, Tools, Nature, Countries, Nationalities and more ...

T&P BOOKS' THEME-BASED DICTIONARIES

The Correct System for Memorizing Foreign Words

Acquiring vocabulary is one of the most important elements of learning a foreign language, because words allow us to express our thoughts, ask questions, and provide answers. An inadequate vocabulary can impede communication with a foreigner and make it difficult to understand a book or movie well.

The pace of activity in all spheres of modern life, including the learning of modern languages, has increased. Today, we need to memorize large amounts of information (grammar rules, foreign words, etc.) within a short period. However, this does not need to be difficult. All you need to do is to choose the right training materials, learn a few special techniques, and develop your individual training system.

Having a system is critical to the process of language learning. Many people fail to succeed in this regard; they cannot master a foreign language because they fail to follow a system comprised of selecting materials, organizing lessons, arranging new words to be learned, and so on. The lack of a system causes confusion and eventually, lowers self-confidence.

T&P Books' theme-based dictionaries can be included in the list of elements needed for creating an effective system for learning foreign words. These dictionaries were specially developed for learning purposes and are meant to help students effectively memorize words and expand their vocabulary.

Generally speaking, the process of learning words consists of three main elements:

- Reception (creation or acquisition) of a training material, such as a word list
- Work aimed at memorizing new words
- Work aimed at reviewing the learned words, such as self-testing

All three elements are equally important since they determine the quality of work and the final result. All three processes require certain skills and a well-thought-out approach.

New words are often encountered quite randomly when learning a foreign language and it may be difficult to include them all in a unified list. As a result, these words remain written on scraps of paper, in book margins, textbooks, and so on. In order to systematize such words, we have to create and continually update a "book of new words." A paper notebook, a netbook, or a tablet PC can be used for these purposes.

This "book of new words" will be your personal, unique list of words. However, it will only contain the words that you came across during the learning process. For example, you might have written down the words "Sunday," "Tuesday," and "Friday." However, there are additional words for days of the week, for example, "Saturday," that are missing, and your list of words would be incomplete. Using a theme dictionary, in addition to the "book of new words," is a reasonable solution to this problem.

The theme-based dictionary may serve as the basis for expanding your vocabulary.

It will be your big "book of new words" containing the most frequently used words of a foreign language already included. There are quite a few theme-based dictionaries available, and you should ensure that you make the right choice in order to get the maximum benefit from your purchase.

Therefore, we suggest using theme-based dictionaries from T&P Books Publishing as an aid to learning foreign words. Our books are specially developed for effective use in the sphere of vocabulary systematization, expansion and review.

Theme-based dictionaries are not a magical solution to learning new words. However, they can serve as your main database to aid foreign-language acquisition. Apart from theme dictionaries, you can have copybooks for writing down new words, flash cards, glossaries for various texts, as well as other resources; however, a good theme dictionary will always remain your primary collection of words.

T&P Books' theme-based dictionaries are specialty books that contain the most frequently used words in a language.

The main characteristic of such dictionaries is the division of words into themes. For example, the *City* theme contains the words "street," "crossroads," "square," "fountain," and so on. The *Talking* theme might contain words like "to talk," "to ask," "question," and "answer".

All the words in a theme are divided into smaller units, each comprising 3–5 words. Such an arrangement improves the perception of words and makes the learning process less tiresome. Each unit contains a selection of words with similar meanings or identical roots. This allows you to learn words in small groups and establish other associative links that have a positive effect on memorization.

The words on each page are placed in three columns: a word in your native language, its translation, and its transcription. Such positioning allows for the use of techniques for effective memorization. After closing the translation column, you can flip through and review foreign words, and vice versa. "This is an easy and convenient method of review – one that we recommend you do often."

Our theme-based dictionaries contain transcriptions for all the foreign words. Unfortunately, none of the existing transcriptions are able to convey the exact nuances of foreign pronunciation. That is why we recommend using the transcriptions only as a supplementary learning aid. Correct pronunciation can only be acquired with the help of sound. Therefore our collection includes audio theme-based dictionaries.

The process of learning words using T&P Books' theme-based dictionaries gives you the following advantages:

- You have correctly grouped source information, which predetermines your success at subsequent stages of word memorization
- Availability of words derived from the same root (lazy, lazily, lazybones), allowing you to memorize word units instead of separate words
- Small units of words facilitate the process of establishing associative links needed for consolidation of vocabulary
- You can estimate the number of learned words and hence your level of language knowledge
- The dictionary allows for the creation of an effective and high-quality revision process
- You can revise certain themes several times, modifying the revision methods and techniques
- Audio versions of the dictionaries help you to work out the pronunciation of words and develop your skills of auditory word perception

The T&P Books' theme-based dictionaries are offered in several variants differing in the number of words: 1.500, 3.000, 5.000, 7.000, and 9.000 words. There are also dictionaries containing 15,000 words for some language combinations. Your choice of dictionary will depend on your knowledge level and goals.

We sincerely believe that our dictionaries will become your trusty assistant in learning foreign languages and will allow you to easily acquire the necessary vocabulary.

TABLE OF CONTENTS

MISCELLANEOUS   245

MAIN 500 VERBS   252

PRONUNCIATION GUIDE

Letter	Estonian example	T&P phonetic alphabet	English example

Vowels

a	vana	[ɑ]	shorter than in park, card
aa	poutaa	[ɑ:]	father, answer
e	ema	[e]	elm, medal
ee	Ameerika	[e:]	longer than in bell
i	ilus	[i]	shorter than in feet
ii+vowel	viia	[i:]	feet, meter
o	orav	[o]	pod, John
oo	antiloop	[o:]	fall, bomb
u	surma	[u]	book
uu	arbuus	[u:]	pool, room
õ	võõras	[ɔu]	rose, window
ä	pärn	[æ]	chess, man
ö	köha	[ø]	eternal, church
ü	üks	[y]	fuel, tuna

Consonants

b	tablett	[b]	baby, book
d	delfiin	[d]	day, doctor
f	faasan	[f]	face, food
g	flamingo	[g]	game, gold
h	haamer	[h]	home, have
j	harjumus	[j]	yes, New York
k	helikopter	[k]	clock, kiss
l	ingel	[l]	lace, people
m	magnet	[m]	magic, milk
n	nöör	[n]	name, normal
p	poolsaar	[p]	pencil, private
r	ripse	[r]	rolled [r]
s	sõprus	[s]	city, boss
š	šotlane	[ʃ]	machine, shark
t	tantsima	[t]	tourist, trip
v	pilves	[ʋ]	vase, winter

Letter	Estonian example	T&P phonetic alphabet	English example
z	zookauplus	[z]	zebra, please
ž	žonglöör	[ʃ], [ʒ]	sharp, azure

ABBREVIATIONS
used in the vocabulary

ab.	-	about
adj	-	adjective
adv	-	adverb
anim.	-	animate
as adj	-	attributive noun used as adjective
e.g.	-	for example
etc.	-	et cetera
fam.	-	familiar
fem.	-	feminine
form.	-	formal
inanim.	-	inanimate
masc.	-	masculine
math	-	mathematics
mil.	-	military
n	-	noun
pl	-	plural
pron.	-	pronoun
sb	-	somebody
sing.	-	singular
sth	-	something
v aux	-	auxiliary verb
vi	-	intransitive verb
vi, vt	-	intransitive, transitive verb
vt	-	transitive verb

BASIC CONCEPTS

Basic concepts. Part 1

1. Pronouns

I, me	mina	[mina]
you	sina	[sina]
he	tema	[təma]
she	tema	[təma]
it	see	[se:]
we	meie	[meje]
you (to a group)	teie	[teje]
they	nemad	[nemad]

2. Greetings. Salutations. Farewells

Hello! (fam.)	Tere!	[tere]
Hello! (form.)	Tere!	[tere]
Good morning!	Tere hommikust!	[tere hommikust]
Good afternoon!	Tere päevast!	[tere pæ:vast]
Good evening!	Tere õhtust!	[tere ihtust]
to say hello	teretama	[teretama]
Hi! (hello)	Tervist!	[tervist]
greeting (n)	tervitus	[tervitus]
to greet (vt)	tervitama	[tervitama]
How are you?	Kuidas läheb?	[kujdas ʎæheb]
What's new?	Mis uudist?	[mis u:dist]
Bye-Bye! Goodbye!	Nägemist!	[nægemist]
See you soon!	Kohtumiseni!	[kohtumiseni]
Farewell!	Hüvasti!	[hyvasti]
to say goodbye	hüvasti jätma	[hyvasti ætma]
So long!	Hüva!	[hyva]
Thank you!	Aitäh!	[ajtəh]
Thank you very much!	Suur tänu!	[su:r tˡænu]
You're welcome	Palun.	[palun]
Don't mention it!	Pole tänu väärt.	[pole tˡænu væ:rt]
It was nothing	Pole tänu väärt.	[pole tˡænu væ:rt]

Excuse me! (fam.)	Vabanda!	[ʋabanda]
Excuse me! (form.)	Vabandage!	[ʋabandage]
to excuse (forgive)	andeks andma	[andeks andma]

to apologize (vi)	vabandama	[ʋabandama]
My apologies	Minu kaastunne	[minu ka:stuŋe]
I'm sorry!	Andke andeks!	[andke andeks]
to forgive (vt)	andeks andma	[andeks andma]
please (adv)	palun	[palun]

Don't forget!	Pidage meeles!	[pidage me:les]
Certainly!	Muidugi!	[mujdugi]
Of course not!	Muidugi mitte!	[mujdugi mitte]
Okay! (I agree)	Ma olen nõus!	[ma olen nɪus]
That's enough!	Aitab küll!	[ajtab kyʎ]

3. How to address

mister, sir	Härra	[hærra]
ma'am	Proua	[proua]
miss	Preili	[prejli]
young man	Noormees	[no:rme:s]
young man (little boy)	Poiss	[pojssʲ]
miss (little girl)	Tüdruk	[tydruk]

4. Cardinal numbers. Part 1

0 zero	null	[nuʎ]
1 one	üks	[yks]
2 two	kaks	[kaks]
3 three	kolm	[koʎm]
4 four	neli	[neli]

5 five	viis	[ʋi:s]
6 six	kuus	[ku:s]
7 seven	seitse	[sejtse]
8 eight	kaheksa	[kaheksa]
9 nine	üheksa	[yheksa]

10 ten	kümme	[kymme]
11 eleven	üksteist	[ykstejst]
12 twelve	kaksteist	[kakstejst]
13 thirteen	kolmteist	[koʎmtejst]
14 fourteen	neliteist	[nelitejst]

15 fifteen	viisteist	[ʋi:stejst]
16 sixteen	kuusteist	[ku:stejst]
17 seventeen	seitseteist	[sejtsetejst]

| 18 eighteen | kaheksateist | [kaheksatejst] |
| 19 nineteen | üheksateist | [yheksatejst] |

20 twenty	kakskümmend	[kakskymmend]
21 twenty-one	kakskümmend üks	[kakskymmend yks]
22 twenty-two	kakskümmend kaks	[kakskymmend kaks]
23 twenty-three	kakskümmend kolm	[kakskymmend koʎm]

30 thirty	kolmkümmend	[koʎmkymmend]
31 thirty-one	kolmkümmend üks	[koʎmkymmend yks]
32 thirty-two	kolmkümmend kaks	[koʎmkymmend kaks]
33 thirty-three	kolmkümmend kolm	[koʎmkymmend koʎm]

40 forty	nelikümmend	[nelikymmend]
41 forty-one	nelikümmend üks	[nelikymmend yks]
42 forty-two	nelikümmend kaks	[nelikymmend kaks]
43 forty-three	nelikümmend kolm	[nelikymmend koʎm]

50 fifty	viiskümmend	[ʋiːskymmend]
51 fifty-one	viiskümmend üks	[ʋiːskymmend yks]
52 fifty-two	viiskümmend kaks	[ʋiːskymmend kaks]
53 fifty-three	viiskümmend kolm	[ʋiːskymmend koʎm]

60 sixty	kuuskümmend	[kuːskymmend]
61 sixty-one	kuuskümmend üks	[kuːskymmend yks]
62 sixty-two	kuuskümmend kaks	[kuːskymmend kaks]
63 sixty-three	kuuskümmend kolm	[kuːskymmend koʎm]

70 seventy	seitsekümmend	[sejtsekymmend]
71 seventy-one	seitsekümmend üks	[sejtsekymmend yks]
72 seventy-two	seitsekümmend kaks	[sejtsekymmend kaks]
73 seventy-three	seitsekümmend kolm	[sejtsekymmend koʎm]

80 eighty	kaheksakümmend	[kaheksakymmend]
81 eighty-one	kaheksakümmend üks	[kaheksakymmend yks]
82 eighty-two	kaheksakümmend kaks	[kaheksakymmend kaks]
83 eighty-three	kaheksakümmend kolm	[kaheksakymmend koʎm]

90 ninety	üheksakümmend	[yheksakymmend]
91 ninety-one	üheksakümmend üks	[yheksakymmend yks]
92 ninety-two	üheksakümmend kaks	[yheksakymmend kaks]
93 ninety-three	üheksakümmend kolm	[yheksakymmend koʎm]

5. Cardinal numbers. Part 2

100 one hundred	sada	[sada]
200 two hundred	kakssada	[kakssada]
300 three hundred	kolmsada	[koʎmsada]
400 four hundred	nelisada	[nelisada]
500 five hundred	viissada	[ʋiːssada]

600 six hundred	**kuussada**	[ku:ssɑdɑ]
700 seven hundred	**seitsesada**	[sejtsesɑdɑ]
800 eight hundred	**kaheksasada**	[kɑheksɑsɑdɑ]
900 nine hundred	**üheksasada**	[yheksɑsɑdɑ]
1000 one thousand	**tuhat**	[tuhɑt]
2000 two thousand	**kaks tuhat**	[kɑks tuhɑt]
3000 three thousand	**kolm tuhat**	[koʌm tuhɑt]
10000 ten thousand	**kümme tuhat**	[kymme tuhɑt]
one hundred thousand	**sada tuhat**	[sɑdɑ tuhɑt]
million	**miljon**	[miʌøn]
billion	**miljard**	[miʌærd]

6. Ordinal numbers

first (adj)	**esimene**	[əsimene]
second (adj)	**teine**	[tejne]
third (adj)	**kolmas**	[koʌmɑs]
fourth (adj)	**neljas**	[neʌæs]
fifth (adj)	**viies**	[ʋi:es]
sixth (adj)	**kuues**	[ku:əs]
seventh (adj)	**seitsmes**	[sejtsmes]
eighth (adj)	**kaheksas**	[kɑheksɑs]
ninth (adj)	**üheksas**	[yheksɑs]
tenth (adj)	**kümnes**	[kymnes]

7. Numbers. Fractions

fraction	**murd**	[murd]
one half	**pool**	[po:ʌ]
one third	**kolmandik**	[koʌmɑndik]
one quarter	**neljandik**	[neʌændik]
one eighth	**kaheksandik**	[kɑheksɑndik]
one tenth	**kümnendik**	[kymnendik]
two thirds	**kaks kolmandikku**	[kɑks koʌmɑndikku]
three quarters	**kolm neljandikku**	[koʌm neʌændikku]

8. Numbers. Basic operations

subtraction	**lahutamine**	[lɑhutɑmine]
to subtract (vi, vt)	**lahutama**	[lɑhutɑmɑ]
division	**jagamine**	[ægɑmine]
to divide (vt)	**jagama**	[ægɑmɑ]
addition	**liitmine**	[li:tmine]

to add up (vt)	liitma	[li:tma]
to add (vi, vt)	lisama	[lisama]
multiplication	korrutamine	[korrutamine]
to multiply (vt)	korrutama	[korrutama]

9. Numbers. Miscellaneous

digit, figure	number	[number]
number	arv	[arʊ]
numeral	arvsõna	[arʊsɪna]
minus sign	miinus	[mi:nus]
plus sign	pluss	[pluss]
formula	valem	[ʊalem]

calculation	arvutamine	[arʊutamine]
to count (vt)	lugema	[lugema]
to count up	arvestama	[arʊestama]
to compare (vt)	võrdlema	[ʊɪrdlema]

How much?	Kui palju?	[kuj paʎjy]
How many?	Mitu?	[mitu]
sum, total	summa	[summa]
result	tulemus	[tulemus]
remainder	jääk	[æek]

a few ...	mõni	[mɪni]
few, little (adv)	natuke	[natuke]
the rest	ülejäänud	[yleæ:nud]
one and a half	poolteist	[po:ʎtejst]
dozen	tosin	[tosin]

in half (adv)	pooleks	[po:leks]
equally (evenly)	võrdselt	[ʊɪrdseʎt]
half	pool	[po:ʎ]
time (three ~s)	üks kord	[yks kord]

10. The most important verbs. Part 1

to advise (vt)	soovitama	[so:ʊitama]
to agree (say yes)	nõustuma	[nɪustuma]
to answer (vi, vt)	vastama	[ʊastama]
to apologize (vi)	vabandama	[ʊabandama]
to arrive (vi)	saabuma	[sa:buma]
to ask (~ oneself)	küsima	[kysima]
to ask (~ sb to do sth)	paluma	[paluma]

to be (vi)	olema	[olema]
to be afraid	kartma	[kartma]

to be hungry	süüa tahtma	[sy:a tahtma]
to be interested in ...	huvi tundma	[huʋi tundma]
to be needed	tarvis olema	[tarʋis olema]
to be surprised	imestama	[imestama]
to be thirsty	juua tahtma	[y:a tahtma]

to begin (vt)	alustama	[alustama]
to belong to ...	kuuluma	[ku:luma]
to boast (vi)	kiitlema	[ki:tlema]
to break (split intc pieces)	murdma	[murdma]

to call (for help)	kutsuma	[kutsuma]
can (v aux)	võima	[ʋɪjma]
to catch (vt)	püüdma	[py:dma]
to change (vt)	muutma	[mu:tma]
to choose (select)	valima	[ʋalima]

to come down	laskuma	[laskuma]
to come in (enter)	sisse tulema	[sisse tulema]
to compare (vt)	võrdlema	[ʋɪrdlema]
to complain (vi, vt)	kaebama	[kaebama]

to confuse (mix up)	segi ajama	[segi aæma]
to continue (vt)	jätkama	[ætkama]
to control (vt)	kontrollima	[kontrollima]
to cook (dinner)	süüa tegema	[sy:a tegema]

to cost (vt)	maksma	[maksma]
to count (add up)	lugema	[lugema]
to count on ...	arvestama	[arʋestama]
to create (vt)	looma	[lo:ma]
to cry (weep)	nutma	[nutma]

11. The most important verbs. Part 2

to deceive (vi, vt)	petma	[petma]
to decorate (tree, street)	ehtima	[əhtima]
to defend (a country, etc.)	kaitsma	[kajtsma]
to demand (request firmly)	nõudma	[nɪudma]

to dig (vt)	kaevama	[kaeʋama]
to discuss (vt)	arutama	[arutama]
to do (vt)	tegema	[tegema]
to doubt (have doubts)	kahtlema	[kahtlema]
to drop (let fall)	pillama	[pillama]

to exist (vi)	olemas olema	[olemas olema]
to expect (foresee)	ette nägema	[ette ɲægema]
to explain (vt)	seletama	[seletama]
to fall (vi)	kukkuma	[kukkuma]

to find (vt)	leidma	[lejdma]
to finish (vt)	lõpetama	[lɪpetama]
to fly (vi)	lendama	[lendama]
to follow ... (come after)	järgnema	[ærgnema]
to forget (vi, vt)	unustama	[unustama]
to forgive (vt)	andeks andma	[andeks andma]
to give (vt)	andma	[andma]
to give a hint	vihjama	[ʋihæma]
to go (on foot)	minema	[minema]
to go for a swim	suplema	[suplema]
to go out (from ...)	välja tulema	[ʋ'æʎæ tulema]
to guess right	ära arvama	[æra aruama]
to have (vt)	omama	[omama]
to have breakfast	hommikust sööma	[hommikust sø:ma]
to have dinner	õhtust sööma	[ɪhtust sø:ma]
to have lunch	lõunat sööma	[lɪunat sø:ma]
to hear (vt)	kuulma	[ku:ʎma]
to help (vt)	aitama	[ajtama]
to hide (vt)	peitma	[pejtma]
to hope (vi, vt)	lootma	[lo:tma]
to hunt (vi, vt)	jahil käima	[æhiʎ k'æjma]
to hurry (vi)	kiirustama	[ki:rustama]

12. The most important verbs. Part 3

to inform (vt)	teavitama	[teaʋitama]
to insist (vi, vt)	nõudma	[nɪudma]
to insult (vt)	solvama	[soʎuama]
to invite (vt)	kutsuma	[kutsuma]
to joke (vi)	nalja tegema	[naʎæ tegema]
to keep (vt)	säilitama	[s'æjlitama]
to keep silent	vaikima	[ʋajkima]
to kill (vt)	tapma	[tapma]
to know (sb)	tundma	[tundma]
to know (sth)	teadma	[teadma]
to laugh (vi)	naerma	[naerma]
to liberate (city, etc.)	vabastama	[ʋabastama]
to like (I like ...)	meeldima	[me:ʎdima]
to look for ... (search)	otsima	[otsima]
to love (sb)	armastama	[armastama]
to make a mistake	eksima	[əksima]
to manage, to run	juhtima	[yhtima]
to mean (signify)	tähendama	[t'æhendama]

to mention (talk about)	meelde tuletama	[meːʎde tuletama]
to miss (school, etc.)	puuduma	[puːduma]
to notice (see)	märkama	[mʲærkama]

to object (vi, vt)	vastu vaidlema	[ʋastu ʋajdlema]
to observe (see)	jälgima	[æʎgima]
to open (vt)	lahti tegema	[lahti tegema]
to order (meal, etc.)	tellima	[tellima]
to order (mil.)	käskima	[kʲæskima]
to own (possess)	valdama	[ʋaʎdama]

to participate (vi)	osa võtma	[osa ʋɨtma]
to pay (vi, vt)	maksma	[maksma]
to permit (vt)	lubama	[lubama]
to plan (vt)	planeerima	[planeːrima]
to play (children)	mängima	[mʲæŋima]

to pray (vi, vt)	palvetama	[palʋetama]
to prefer (vt)	eelistama	[eelistama]
to promise (vt)	lubama	[lubama]
to pronounce (vt)	hääldama	[hæːʎdama]
to propose (vt)	pakkuma	[pakkuma]
to punish (vt)	karistama	[karistama]

to read (vi, vt)	lugema	[lugema]
to recommend (vt)	soovitama	[soːʋitama]
to refuse (vi, vt)	keelduma	[keːʎduma]
to regret (be sorry)	kahetsema	[kahetsema]

to rent (sth from sb)	üürima	[yːrima]
to repeat (say again)	kordama	[kordama]
to reserve, to book	reserveerima	[reserʋeːrima]
to run (vi)	jooksma	[joːksma]

13. The most important verbs. Part 4

to save (rescue)	päästma	[pæːstma]
to say (~ thank you)	ütlema	[ytlema]
to scold (vt)	sõimama	[sɨjmama]
to see (vt)	nägema	[nægema]
to sell (vt)	müüma	[myːma]
to send (vt)	saatma	[saːtma]

to shoot (vi)	tulistama	[tulistama]
to shout (vi)	karjuma	[karjyma]
to show (vt)	näitama	[næjtama]
to sign (document)	allkirjastama	[aʎkirʲæstama]
to sit down (vi)	istuma	[istuma]
to smile (vi)	naeratama	[naeratama]
to speak (vi, vt)	rääkima	[ræːkima]

| to steal (money, etc.) | varastama | [ʋarastama] |
| to stop (please ~ calling me) | katkestama | [katkestama] |

to stop (for pause, etc.)	peatuma	[peatuma]
to study (vt)	uurima	[uːrima]
to swim (vi)	ujuma	[uyma]

to take (vt)	võtma	[ʋʊtma]
to think (vi, vt)	mõtlema	[mɪtlema]
to threaten (vt)	ähvardama	[əhʋardama]
to touch (with hands)	puudutama	[puːdutama]
to translate (vt)	tõlkima	[tɪʎkima]
to trust (vt)	usaldama	[usaʎdama]
to try (attempt)	proovima	[proːʋima]
to turn (~ to the left)	pöörama	[pøːrama]

to underestimate (vt)	alahindama	[alahindama]
to understand (vt)	aru saama	[aru saːma]
to unite (vt)	ühendama	[yhendama]

to wait (vt)	ootama	[oːtama]
to want (wish, desire)	tahtma	[tahtma]
to warn (vt)	hoiatama	[hojatama]
to work (vi)	töötama	[tøːtama]
to write (vt)	kirjutama	[kirjytama]
to write down	üles kirjutama	[yles kirjytama]

14. Colors

color	värv	[ʋˈæru]
shade (tint)	varjund	[ʋarjynd]
hue	toon	[toːn]
rainbow	vikerkaar	[ʋikerkaːr]

white (adj)	valge	[ʋalge]
black (adj)	must	[must]
gray (adj)	hall	[haʎ]

green (adj)	roheline	[roheline]
yellow (adj)	kollane	[kollane]
red (adj)	punane	[punane]

blue (adj)	sinine	[sinine]
light blue (adj)	helesinine	[helesinine]
pink (adj)	roosa	[roːsa]
orange (adj)	oranž	[oranʒ]
violet (adj)	violetne	[ʋioletne]
brown (adj)	pruun	[pruːn]
golden (adj)	kuldne	[kuʎdne]
silvery (adj)	hõbedane	[hɪbedane]

beige (adj)	beež	[be:ʒ]
cream (adj)	kreemjas	[kre:mʲæs]
turquoise (adj)	türkiissinine	[tyrki:ssinine]
cherry red (adj)	kirsipunane	[kirsipunɑne]
lilac (adj)	lilla	[lillɑ]
crimson (adj)	vaarikpunane	[ʋɑ:rikpunɑne]

light (adj)	hele	[hele]
dark (adj)	tume	[tume]
bright, vivid (adj)	erk	[ərk]

colored (pencils)	värvipliiats	[ʋʲærʋipli:ɑts]
color (e.g., ~ film)	värvi-	[ʋʲærʋi]
black-and-white (adj)	must-valge	[must ʋɑlge]
plain (one-colored)	ühevärviline	[yheʋʲærʋiline]
multicolored (adj)	mitmevärviline	[mitmeʋʲærʋiline]

15. Questions

Who?	Kes?	[kes]
What?	Mis?	[mis]
Where? (at, in)	Kus?	[kus]
Where (to)?	Kuhu?	[kuhu]
From where?	Kust?	[kust]
When?	Millal?	[millaʎ]
Why? (What for?)	Milleks?	[milleks]
Why? (reason)	Miks?	[miks]

What for?	Mille jaoks?	[mille æoks]
How? (in what way)	Kuidas?	[kujdɑs]
What? (What kind of ...?)	Missugune?	[missugune]
Which?	Mis?	[mis]

To whom?	Kellele?	[kellele]
About whom?	Kellest?	[kellest]
About what?	Millest?	[millest]
With whom?	Kellega?	[kellegɑ]

How many?	Mitu?	[mitu]
How much?	Kui palju?	[kuj pɑʎjy]
Whose?	Kelle?	[kelle]

16. Prepositions

with (accompanied by)	koos	[ko:s]
without	ilma	[iʎmɑ]
to (indicating direction)	sisse	[sisse]
about (talking ~ ...)	kohta	[kohtɑ]

before (in time)	enne	[əŋe]
in front of ...	ees	[əes]

under (beneath, below)	all	[ɑʎ]
above (over)	kohal	[kohɑʎ]
on (atop)	peal	[peɑʎ]
from (off, out of)	seest	[se:st]
of (made from)	millest tehtud	[millest təhtud]

in (e.g., ~ ten minutes)	pärast	[pʲærɑst]
over (across the top of)	läbi	[ʎæbi]

17. Function words. Adverbs. Part 1

Where? (at, in)	Kus?	[kus]
here (adv)	siin	[si:n]
there (adv)	seal	[seɑʎ]

somewhere (to be)	kuskil	[kuskiʎ]
nowhere (not anywhere)	mitte kuskil	[mitte kuskiʎ]

by (near, beside)	juures	[y:res]
by the window	akna juures	[ɑknɑ y:res]

Where (to)?	Kuhu?	[kuhu]
here (e.g., come ~!)	siia	[si:æ]
there (e.g., to go ~)	sinna	[siŋɑ]
from here (adv)	siit	[si:t]
from there (adv)	sealt	[seɑʎt]

close (adv)	lähedal	[ʎæhedɑʎ]
far (adv)	kaugel	[kɑugeʎ]

near (e.g., ~ Paris)	kõrval	[kɪrʋɑʎ]
nearby (adv)	lähedal	[ʎæhedɑʎ]
not far (adv)	lähedale	[ʎæhedɑle]

left (adj)	vasak	[ʋɑsɑk]
on the left	vasakul	[ʋɑsɑkuʎ]
to the left	vasakule	[ʋɑsɑkule]

right (adj)	parem	[pɑrem]
on the right	paremal	[pɑremɑʎ]
to the right	paremale	[pɑrəmɑle]

in front (adv)	eest	[əest]
front (as adj)	eesmine	[əesmine]
ahead (look ~)	edasi	[ədɑsi]
behind (adv)	taga	[tɑgɑ]
from behind	tagant	[tɑgɑnt]

back (towards the rear)	**tagasi**	[tɑgɑsi]
middle	**keskkoht**	[keskkoht]
in the middle	**keskel**	[keskeʎ]
at the side	**kõrvalt**	[kɪrʊɑʎt]
everywhere (adv)	**igal pool**	[igɑʎ po:ʎ]
around (in all directions)	**ümberringi**	[ymberriŋi]
from inside	**seest**	[se:st]
somewhere (to go)	**kuhugi**	[kuhugi]
straight (directly)	**otse**	[otse]
back (e.g., come ~)	**tagasi**	[tɑgɑsi]
from anywhere	**kuskilt**	[kuskiʎt]
from somewhere	**kuskilt**	[kuskiʎt]
firstly (adv)	**esiteks**	[əsiteks]
secondly (adv)	**teiseks**	[tejseks]
thirdly (adv)	**kolmandaks**	[koʎmɑndɑks]
suddenly (adv)	**äkki**	[əkki]
at first (adv)	**alguses**	[ɑʎguses]
for the first time	**esimest korda**	[əsimest kordɑ]
long before …	**ammu enne**	[ɑmmu əŋe]
anew (over again)	**uuesti**	[u:əsti]
for good (adv)	**päriseks**	[pʲæriseks]
never (adv)	**mitte kunagi**	[mitte kunɑgi]
again (adv)	**jälle**	[ælle]
now (adv)	**nüüd**	[ny:d]
often (adv)	**sageli**	[sɑgeli]
then (adv)	**siis**	[si:s]
urgently (quickly)	**kiiresti**	[ki:resti]
usually (adv)	**tavaliselt**	[tɑʊɑliseʎt]
by the way, …	**muide**	[mujde]
possible (that is ~)	**võimalik**	[ʊɪjmɑlik]
probably (adv)	**tõenäoliselt**	[tɪːɲæoliseʎt]
maybe (adv)	**võib olla**	[ʊɪjb ollɑ]
besides …	**peale selle …**	[peɑle selle]
that's why …	**sellepärast**	[sellepʲærɑst]
in spite of …	**… vaatamata**	[ʊɑ:tɑmɑtɑ]
thanks to …	**tänu …**	[tʲænu]
what (pron.)	**mis**	[mis]
that (conj.)	**et**	[ət]
something	**miski**	[miski]
anything (something)	**miski**	[miski]
nothing	**mitte midagi**	[mitte midɑgi]
who (pron.)	**kes**	[kes]
someone	**keegi**	[ke:gi]

somebody	keegi	[ke:gi]
nobody	mitte keegi	[mitte ke:gi]
nowhere (a voyage to ~)	mitte kuhugi	[mitte kuhugi]
nobody's	ei kellegi oma	[əj kellegi oma]
somebody's	kellegi oma	[kellegi oma]

so (I'm ~ glad)	nii	[ni:]
also (as well)	samuti	[samuti]
too (as well)	ka	[ka]

18. Function words. Adverbs. Part 2

Why?	Miks?	[miks]
for some reason	millegi pärast	[millegi pʲærast]
because ...	sest ...	[sest]
for some purpose	millekski	[millekski]

and	ja	[æ]
or	või	[uɪj]
but	kuid	[kujd]
for (e.g., ~ me)	jaoks	[æoks]

too (~ many people)	liiga	[li:ga]
only (exclusively)	ainult	[ajnuʌt]
exactly (adv)	täpselt	[tʲæpseʌt]
about (more or less)	umbes	[umbes]

approximately (adv)	ligikaudu	[ligikaudu]
approximate (adj)	ligikaudne	[ligikaudne]
almost (adv)	peaaegu	[pea:əgu]
the rest	ülejäänud	[yleæ:nud]

each (adj)	iga	[iga]
any (no matter which)	mis tahes	[mis tahes]
many, much (a lot of)	palju	[paʌjy]
many people	paljud	[paʌjyd]
all (everyone)	kõik	[kɪjk]

in return for ...	... vastu	[uastu]
in exchange (adv)	asemele	[asemele]
by hand (made)	käsitsi	[kʲæsitsi]
hardly (negative opinion)	vaevalt	[uaəuaʌt]

probably (adv)	vist	[uist]
on purpose (adv)	meelega	[me:lega]
by accident (adv)	juhuslikult	[yhuslikuʌt]

very (adv)	väga	[uʲæga]
for example (adv)	näiteks	[næjteks]
between	vahel	[uaheʌ]

among	**keskel**	[keskeʎ]
so much (such a lot)	**niipalju**	[niːpɑʎjy]
especially (adv)	**eriti**	[əriti]

Basic concepts. Part 2

19. Weekdays

Monday	esmaspäev	[əsmɑspæ:ʊ]
Tuesday	teisipäev	[tejsipæ:ʊ]
Wednesday	kolmapäev	[koʎmɑpæ:ʊ]
Thursday	neljapäev	[neʎæpæ:ʊ]
Friday	reede	[re:de]
Saturday	laupäev	[lɑupæ:ʊ]
Sunday	pühapäev	[pyhɑpæ:ʊ]
today (adv)	täna	[tⁱænɑ]
tomorrow (adv)	homme	[homme]
the day after tomorrow	ülehomme	[ylehomme]
yesterday (adv)	eile	[əjle]
the day before yesterday	üleeile	[yle:jle]
day	päev	[pæ:ʊ]
working day	tööpäev	[tø:pæ:ʊ]
public holiday	pidupäev	[pidupæ:ʊ]
day off	puhkepäev	[puhkepæ:ʊ]
weekend	nädalavahetus	[ɲædɑlɑʊɑhetus]
all day long	terve päev	[terʊe pæ:ʊ]
next day (adv)	järgmiseks päevaks	[ærgmiseks pæ:ʊɑks]
two days ago	kaks päeva tagasi	[kaks pæ:ʊɑ tɑgɑsi]
the day before	eile õhtul	[əjle ıhtuʎ]
daily (adj)	igapäevane	[igɑpæ:ʊɑne]
every day (adv)	iga päev	[igɑ pæ:ʊ]
week	nädal	[ɲædɑʎ]
last week (adv)	möödunud nädalal	[mø:dunud ɲædɑlɑʎ]
next week (adv)	järgmisel nädalal	[ærgmiseʎ ɲædɑlɑʎ]
weekly (adj)	iganädalane	[igɑɲædɑlɑne]
every week (adv)	igal nädalal	[igɑʎ ɲædɑlɑʎ]
twice a week	kaks korda nädalas	[kaks kordɑ ɲædɑlɑs]
every Tuesday	igal teisipäeval	[igɑʎ tejsipæ:ʊɑʎ]

20. Hours. Day and night

morning	hommik	[hommik]
in the morning	hommikul	[hommikuʎ]
noon, midday	keskpäev	[keskpæ:ʊ]

in the afternoon	pärast lõunat	[pʲærɑst lɪunɑt]
evening	õhtu	[ɪhtu]
in the evening	õhtul	[ɪhtuʎ]
night	öö	[ø:]
at night	öösel	[ø:seʎ]
midnight	kesköö	[keskø:]

second	sekund	[sekund]
minute	minut	[minut]
hour	tund	[tuɳd]
half an hour	pool tundi	[po:ʎ tundi]
quarter of an hour	veerand tundi	[ʋeːrɑnd tundi]
fifteen minutes	viisteist minutit	[ʋiːstəjst minutit]
24 hours	ööpäev	[ø:pæ:ʋ]

sunrise	päikesetõus	[pʲæjkesetɪus]
dawn	koit	[kojt]
early morning	varahommik	[ʋɑrɑhommik]
sunset	loojang	[lo:æŋ]

early in the morning	hommikul vara	[hommikuʎ ʋɑrɑ]
this morning	täna hommikul	[tʲænɑ hommikuʎ]
tomorrow morning	homme hommikul	[homme hommikuʎ]

this afternoon	täna päeval	[tʲænɑ pæ:ʋɑʎ]
in the afternoon	pärast lõunat	[pʲærɑst lɪunɑt]
tomorrow afternoon	homme pärast lõunat	[homme pʲærɑst lɪunɑt]

| tonight (this evening) | täna õhtul | [tʲænɑ ɪhtuʎ] |
| tomorrow night | homme õhtul | [homme ɪhtuʎ] |

at 3 o'clock sharp	täpselt kell kolm	[tʲæpseʎt keʎ koʎm]
about 4 o'clock	umbes kell neli	[umbes keʎ neli]
by 12 o'clock	kella kaheteistkümneks	[kellɑ kɑhetejstkymneks]

| in 20 minutes | kahekümne minuti pärast | [kɑhekymne minuti pʲærɑst] |

| in an hour | tunni aja pärast | [tuɳi ɑæ pʲærɑst] |
| on time (adv) | õigeks ajaks | [ɪjgeks ɑæks] |

a quarter of ...	kolmveerand	[koʎmʋe:rɑnd]
within an hour	tunni aja jooksul	[tuɳi ɑæ jo:ksul]
every 15 minutes	iga viieteist minuti tagant	[igɑ ʋiːətəjst minuti tɑgɑnt]

| round the clock | terve ööpäev | [terʋe ø:pæ:ʋ] |

21. Months. Seasons

| January | jaanuar | [æ:nuɑr] |
| February | veebruar | [ʋeːbruɑr] |

March	märts	[mˈærts]
April	aprill	[apriʎ]
May	mai	[maj]
June	juuni	[yuni]

July	juuli	[yuli]
August	august	[august]
September	september	[september]
October	oktoober	[oktoːber]
November	november	[noʋember]
December	detsember	[detsember]

spring	kevad	[keʋad]
in spring	kevadel	[keʋadeʎ]
spring (as adj)	kevadine	[keʋadine]

summer	suvi	[suʋi]
in summer	suvel	[suʋeʎ]
summer (as adj)	suvine	[suʋine]

fall	sügis	[sygis]
in fall	sügisel	[sygiseʎ]
fall (as adj)	sügisene	[sygisene]

winter	talv	[taʎʊ]
in winter	talvel	[taʎʋeʎ]
winter (as adj)	talvine	[taʎʋine]

month	kuu	[kuː]
this month	selles kuus	[selles kuːs]
next month	järgmises kuus	[ærgmises kuːs]
last month	möödunud kuus	[møːdunud kuːs]

a month ago	kuu aega tagasi	[kuː aega tagasi]
in a month	kuu aja pärast	[kuː aæ pˈærast]
in two months	kahe kuu pärast	[kahe kuː pˈærast]
the whole month	terve kuu	[terʋe kuː]
all month long	terve kuu	[terʋe kuː]

monthly (~ magazine)	igakuine	[igakujne]
monthly (adv)	igas kuus	[igas kuːs]
every month	iga kuu	[iga kuː]
twice a month	kaks korda kuus	[kaks korda kuːs]

year	aasta	[aːsta]
this year	sel aastal	[seʎ aːstaʎ]
next year	järgmisel aastal	[ærgmiseʎ aːstaʎ]
last year	möödunud aastal	[møːdunud aːstaʎ]

a year ago	aasta tagasi	[aːsta tagasi]
in a year	aasta pärast	[aːsta pˈærast]
in two years	kahe aasta pärast	[kahe aːsta pˈærast]

| the whole year | kogu aasta | [kogu ɑːstɑ] |
| all year long | terve aasta | [terʋe ɑːstɑ] |

every year	igal aastal	[igɑʎ ɑːstɑʎ]
annual (adj)	iga-aastane	[igɑ ɑːstɑne]
annually (adv)	igal aastal	[igɑʎ ɑːstɑʎ]
4 times a year	neli korda aastas	[neli kordɑ ɑːstɑs]

date (e.g., today's ~)	kuupäev	[kuːpæːʋ]
date (e.g., ~ of birth)	kuupäev	[kuːpæːʋ]
calendar	kalender	[kɑlender]

half a year	pool aastat	[poːʎ ɑːstɑt]
six months	poolaasta	[poːʎɑːstɑ]
season (summer, etc.)	hooaeg	[hoːɑeg]
century	sajand	[sɑænd]

22. Time. Miscellaneous

time	aeg	[ɑeg]
instant (n)	hetk	[hetk]
moment	silmapilk	[siʎmɑpiʎk]
instant (adj)	silmapilkselt	[siʎmɑpiʎkseʎt]
lapse (of time)	ajavahemik	[ɑæʋɑhemik]
life	elu	[əlu]
eternity	igavik	[igɑʋik]

epoch	ajastu	[ɑæstu]
era	ajajärk	[ɑæːrk]
cycle	tsükkel	[tsykkeʎ]
period	periood	[perioːd]
term (short-~)	tähtaeg	[tʲæhtɑeg]

the future	tulevik	[tuleʋik]
future (as adj)	tulevane	[tuleʋɑne]
next time	järgmine kord	[ærgmine kord]
the past	minevik	[mineʋik]
past (recent)	möödunud	[møːdunud]
last time	eelmine kord	[əeʎmine kord]

later (adv)	hiljem	[hiʎjem]
after (prep.)	pärast	[pʲærɑst]
nowadays (adv)	praegu	[prɑegu]
now (adv)	nüüd	[nyːd]
immediately (adv)	kohe	[kohe]
soon (adv)	varsti	[ʋɑrsti]
in advance (beforehand)	varakult	[ʋɑrɑkuʎt]

| a long time ago | ammu | [ɑmmu] |
| recently (adv) | hiljuti | [hiʎjyti] |

destiny	saatus	[sɑːtus]
memories (childhood ~)	mälestused	[mʲælestused]
archives	arhiiv	[ɑrhiːʊ]

during ...	... ajal	[ɑæʎ]
long, a long time (adv)	kaua	[kɑuɑ]
not long (adv)	lühikest aega	[lyhikest ɑəgɑ]
early (in the morning)	vara	[ʊɑrɑ]
late (not early)	hilja	[hiʎæ]

forever (for good)	alatiseks	[ɑlɑtiseks]
to start (begin)	alustama	[ɑlustɑmɑ]
to postpone (vt)	edasi lükkama	[ədɑsi lykkɑmɑ]

at the same time	üheaegselt	[yheɑəgseʎt]
permanently (adv)	pidevalt	[pideʊɑʎt]
constant (noise, pain)	pidev	[pideʊ]
temporary (adj)	ajutine	[ɑytine]

sometimes (adv)	mõnikord	[mɪnikord]
rarely (adv)	harva	[hɑrʊɑ]
often (adv)	sageli	[sɑgeli]

23. Opposites

| rich (adj) | rikas | [rikɑs] |
| poor (adj) | vaene | [ʊɑəne] |

| ill, sick (adj) | haige | [hɑjge] |
| healthy (adj) | terve | [terʊe] |

| big (adj) | suur | [suːr] |
| small (adj) | väike | [ʊʲæjke] |

| quickly (adv) | kiiresti | [kiːresti] |
| slowly (adv) | aeglaselt | [ɑəglɑseʎt] |

| fast (adj) | kiire | [kiːre] |
| slow (adj) | aeglane | [ɑəglɑne] |

| cheerful (adj) | lõbus | [lɪbus] |
| sad (adj) | kurb | [kurb] |

| together (adv) | koos | [koːs] |
| separately (adv) | eraldi | [ərɑʎdi] |

aloud (to read)	valjusti	[ʊɑʎjysti]
silently (to oneself)	omaette	[omɑətte]
tall (adj)	kõrge	[kɪrge]
low (adj)	madal	[mɑdɑʎ]

| deep (adj) | sügav | [sygɑʋ] |
| shallow (adj) | madal | [mɑdɑʎ] |

| yes | jaa | [æ:] |
| no | ei | [əj] |

| distant (in space) | kauge | [kɑuge] |
| nearby (adj) | lähedane | [ʎæhedɑne] |

| far (adv) | kaugel | [kɑugeʎ] |
| nearby (adv) | lähedal | [ʎæhedɑʎ] |

| long (adj) | pikk | [pikk] |
| short (adj) | lühike | [lyhike] |

| good (kindhearted) | hea | [heɑ] |
| evil (adj) | kuri | [kuri] |

| married (adj) | abielus | [ɑbiəlus] |
| single (adj) | vallaline | [ʋɑllɑline] |

| to forbid (vt) | keelama | [ke:lɑmɑ] |
| to permit (vt) | lubama | [lubɑmɑ] |

| end | lõpp | [lɪpp] |
| beginning | algus | [ɑlgus] |

| left (adj) | vasak | [ʋɑsɑk] |
| right (adj) | parem | [pɑrem] |

| first (adj) | esimene | [əsimene] |
| last (adj) | viimane | [ʋi:mɑne] |

| crime | kuritegu | [kuritəgu] |
| punishment | karistus | [kɑristus] |

| to order (vt) | käskima | [kʲæskimɑ] |
| to obey (vi, vt) | alluma | [ɑllumɑ] |

| straight (adj) | sirge | [sirge] |
| curved (adj) | kõver | [kɪʋer] |

| paradise | paradiis | [pɑrɑdi:s] |
| hell | põrgu | [pɪrgu] |

| to be born | sündima | [syndimɑ] |
| to die (vi) | surema | [suremɑ] |

strong (adj)	tugev	[tugeʋ]
weak (adj)	nõrk	[nɪrk]
old (adj)	vana	[ʋɑnɑ]
young (adj)	noor	[no:r]

| old (adj) | vana | [ʋɑnɑ] |
| new (adj) | uus | [u:s] |

| hard (adj) | kõva | [kɪʋɑ] |
| soft (adj) | pehme | [pehme] |

| warm (adj) | soe | [soə] |
| cold (adj) | külm | [kyʌm] |

| fat (adj) | paks | [pɑks] |
| thin (adj) | kõhn | [kɪhn] |

| narrow (adj) | kitsas | [kitsɑs] |
| wide (adj) | lai | [lɑj] |

| good (adj) | hea | [heɑ] |
| bad (adj) | halb | [hɑʌb] |

| brave (adj) | vapper | [ʋɑpper] |
| cowardly (adj) | arg | [ɑrg] |

24. Lines and shapes

square	ruut	[ru:t]
square (as adj)	kandiline	[kɑndiline]
circle	ring	[riŋ]
round (adj)	ümmargune	[ymmɑrgune]
triangle	kolmnurk	[koʌmnurk]
triangular (adj)	kolmnurkne	[koʌmnurkne]

oval	ovaal	[oʋɑ:ʌ]
oval (as adj)	ovaalne	[oʋɑ:ʌne]
rectangle	ristkülik	[ristkylik]
rectangular (adj)	ristkülikuline	[ristkylikuline]

pyramid	püramiid	[pyrɑmi:d]
rhombus	romb	[romb]
trapezoid	trapets	[trɑpets]
cube	kuup	[ku:p]
prism	prisma	[prismɑ]

circumference	ringjoon	[riŋjo:n]
sphere	sfäär	[sfæ:r]
ball (solid sphere)	kera	[kerɑ]
diameter	diameeter	[diɑme:ter]
radius	raadius	[rɑ:dius]
perimeter (circle's ~)	ümbermõõt	[ymbermɪ:t]
center	keskpunkt	[keskpuŋkt]
horizontal (adj)	horisontaalne	[horisontɑ:ʌne]
vertical (adj)	vertikaalne	[ʋertikɑ:ʌne]

| parallel (n) | **paralleel** | [parɑlleːʎ] |
| parallel (as adj) | **paralleelne** | [parɑlleːʎne] |

line	**joon**	[joːn]
stroke	**joon**	[joːn]
straight line	**sirgjoon**	[sirgjoːn]
curve (curved line)	**kõver**	[kɪʊer]
thin (line, etc.)	**peenike**	[peːnike]
contour (outline)	**kontuur**	[kontuːr]

intersection	**läbilõige**	[ʎæbilɪjge]
right angle	**täisnurk**	[tʲæjsnurk]
segment	**segment**	[segment]
sector	**sektor**	[sektor]
side (of triangle)	**külg**	[kyʎg]
angle	**nurk**	[nurk]

25. Units of measurement

weight	**kaal**	[kɑːl]
length	**pikkus**	[pikkus]
width	**laius**	[lɑjus]
height	**kõrgus**	[kɪrgus]
depth	**sügavus**	[sygɑʋus]
volume	**maht**	[mɑht]
area	**pindala**	[pindɑlɑ]

gram	**gramm**	[grɑmm]
milligram	**milligramm**	[milligrɑmm]
kilogram	**kilogramm**	[kilogrɑmm]
ton	**tonn**	[tonʲ]
pound	**nael**	[nɑəʎ]
ounce	**unts**	[unʦ]

meter	**meeter**	[meːter]
millimeter	**millimeeter**	[millimeːter]
centimeter	**sentimeeter**	[sentimeːter]
kilometer	**kilomeeter**	[kilomeːter]
mile	**miil**	[miːʎ]

inch	**toll**	[toʎ]
foot	**jalg**	[ælg]
yard	**jard**	[ærd]

| square meter | **ruutmeeter** | [ruːtmeːter] |
| hectare | **hektar** | [hektɑr] |

liter	**liiter**	[liːter]
degree	**kraad**	[krɑːd]
volt	**volt**	[ʋoʎt]

| ampere | amper | [amper] |
| horsepower | hobujõud | [hobujɪud] |

quantity	hulk	[huʌk]
a little bit of ...	natuke	[natuke]
half	pool	[poːʌ]
dozen	tosin	[tosin]
piece (item)	tükk	[tykk]

| size | suurus | [suːrus] |
| scale (map ~) | mastaap | [mastaːp] |

minimal (adj)	minimaalne	[minimaːʌne]
the smallest (adj)	kõige väiksem	[kɪjge ʋˈæjksem]
medium (adj)	keskmine	[keskmine]
maximal (adj)	maksimaalne	[maksimaːʌne]
the largest (adj)	kõige suurem	[kɪjge suːrem]

26. Containers

jar (glass)	purk	[purk]
can	purk	[purk]
bucket	ämber	[əmber]
barrel	tünn	[tyŋʲ]

basin (for washing)	pesukauss	[pesukaussʲ]
tank (for liquid, gas)	paak	[paːk]
hip flask	plasku	[plasku]
jerrycan	kanister	[kanister]
cistern (tank)	tsistern	[ʦistern]

mug	kruus	[kruːs]
cup (of coffee, etc.)	tass	[tassʲ]
saucer	alustass	[alustassʲ]
glass (tumbler)	klaas	[klaːs]
wineglass	veiniklaas	[ʋejniklaːs]
saucepan	pott	[pottʲ]

| bottle (~ of wine) | pudel | [pudeʌ] |
| neck (of the bottle) | pudelikael | [pudelikaeʌ] |

carafe	karahvin	[karahʋin]
pitcher (earthenware)	kann	[kaŋʲ]
vessel (container)	nõu	[nɪu]
pot (crock)	pott	[pottʲ]
vase	vaas	[ʋaːs]

bottle (~ of perfume)	pudel	[pudeʌ]
vial, small bottle	rohupudel	[rohupudeʌ]
tube (of toothpaste)	tuub	[tuːb]

sack (bag)	kott	[kottʲ]
bag (paper ~, plastic ~)	kilekott	[kilekottʲ]
pack (of cigarettes, etc.)	pakk	[pɑkk]

box (e.g., shoebox)	karp	[kɑrp]
crate	kast	[kɑstʲ]
basket	korv	[korʋ]

27. Materials

material	materjal	[materʲæl]
wood	puu	[pu:]
wooden (adj)	puust	[pu:stʲ]

| glass (n) | klaas | [klɑ:s] |
| glass (as adj) | klaas- | [klɑ:s] |

| stone (n) | kivi | [kiʋi] |
| stone (as adj) | kivist | [kiʋistʲ] |

plastic (n)	plastik	[plɑstik]
plastic (as adj)	plastik-	[plɑstik]
rubber (n)	kumm	[kumm]
rubber (as adj)	kummi-	[kummi]

| cloth, fabric (n) | kangas | [kɑŋɑs] |
| fabric (as adj) | riidest | [ri:destʲ] |

paper (n)	paber	[pɑber]
paper (as adj)	paber-	[pɑberi]
cardboard (n)	papp	[pɑpp]
cardboard (as adj)	papp-	[pɑpp]

polyethylene	polüetüleen	[polyetyle:n]
cellophane	tsellofaan	[tsellofɑ:n]
plywood	vineer	[ʋine:r]

porcelain (n)	portselan	[portselɑn]
porcelain (as adj)	portselan-	[portselɑn]
clay (n)	savi	[sɑʋi]
clay (as adj)	savi-	[sɑʋi]
ceramics (n)	keraamika	[kerɑ:mikɑ]
ceramic (as adj)	keraamiline	[kerɑ:miline]

28. Metals

| metal (n) | metall | [metɑʎ] |
| metal (as adj) | metall- | [metɑʎ] |

alloy (n)	sulam	[sulɑm]
gold (n)	kuld	[kuʎd]
gold, golden (adj)	kuldne	[kuʎdne]
silver (n)	hõbe	[hɪbe]
silver (as adj)	hõbedane	[hɪbedɑne]

iron (n)	raud	[rɑud]
iron (adj), made of iron	raudne	[rɑudne]
steel (n)	teras	[terɑs]
steel (as adj)	teras-	[terɑs]
copper (n)	vask	[ʋɑsʲk]
copper (as adj)	vaskne	[ʋɑsʲkne]

aluminum (n)	alumiinium	[ɑlumiːnium]
aluminum (as adj)	alumiinium-	[ɑlumiːnium]
bronze (n)	pronks	[proŋks]
bronze (as adj)	pronks-	[proŋks]

brass	valgevask	[ʋɑlgeʋɑsʲk]
nickel	nikkel	[nikkeʎ]
platinum	plaatina	[plɑːtinɑ]
mercury	elavhõbe	[elɑʋhɪbe]
tin	tina	[tinɑ]
lead	seatina	[seɑtinɑ]
zinc	tsink	[ʦiŋk]

HUMAN BEING

Human being. The body

29. Humans. Basic concepts

human being	**inimene**	[inimene]
man (adult male)	**mees**	[me:s]
woman	**naine**	[nɑjne]
child	**laps**	[lɑps]
girl	**tüdruk**	[tydruk]
boy	**poiss**	[pojssʲ]
teenager	**nooruk**	[no:ruk]
old man	**vanamees**	[ʋɑnɑme:s]
old woman	**vanaeit**	[ʋɑnɑejt]

30. Human anatomy

organism	**organism**	[organism]
heart	**süda**	[sydɑ]
blood	**veri**	[ʋeri]
artery	**arter**	[ɑrter]
vein	**veen**	[ʋe:n]
brain	**aju**	[ɑy]
nerve	**närv**	[ɲæruʊ]
nerves	**närvid**	[ɲæruʊid]
vertebra	**selgroolüli**	[selgro:lyli]
spine	**selgroog**	[selgro:g]
stomach (organ)	**magu**	[mɑgu]
intestines, bowel	**soolestik**	[so:lestik]
intestine (e.g., large ~)	**soolikas**	[so:likɑs]
liver	**maks**	[mɑks]
kidney	**neer**	[ne:r]
bone	**luu**	[lu:]
skeleton	**luukere**	[lu:kere]
rib	**roie**	[roje]
skull	**pealuu**	[peɑlu:]
muscle	**lihas**	[lihɑs]
biceps	**biitseps**	[bi:tseps]

tendon	kõõlus	[kɪ:lus]
joint	liiges	[li:ges]
lungs	kops	[kops]
genitals	suguelundid	[suguəlundid]
skin	nahk	[nɑhk]

31. Head

head	pea	[peɑ]
face	nägu	[ɲægu]
nose	nina	[ninɑ]
mouth	suu	[su:]

eye	silm	[siʎm]
eyes	silmad	[siʎmɑd]
pupil	silmatera	[siʎmɑterɑ]
eyebrow	kulm	[kuʎm]
eyelash	ripse	[ripse]
eyelid	silmalaug	[siʎmɑlɑug]

tongue	keel	[ke:ʎ]
tooth	hammas	[hɑmmɑs]
lips	huuled	[hu:led]
cheekbones	põsesarnad	[pɪsəsɑrnɑd]
gum	ige	[ige]
palate	suulagi	[su:lɑgi]

nostrils	sõõrmed	[sɪ:rmed]
chin	lõug	[lɪug]
jaw	lõualuu	[lɪuɑlu:]
cheek	põsk	[pɪsk]

forehead	laup	[lɑup]
temple	meelekoht	[me:lekoht]
ear	kõrv	[kɪrʊ]
back of the head	kukal	[kukɑʎ]
neck	kael	[kɑəʎ]
throat	kõri	[kɪri]

hair	juuksed	[y:ksed]
hairstyle	soeng	[soəŋ]
haircut	juukselõikus	[y:kselɪjkus]
wig	parukas	[pɑrukɑs]

mustache	vuntsid	[ʊuntsid]
beard	habe	[hɑbe]
to have (a beard, etc.)	kandma	[kɑndmɑ]
braid	pats	[pɑtsʲ]
sideburns	bakenbardid	[bɑkenbɑrdid]
red-haired (adj)	punapea	[punɑpeɑ]

gray (hair)	**hall**	[hɑʎ]
bald (adj)	**kiilas**	[ki:lɑs]
bald patch	**kiilaspea**	[ki:lɑspeɑ]
ponytail	**hobusesaba**	[hobusesɑbɑ]
bangs	**tukk**	[tukk]

32. Human body

hand	**käelaba**	[kæ:lɑbɑ]
arm	**käsi**	[kʲæsi]
finger	**sõrm**	[sɪrm]
thumb	**pöial**	[pøjæʎ]
little finger	**väike sõrm**	[ʋʲæjke sɪrm]
nail	**küüs**	[ky:s]
fist	**rusikas**	[rusikɑs]
palm	**peopesa**	[peopesɑ]
wrist	**ranne**	[rɑŋe]
forearm	**küünarvars**	[ky:nɑrʋɑrs]
elbow	**küünarnukk**	[ky:nɑrnukk]
shoulder	**õlg**	[ɪʎg]
leg	**säär**	[sæ:r]
foot	**jalalaba**	[ælɑlɑbɑ]
knee	**põlv**	[pɪʎʋ]
calf (part of leg)	**sääremari**	[sæ:remɑri]
hip	**puus**	[pu:s]
heel	**kand**	[kɑnd]
body	**keha**	[kehɑ]
stomach	**kõht**	[kɪht]
chest	**rind**	[rind]
breast	**rind**	[rind]
flank	**külg**	[kyʎg]
back	**selg**	[seʎg]
lower back	**ristluud**	[ristlu:d]
waist	**talje**	[tɑʎje]
navel	**naba**	[nɑbɑ]
buttocks	**tuharad**	[tuhɑrɑd]
bottom	**tagumik**	[tɑgumik]
beauty mark	**sünnimärk**	[syŋimʲærk]
tattoo	**tätoveering**	[tʲætoʋe:riŋ]
scar	**arm**	[ɑrm]

Clothing & Accessories

33. Outerwear. Coats

clothes	riided	[ri:ded]
outer clothes	üleriided	[yleri:ded]
winter clothes	talveriided	[talʋeri:ded]

overcoat	mantel	[manteʎ]
fur coat	kasukas	[kasukas]
fur jacket	poolkasukas	[po:ʎkasukas]
down coat	sulejope	[suleøpe]

jacket (e.g., leather ~)	jope	[øpe]
raincoat	vihmamantel	[ʋihmamanteʎ]
waterproof (adj)	veekindel	[ʋe:kindeʎ]

34. Men's & women's clothing

shirt	särk	[sʲærk]
pants	püksid	[pyksid]
jeans	teksapüksid	[teksapyksid]
jacket (of man's suit)	pintsak	[pintsak]
suit	ülikond	[ylikond]

dress (frock)	kleit	[klejt]
skirt	seelik	[se:lik]
blouse	pluus	[plu:s]
knitted jacket	jakk	[ækk]
jacket (of woman's suit)	jakk	[ækk]

T-shirt	T-särk	[te: sʲærk]
shorts (short trousers)	põlvpüksid	[pɪʎʋpyksid]
tracksuit	dress	[dress]
bathrobe	hommikumantel	[hommikumanteʎ]
pajamas	pidžaama	[pidʒa:ma]

| sweater | sviiter | [sʋi:tər] |
| pullover | pullover | [pulloʋer] |

vest	vest	[ʋest]
tailcoat	frakk	[frakk]
tuxedo	smoking	[smokiŋ]
uniform	vormiriietus	[ʋormiri:etus]

workwear	**tööriietus**	[tø:ri:etus]
overalls	**kombinesoon**	[kombineso:n]
coat (e.g., doctor's smock)	**kittel**	[kitteʎ]

35. Clothing. Underwear

underwear	**pesu**	[pesu]
undershirt (A-shirt)	**alussärk**	[alussʲærk]
socks	**sokid**	[sokid]

nightgown	**öösärk**	[ø:sʲærk]
bra	**rinnahoidja**	[riŋahojdʲæ]
knee highs	**põlvikud**	[pɪʎʋikud]
tights	**sukkpüksid**	[sukkpyksid]
stockings (thigh highs)	**sukad**	[sukɑd]
bathing suit	**trikoo**	[triko:]

36. Headwear

hat	**müts**	[myʦ]
fedora	**kaabu**	[kɑ:bu]
baseball cap	**pesapallimüts**	[pesapallimyʦ]
flatcap	**soni**	[soni]

beret	**barett**	[baret]
hood	**kapuuts**	[kapu:ʦ]
panama hat	**panama**	[panama]
knitted hat	**kootud müts**	[ko:tud myʦ]

| headscarf | **rätik** | [rʲætik] |
| women's hat | **kübar** | [kybɑr] |

hard hat	**kiiver**	[ki:ʋer]
garrison cap	**pilotka**	[pilotkɑ]
helmet	**lendurimüts**	[lendurimyʦ]

| derby | **kübar** | [kybɑr] |
| top hat | **silinder** | [silinder] |

37. Footwear

footwear	**jalatsid**	[ælɑʦid]
ankle boots	**poolsaapad**	[po:ʎsɑ:pɑd]
shoes (low-heeled ~)	**kingad**	[kiŋɑd]
boots (cowboy ~)	**saapad**	[sɑ:pɑd]
slippers	**sussid**	[sussid]

tennis shoes	**tossud**	[tossud]
sneakers	**ketsid**	[ketsid]
sandals	**sandaalid**	[sandɑ:lid]

cobbler	**kingsepp**	[kiŋsepp]
heel	**konts**	[konts]
pair (of shoes)	**paar**	[pɑ:r]

shoestring	**kingapael**	[kiŋapaeʎ]
to lace (vt)	**kingapaelu siduma**	[kiŋapaelu siduma]
shoehorn	**kingalusikas**	[kiŋalusikas]
shoe polish	**kingakreem**	[kiŋakre:m]

38. Textile. Fabrics

cotton (n)	**puuvill**	[pu:ʋiʎ]
cotton (as adj)	**puuvillane**	[pu:ʋillane]
flax (n)	**lina**	[lina]
flax (as adj)	**linane**	[linane]

silk (n)	**siid**	[si:d]
silk (as adj)	**siidi-**	[si:di]
wool (n)	**vill**	[ʋiʎ]
woolen (adj)	**villane**	[ʋillane]

velvet	**samet**	[samet]
suede	**seemisnahk**	[se:misnahk]
corduroy	**velvet**	[ʋeʎʋet]

nylon (n)	**nailon**	[najlon]
nylon (as adj)	**nailonist**	[najlonist]
polyester (n)	**polüester**	[polyester]
polyester (as adj)	**polüestrist**	[polyestrist]

leather (n)	**nahk**	[nahk]
leather (as adj)	**nahast**	[nahast]
fur (n)	**karusnahk**	[karusnahk]
fur (e.g., ~ coat)	**karusnahkne**	[karusnahkne]

39. Personal accessories

gloves	**sõrmkindad**	[sɪrmkindad]
mittens	**labakindad**	[labakindad]
scarf (muffler)	**sall**	[saʎ]

glasses	**prillid**	[prillid]
frame (eyeglass ~)	**prilliraamid**	[prillirɑ:mid]
umbrella	**vihmavari**	[ʋihmamʋari]

walking stick	jalutuskepp	[ælutuskepp]
hairbrush	juuksehari	[y:ksəhari]
fan	lehvik	[lehʋik]

necktie	lips	[lips]
bow tie	kikilips	[kikilips]
suspenders	traksid	[trɑksid]
handkerchief	taskurätik	[tɑskurˈætik]

comb	kamm	[kɑmm]
barrette	juukseklamber	[y:kseklɑmber]
hairpin	juuksenõel	[y:ksenɪːʎ]
buckle	pannal	[pɑŋɑʎ]

| belt | vöö | [ʋøː] |
| shoulder strap | rihm | [rihm] |

bag (handbag)	kott	[kottʲ]
purse	käekott	[kʲæekottʲ]
backpack	seljakott	[seʎækottʲ]

40. Clothing. Miscellaneous

fashion	mood	[moːd]
in vogue (adj)	moodne	[moːdne]
fashion designer	moekunstnik	[moəkunstnik]

collar	krae	[krɑə]
pocket	tasku	[tɑsku]
pocket (as adj)	tasku-	[tɑsku]
sleeve	varrukas	[ʋɑrrukɑs]
hanging loop	tripp	[tripp]
fly (on trousers)	püksiauk	[pyksiɑuk]

zipper (fastener)	tõmblukk	[tɪmblukk]
fastener	kinnis	[kiŋis]
button	nööp	[nøːp]
buttonhole	nööpauk	[nøːpɑuk]
to come off (ab. button)	eest ära tulema	[əest æra tulemɑ]

to sew (vi, vt)	õmblema	[ɪmblemɑ]
to embroider (vi, vt)	tikkima	[tikkimɑ]
embroidery	tikkimine	[tikkimine]
sewing needle	nõel	[nɪːʎ]
thread	niit	[niːt]
seam	õmblus	[ɪmblus]

to get dirty (vi)	ära määrima	[əra mæːrimɑ]
stain (mark, spot)	plekk	[plekk]
to crease, crumple (vi)	kortsu minema	[kortsu minemɑ]

| to tear (vt) | katki minema | [kat'ki minema] |
| clothes moth | koi | [koj] |

41. Personal care. Cosmetics

toothpaste	hambapasta	[hɑmbɑpɑstɑ]
toothbrush	hambahari	[hɑmbɑhɑri]
to brush one's teeth	hambaid pesema	[hɑmbɑjd pesəmɑ]

razor	pardel	[pɑrdəʎ]
shaving cream	habemeajamiskreem	[hɑbemeɑæmiskre:m]
to shave (vi)	habet ajama	[hɑbet ɑæmɑ]

| soap | seep | [se:p] |
| shampoo | šampoon | [ʃɑmpo:n] |

scissors	käärid	[kæ:rid]
nail file	küüneviil	[ky:neʋi:ʎ]
nail clippers	küünekäärid	[ky:nekæ:rid]
tweezers	pintsett	[pintsett]

cosmetics	kosmeetika	[kosme:tikɑ]
face mask	mask	[mɑs'k]
manicure	maniküür	[mɑniky:r]
to have a manicure	maniküüri tegema	[mɑniky:ri tegemɑ]
pedicure	pediküür	[pediky:r]

make-up bag	kosmeetikakott	[kosme:tikɑkott']
face powder	puuder	[pu:der]
powder compact	puudritoos	[pu:drito:s]
blusher	põsepuna	[pɪsəpunɑ]

perfume (bottled)	lõhnaõli	[lɪhnɑɪli]
toilet water (perfume)	tualettvesi	[tuɑlettʋesi]
lotion	näovesi	[næoʋesi]
cologne	odekolonn	[odekoloŋ']

eyeshadow	lauvärv	[lɑuʋ'ærʋ]
eyeliner	silmapliiats	[siʎmɑpli:ɑts]
mascara	ripsmetušš	[ripsmetuʃ]

lipstick	huulepulk	[hu:lepuʎk]
nail polish, enamel	küünelakk	[ky:nelɑkk]
hair spray	juukselakk	[y:kselɑkk]
deodorant	desodorant	[desodorɑnt]

cream	kreem	[kre:m]
face cream	näokreem	[næokre:m]
hand cream	kätekreem	[k'ætəkre:m]
anti-wrinkle cream	kortsudevastane kreem	[kortsudeʋɑstɑne kre:m]

| day (as adj) | päevane | [pæːʋɑne] |
| night (as adj) | öökreem | [øːkreːm] |

tampon	tampoon	[tɑmpoːn]
toilet paper	tualettpaber	[tuɑlettpɑber]
hair dryer	föön	[føːn]

42. Jewelry

jewelry	väärtesemed	[ʋæːrtəsemed]
precious (e.g., ~ stone)	väärtuslik	[ʋʲæertuslik]
hallmark	proov	[proːʋ]
ring	sõrmus	[sɪrmus]
wedding ring	laulatussõrmus	[lɑulɑtussɪrmus]
bracelet	käevõru	[kæːʋɪru]

earrings	kõrvarõngad	[kɪrʋɑrɪŋɑd]
necklace (~ of pearls)	kaelakee	[kɑəlɑkeː]
crown	kroon	[kroːn]
bead necklace	helmed	[heʎmed]

diamond	briljant	[briʎænt]
emerald	smaragd	[smɑrɑgd]
ruby	rubiin	[rubiːn]
sapphire	safiir	[sɑfiːr]
pearl	pärlid	[pʲærlid]
amber	merevaik	[mereʋɑjk]

43. Watches. Clocks

watch (wristwatch)	käekell	[kæːkeʎ]
dial	sihverplaat	[sihʋerplɑːt]
hand (of clock, watch)	osuti	[osuti]
metal watch band	kellarihm	[kellɑrihm]
watch strap	kellarihm	[kellɑrihm]

battery	patarei	[pɑtɑrej]
to be dead (battery)	tühjaks saama	[tyɦæks sɑːmɑ]
to change a battery	patareid vahetama	[pɑtɑrejd ʋɑhetɑmɑ]
to run fast	ette käima	[ətte kʲæjmɑ]
to run slow	taha jääma	[tɑhɑ æːmɑ]

wall clock	seinakell	[sejnɑkeʎ]
hourglass	liivakell	[liːʋɑkeʎ]
sundial	päiksekell	[pʲæjksekeʎ]
alarm clock	äratuskell	[ərɑtuskeʎ]
watchmaker	kellassepp	[kellɑssepp]
to repair (vt)	parandama	[pɑrɑndɑmɑ]

Food. Nutricion

44. Food

meat	liha	[liha]
chicken	kana	[kana]
young chicken	kanapoeg	[kanapoeg]
duck	part	[part]
goose	hani	[hani]
game	metslinnud	[metsliŋud]
turkey	kalkun	[kalkun]

pork	sealiha	[sealiha]
veal	vasikaliha	[ʋasikaliha]
lamb	lambaliha	[lambaliha]
beef	loomaliha	[loːmaliha]
rabbit	küülik	[kyːlik]

sausage (salami, etc.)	vorst	[ʋorst]
vienna sausage	viiner	[ʋiːner]
bacon	peekon	[peːkon]
ham	sink	[siŋk]
gammon (ham)	sink	[siŋk]

pâté	pasteet	[pasteːt]
liver	maks	[maks]
lard	pekk	[pekk]
ground beef	hakkliha	[hakkliha]
tongue	keel	[keːʎ]

egg	muna	[muna]
eggs	munad	[munad]
egg white	munavalge	[munaʋalge]
egg yolk	munakollane	[munakollane]

fish	kala	[kala]
seafood	mereannid	[mereaŋid]
caviar	kalamari	[kalamari]

crab	krabi	[krabi]
shrimp	krevett	[kreʋett]
oyster	auster	[auster]
spiny lobster	langust	[laŋust]
octopus	kaheksajalg	[kaheksaæ|g]
squid	kalmaar	[kalmaːr]
sturgeon	tuurakala	[tuːrakala]

salmon	lõhe	[lıhe]
halibut	paltus	[paltus]
cod	tursk	[tursk]
mackerel	skumbria	[skumbriæ]
tuna	tuunikala	[tu:nikala]
eel	angerjas	[aɲerˈæs]

trout	forell	[foreʎ]
sardine	sardiin	[sardi:n]
pike	haug	[haug]
herring	heeringas	[he:riŋas]

bread	leib	[lejb]
cheese	juust	[y:st]
sugar	suhkur	[suhkur]
salt	sool	[so:ʎ]

rice	riis	[ri:s]
pasta	makaronid	[makaronid]
noodles	lintnuudlid	[lintnu:dlid]

butter	või	[ʊıj]
vegetable oil	taimeõli	[tajmeıli]
sunflower oil	päevalilleõli	[pæ:ʊalilleıli]
margarine	margariin	[margari:n]
olives	oliivid	[oli:ʊid]
olive oil	oliivõli	[oli:ʊıli]

milk	piim	[pi:m]
condensed milk	kondenspiim	[kondenspi:m]
yogurt	jogurt	[øgurt]
sour cream	hapukoor	[hapuko:r]
cream (of milk)	koor	[ko:r]

| mayonnaise | majonees | [maøne:s] |
| buttercream | kreem | [kre:m] |

cereal grain (wheat, ǝtc.)	tangud	[taŋud]
flour	jahu	[æhu]
canned food	konservid	[konserʊid]
cornflakes	maisihelbed	[majsiheʎbed]
honey	mesi	[mesi]
jam	džemm	[dʒemm]
chewing gum	närimiskumm	[ɲærimiskumm]

45. Drinks

water	vesi	[ʊesi]
drinking water	joogivesi	[jo:giʊesi]
mineral water	mineraalvesi	[minera:ʎʊesi]

still (adj)	gaasita	[gɑ:sitɑ]
carbonated (adj)	gaseeritud	[gɑse:ritud]
sparkling (adj)	gaasiga	[gɑ:sigɑ]

| ice | jää | [æ:] |
| with ice | jääga | [æ:gɑ] |

non-alcoholic (adj)	alkoholivaba	[ɑlkoholiʋɑbɑ]
soft drink	alkoholivaba jook	[ɑlkoholiʋɑbɑ jo:k]
cool soft drink	karastusjook	[kɑrɑstusjo:k]
lemonade	limonaad	[limonɑ:d]

| liquor | alkoholsed joogid | [ɑlkoho:ʎsed jo:gid] |
| wine | vein | [ʋejn] |

| white wine | valge vein | [ʋɑlge ʋejn] |
| red wine | punane vein | [punɑne ʋejn] |

liqueur	liköör	[likø:r]
champagne	šampus	[ʃɑmpus]
vermouth	vermut	[ʋermut]

whisky	viski	[ʋiski]
vodka	viin	[ʋi:n]
gin	džinn	[dʒiŋ]

| cognac | konjak | [koɲæk] |
| rum | rumm | [rumm] |

coffee	kohv	[kohʋ]
black coffee	must kohv	[must kohʋ]
coffee with milk	piimaga kohv	[pi:mɑgɑ kohʋ]

| cappuccino | koorega kohv | [ko:regɑ kohʋ] |
| instant coffee | lahustuv kohv | [lɑhustuʋ kohʋ] |

milk	piim	[pi:m]
cocktail	kokteil	[koktejʎ]
milk shake	piimakokteil	[pi:mɑkoktejʎ]

juice	mahl	[mɑhl]
tomato juice	tomatimahl	[tomɑtimɑhl]
orange juice	apelsinimahl	[apeʎsinimɑhl]
freshly squeezed juice	värskelt pressitud mahl	[ʋ'ærskeʎt pressitud mɑhl]

beer	õlu	[ɪlu]
light beer	hele õlu	[hele ɪlu]
dark beer	tume õlu	[tume ɪlu]

tea	tee	[te:]
black tea	must tee	[must te:]
green tea	roheline tee	[roheline te:]

46. Vegetables

vegetables	**juurviljad**	[yːrʋiʎæd]
greens	**maitseroheline**	[mɑjtseroheline]
tomato	**tomat**	[tomɑt]
cucumber	**kurk**	[kurk]
carrot	**porgand**	[porgɑnd]
potato	**kartul**	[kɑrtuʎ]
onion	**sibul**	[sibuʎ]
garlic	**küüslauk**	[kyːslɑuk]
cabbage	**kapsas**	[kɑpsɑs]
cauliflower	**lillkapsas**	[liʎkɑpsɑs]
Brussels sprouts	**brüsseli kapsas**	[brysseli kɑpsɑs]
broccoli	**brokkoli**	[brokkoli]
beetroot	**peet**	[peːt]
eggplant	**baklažaan**	[bɑklɑʒɑːn]
zucchini	**kabatšokk**	[kɑbɑtʃokk]
pumpkin	**kõrvits**	[kɪrʋits]
turnip	**naeris**	[nɑəris]
parsley	**petersell**	[peterseʎ]
dill	**till**	[tiʎ]
lettuce	**salat**	[sɑlɑt]
celery	**seller**	[seller]
asparagus	**aspar**	[ɑspɑr]
spinach	**spinat**	[spinɑt]
pea	**hernes**	[hernes]
beans	**oad**	[oɑd]
corn (maize)	**mais**	[mɑjs]
kidney bean	**aedoad**	[ɑedoɑd]
pepper	**pipar**	[pipɑr]
radish	**redis**	[redis]
artichoke	**artišokk**	[ɑrtiʃok]

47. Fruits. Nuts

fruit	**puuvili**	[puːʋili]
apple	**õun**	[ɪun]
pear	**pirn**	[pirn]
lemon	**sidrun**	[sidrun]
orange	**apelsin**	[ɑpeʎsin]
strawberry	**aedmaasikas**	[ɑədmɑːsikɑs]
mandarin	**mandariin**	[mɑndɑriːn]
plum	**ploom**	[ploːm]

peach	virsik	[ʋirsik]
apricot	aprikoos	[apriko:s]
raspberry	vaarikas	[ʋa:rikas]
pineapple	ananass	[ananas]

banana	banaan	[bana:n]
watermelon	arbuus	[arbu:s]
grape	viinamarjad	[ʋi:namarʲæd]
sour cherry	kirss	[kirss]
sweet cherry	murel	[mureʎ]
melon	melon	[melon]

grapefruit	greip	[grejp]
avocado	avokaado	[aʋoka:do]
papaya	papaia	[papaja]
mango	mango	[maŋo]
pomegranate	granaatõun	[grana:tɪun]

redcurrant	punane sõstar	[punane sɪstar]
blackcurrant	must sõstar	[must sɪstar]
gooseberry	karusmari	[karusmari]
bilberry	mustikas	[mustikas]
blackberry	põldmari	[pɪʎdmari]

raisin	rosinad	[rosinad]
fig	ingver	[iŋʋer]
date	dattel	[datteʎ]

peanut	maapähkel	[ma:pʲæhkeʎ]
almond	mandlipähkel	[mandlipʲæhkeʎ]
walnut	kreeka pähkel	[kre:ka pʲæhkeʎ]
hazelnut	sarapuupähkel	[sarapu:pʲæhkeʎ]
coconut	kookospähkel	[ko:kospʲæhkeʎ]
pistachios	pistaatsiapähkel	[pista:tsiapʲæhkeʎ]

48. Bread. Candy

confectionery (pastry)	kondiitritooted	[kondi:trito:ted]
bread	leib	[lejb]
cookies	küpsis	[kypsis]

chocolate (n)	šokolaad	[ʃokola:d]
chocolate (as adj)	šokolaadi-	[ʃokola:di]
candy	komm	[komm]
cake (e.g., cupcake)	kook	[ko:k]
cake (e.g., birthday ~)	tort	[tort]

pie (e.g., apple ~)	pirukas	[pirukas]
filling (for cake, pie)	täidis	[tʲæjdis]
whole fruit jam	moos	[mo:s]

marmalade	**marmelaad**	[marmela:d]
waffle	**vahvlid**	[ʋahʋlid]
ice-cream	**jäätis**	[æ:tis]

49. Cooked dishes

course, dish	**roog**	[ro:g]
cuisine	**köök**	[kø:k]
recipe	**retsept**	[retsept]
portion	**portsjon**	[portsøn]

| salad | **salat** | [salat] |
| soup | **supp** | [supp] |

clear soup (broth)	**puljong**	[puʎoŋ]
sandwich (bread)	**võileib**	[ʋɨjlejb]
fried eggs	**munaroog**	[munaro:g]

cutlet (croquette)	**kotlett**	[kotlett]
hamburger (beefburger)	**hamburger**	[hamburger]
beefsteak	**biifsteek**	[bi:fste:k]
stew	**praad**	[pra:d]

side dish	**lisand**	[lisand]
spaghetti	**spagetid**	[spagetid]
mashed potatoes	**kartulipüree**	[kartulipyre:]
pizza	**pitsa**	[pitsa]
porridge (oatmeal, etc.)	**puder**	[puder]
omelet	**omlett**	[omlet]

boiled (e.g., ~ beef)	**keedetud**	[ke:detud]
smoked (adj)	**suitsutatud**	[sujtsutatud]
fried (adj)	**praetud**	[praetud]
dried (adj)	**kuivatatud**	[kujʋatatud]
frozen (adj)	**külmutatud**	[kyʎmutatud]
pickled (adj)	**marineeritud**	[marine:ritud]

sweet (sugary)	**magus**	[magus]
salty (adj)	**soolane**	[so:lane]
cold (adj)	**külm**	[kyʎm]
hot (adj)	**kuum**	[ku:m]
bitter (adj)	**mõru**	[mɪru]
tasty (adj)	**maitsev**	[majtseʋ]

to cook in boiling water	**keetma**	[ke:tma]
to cook (dinner)	**süüa tegema**	[sy:a tegema]
to fry (vt)	**praadima**	[pra:dima]
to heat up (food)	**soojendama**	[so:endama]
to salt (vt)	**soolama**	[so:lama]
to pepper (vt)	**pipardama**	[pipardama]

to grate (vt)	riivima	[riːʋima]
peel (n)	koor	[koːr]
to peel (vt)	koorima	[koːrima]

50. Spices

salt	sool	[soːʎ]
salty (adj)	soolane	[soːlane]
to salt (vt)	soolama	[soːlama]

black pepper	must pipar	[must pipar]
red pepper	punane pipar	[punane pipar]
mustard	sinep	[sinep]
horseradish	mädaroigas	[mˈædarɪjgas]

condiment	maitseaine	[majʦeajne]
spice	vürts	[ʋyrʦ]
sauce	kaste	[kaste]
vinegar	äädikas	[æːdikas]

anise	aniis	[aniːs]
basil	basiilik	[basiːlik]
cloves	nelk	[neʎk]
ginger	ingver	[iŋʋer]
coriander	koriander	[koriander]
cinnamon	kaneel	[kaneːʎ]

sesame	seesamiseemned	[seːsamiseːmned]
bay leaf	loorber	[loːrber]
paprika	paprika	[paprika]
caraway	köömned	[køːmned]
saffron	safran	[safran]

51. Meals

food	söök	[søːmine]
to eat (vi, vt)	sööma	[søːma]

breakfast	hommikusöök	[hommikusøːk]
to have breakfast	hommikust sööma	[hommikust søːma]
lunch	lõuna	[lɪuna]
to have lunch	lõunat sööma	[lɪunat søːma]
dinner	õhtusöök	[ɪhtusøːk]
to have dinner	õhtust sööma	[ɪhtust søːma]

appetite	söögiisu	[søːgiːsu]
Enjoy your meal!	Head isu!	[head isu]
to open (~ a bottle)	avama	[aʋama]

| to spill (liquid) | maha valama | [mɑhɑ ʋɑlɑmɑ] |
| to spill out (vi) | maha voolama | [mɑhɑ ʋo:lɑmɑ] |

to boil (vi)	keema	[ke:mɑ]
to boil (vt)	keetma	[ke:tmɑ]
boiled (~ water)	keedetud	[ke:detud]
to chill, cool down (vt)	jahutama	[æhutɑmɑ]
to chill (vi)	jahtuma	[æhtumɑ]

| taste, flavor | maitse | [mɑjtse] |
| aftertaste | kõrvalmaitse | [kɪrʋɑlmɑjtse] |

to be on a diet	kaalus alla võtma	[kɑ:lus ɑllɑ ʋɪtmɑ]
diet	dieet	[die:t]
vitamin	vitamiin	[ʋitɑmi:n]
calorie	kalor	[kɑlor]
vegetarian (n)	taimetoitlane	[tɑjmetojtlɑne]
vegetarian (adj)	taimetoitluslik	[tɑjmetojtluslik]

fats (nutrient)	rasvad	[rɑsʋɑd]
proteins	valgud	[ʋɑlgud]
carbohydrates	süsivesikud	[sysiʋesikud]
slice (of lemon, ham)	viil	[ʋi:ʎ]
piece (of cake, pie)	tükk	[tykk]
crumb (of bread)	puru	[puru]

52. Table setting

spoon	lusikas	[lusikɑs]
knife	nuga	[nugɑ]
fork	kahvel	[kɑhʋeʎ]

cup (of coffee)	tass	[tɑssʲ]
plate (dinner ~)	taldrik	[tɑldrik]
saucer	alustass	[ɑlustɑssʲ]
napkin (on table)	salvrätik	[sɑlʋrʲætik]
toothpick	hambaork	[hɑmbɑork]

53. Restaurant

restaurant	restoran	[restorɑn]
coffee house	kohvituba	[kohʋitubɑ]
pub, bar	baar	[bɑ:r]
tearoom	teesalong	[te:sɑloŋ]

waiter	kelner	[keʎner]
waitress	ettekandja	[ettekɑndʲæ]
bartender	baarimees	[bɑ:rime:s]

menu	menüü	[menyu]
wine list	veinikaart	[ʋejnikaːrt]
to book a table	lauda kinni panema	[lauda kiŋi panema]

course, dish	roog	[roːg]
to order (meal)	tellima	[tellima]
to make an order	tellimust andma	[tellimust andma]

aperitif	aperitiiv	[aperitiːʋ]
appetizer	suupiste	[suːpiste]
dessert	magustoit	[magustojt]

check	arve	[arʋe]
to pay the check	arvet maksma	[arʋet maksma]
to give change	raha tagasi andma	[raha tagasi andma]
tip	jootraha	[joːtraha]

Family, relatives and friends

54. Personal information. Forms

name, first name	**eesnimi**	[əesnimi]
family name	**perekonnnimi**	[perekoŋanimi]
date of birth	**sünniaeg**	[syŋiaəg]
place of birth	**sünnikoht**	[syŋikoht]
nationality	**rahvus**	[rahʋus]
place of residence	**elukoht**	[əlukoht]
country	**riik**	[riːk]
profession (occupation)	**elukutse**	[əlukutse]
gender, sex	**sugu**	[sugu]
height	**kasv**	[kasʋ]
weight	**kaal**	[kɑːl]

55. Family members. Relatives

mother	**ema**	[əma]
father	**isa**	[isa]
son	**poeg**	[poəg]
daughter	**tütar**	[tytar]
younger daughter	**noorem tütar**	[noːrem tytar]
younger son	**noorem poeg**	[noːrem poəg]
eldest daughter	**vanem tütar**	[ʋanem tytar]
eldest son	**vanem poeg**	[ʋanem poəg]
brother	**vend**	[ʋend]
sister	**õde**	[ɪde]
cousin (masc.)	**onupoeg**	[onupoəg]
cousin (fem.)	**onutütar**	[onutytar]
mom	**mamma**	[mamma]
dad, daddy	**papa**	[papa]
parents	**vanemad**	[ʋanemad]
child	**laps**	[laps]
children	**lapsed**	[lapsed]
grandmother	**vanaema**	[ʋanaəma]
grandfather	**vanaisa**	[ʋanaisa]
grandson	**lapselaps**	[lapselaps]

| granddaughter | lapselaps | [lɑpselɑps] |
| grandchildren | lapselapsed | [lɑpselɑpsed] |

uncle	onu	[onu]
aunt	tädi	[tʲædi]
nephew	vennapoeg	[ʋeŋɑpoeg]
niece	vennatütar	[ʋeŋɑtytɑr]

mother-in-law (wife's mother)	ämm	[əmm]
father-in-law (husband's father)	äi	[æj]
son-in-law (daughter's husband)	väimees	[ʋʲæjmeːs]
stepmother	võõrasema	[ʋɪːrɑsemɑ]
stepfather	võõrasisa	[ʋɪːrɑsisɑ]

infant	rinnalaps	[riŋɑlɑps]
baby (infant)	imik	[imik]
little boy, kid	väikelaps	[ʋʲæjkelɑps]

wife	naine	[nɑjne]
husband	mees	[meːs]
spouse (husband)	abikaasa	[ɑbikɑːsɑ]
spouse (wife)	abikaasa	[ɑbikɑːsɑ]

married (masc.)	abielus	[ɑbielus]
married (fem.)	abielus	[ɑbielus]
single (unmarried)	vallaline	[ʋɑllɑline]
bachelor	vanapoiss	[ʋɑnɑpojssʲ]
divorced (masc.)	lahutatud	[lɑhutɑtud]
widow	lesk	[lesk]
widower	lesk	[lesk]

relative	sugulane	[sugulɑne]
close relative	lähedane sugulane	[ʎæhedɑne sugulɑne]
distant relative	kaugelt sugulane	[kɑugeʎt sugulɑne]
relatives	sugulased	[sugulɑsed]

orphan (boy or girl)	orb	[orb]
guardian (of minor)	eestkostja	[eestkostʲæ]
to adopt (a boy)	lapsendama	[lɑpsendɑmɑ]
to adopt (a girl)	lapsendama	[lɑpsendɑmɑ]

56. Friends. Coworkers

friend (masc.)	sõber	[sɪber]
friend (fem.)	sõbranna	[sɪbrɑŋɑ]
friendship	sõprus	[sɪprus]
to be friends	sõber olla	[sɪber ollɑ]

buddy (masc.)	sõber	[sɪber]
buddy (fem.)	sõbranna	[sɪbraŋa]
partner	partner	[partner]

chief (boss)	šeff	[ʃəf]
superior	ülemus	[ylemus]
subordinate	alluv	[alluʋ]
colleague	kolleeg	[kolle:g]

acquaintance (person)	tuttav	[tuttaʋ]
fellow traveler	teekaaslane	[te:ka:slane]
classmate	klassikaaslane	[klassika:slane]

neighbor (masc.)	naaber	[na:ber]
neighbor (fem.)	naabrinaine	[na:brinajne]
neighbors	naabrid	[na:brid]

57. Man. Woman

woman	naine	[najne]
girl (young woman)	tütarlaps	[tytarlaps]
bride	pruut	[pru:t]

beautiful (adj)	ilus	[ilus]
tall (adj)	pikka kasvu	[pikka kasuu]
slender (adj)	sale	[sale]
short (adj)	lühikest kasvu	[lyhikest kasuu]

blonde (n)	blondiin	[blondi:n]
brunette (n)	brünett	[brynett]
ladies' (adj)	daamide	[da:mide]
virgin (girl)	neitsi	[nejtsi]
pregnant (adj)	rase	[rase]

man (adult male)	mees	[me:s]
blond (n)	blondiin	[blondi:n]
brunet (n)	brünett	[brynett]
tall (adj)	pikka kasvu	[pikka kasuu]
short (adj)	lühikest kasvu	[lyhikest kasuu]

rude (rough)	jõhker	[jɪhker]
stocky (adj)	jässakas	[æssakas]
robust (adj)	vastupidav	[ʋastupidaʋ]
strong (adj)	tugev	[tugeʋ]
strength	jõud	[jiud]

stout, fat (adj)	täidlane	[tʲæjdlane]
swarthy (adj)	tõmmu	[tɪmmu]
well-built (adj)	sihvakas	[sihʋakas]
elegant (adj)	elegantne	[əlegantne]

58. Age

age	vanus	[ʋɑnus]
youth (young age)	noorus	[noːrus]
young (adj)	noor	[noːr]
younger (adj)	noorem	[noːrem]
older (adj)	vanem	[ʋɑnem]
young man	noormees	[noːrmeːs]
teenager	nooruk	[noːruk]
guy, fellow	poiss	[pojssʲ]
old man	vanamees	[ʋɑnɑmeːs]
old woman	vanaeit	[ʋɑnɑejt]
adult	täiskasvanud	[tʲæjskɑsʋɑnud]
middle-aged (adj)	keskealine	[keskəɑline]
elderly (adj)	eakas	[əɑkɑs]
old (adj)	vana	[ʋɑnɑ]
retirement	pension	[pensʲon]
to retire (from job)	pensionile minema	[pensʲonile minemɑ]
retiree	pensionär	[pensʲoɲær]

59. Children

child	laps	[lɑps]
children	lapsed	[lɑpsed]
twins	kaksikud	[kɑksikud]
cradle	häll	[hæʎ]
rattle	kõristi	[kıristi]
diaper	mähe	[mʲæhe]
pacifier	lutt	[luttʲ]
baby carriage	lapsevanker	[lɑpseʋɑŋker]
kindergarten	lasteaed	[lɑsteɑed]
babysitter	lapsehoidja	[lɑpsehojdʲæ]
childhood	lapsepõlv	[lɑpsepıʎʋ]
doll	nukk	[nukk]
toy	mänguasi	[mʲæŋuɑsi]
construction set	konstruktor	[konstruktor]
well-bred (adj)	hästikasvatatud	[hæstikɑsʋɑtɑtud]
ill-bred (adj)	kasvatamatu	[kɑsʋɑtɑmɑtu]
spoiled (adj)	hellitatud	[hellitɑtud]
to be naughty	mürama	[myrɑmɑ]

mischievous (adj)	**vallatu**	[ʋallatu]
mischievousness	**vallatus**	[ʋallatus]
mischievous child	**vallatu jõmpsikas**	[ʋallatu jɪmpsikas]
obedient (adj)	**kuulekas**	[ku:lekas]
disobedient (adj)	**sõnakuulmatu**	[sɪnaku:lmatu]
docile (adj)	**mõistlik**	[mɪjstlik]
clever (smart)	**tark**	[tark]
child prodigy	**imelaps**	[imelaps]

60. Married couples. Family life

to kiss (vt)	**suudlema**	[su:dlema]
to kiss (vi)	**suudlema**	[su:dlema]
family (n)	**perekond**	[perekond]
family (as adj)	**perekondlik**	[perekondlik]
couple	**abielupaar**	[abielupɑ:r]
marriage (state)	**abielu**	[abielu]
hearth (home)	**kodukolle**	[kodukolle]
dynasty	**dünastia**	[dynastia]
date	**kohtamine**	[kohtamine]
kiss	**suudlus**	[su:dlus]
love (for sb)	**armastus**	[armastus]
to love (sb)	**armastama**	[armastama]
beloved	**kallim**	[kallim]
tenderness	**õrnus**	[ɪrnus]
tender (affectionate)	**õrn**	[ɪrn]
faithfulness	**truudus**	[tru:dus]
faithful (adj)	**truu**	[tru:]
care (attention)	**hoolitsus**	[ho:litsus]
caring (~ father)	**hoolitsev**	[ho:litseʋ]
newlyweds	**pruutpaar**	[pru:tpɑ:r]
honeymoon	**mesinädalad**	[mesiɲædalad]
to get married (ab. woman)	**mehele minema**	[mehele minema]
to get married (ab. man)	**naist võtma**	[najst ʋɪtma]
wedding	**pulmad**	[puʌmad]
golden wedding	**kuldpulm**	[kuʌdpuʌm]
anniversary	**aastapäev**	[a:stapæ:ʋ]
lover (masc.)	**armuke**	[armuke]
mistress	**armuke**	[armuke]
adultery	**petmine**	[petmine]
to cheat on ... (commit adultery)	**petma**	[petma]

jealous (adj)	armukade	[ɑrmukɑde]
to be jealous	armukadetsema	[ɑrmukɑdetsemɑ]
divorce	lahutus	[lɑhutus]
to divorce (vi)	lahutama	[lɑhutɑmɑ]

to quarrel (vi)	tülitsema	[tylitsemɑ]
to be reconciled	leppima	[leppimɑ]
together (adv)	koos	[ko:s]
sex	seks	[seks]

happiness	õnn	[ɪŋʲ]
happy (adj)	õnnelik	[ɪŋelik]
misfortune (accident)	õnnetus	[ɪŋetus]
unhappy (adj)	õnnetu	[ɪŋetu]

Character. Feelings. Emotions

61. Feelings. Emotions

feeling (emotion)	tunne	[tuŋe]
feelings	tunded	[tunded]
hunger	nälg	[ɲæʌg]
to be hungry	süüa tahtma	[syːɑ tɑhtmɑ]
thirst	janu	[ænu]
to be thirsty	juua tahtma	[yːɑ tɑhtmɑ]
sleepiness	unisus	[unisus]
to feel sleepy	magada tahtma	[mɑgɑdɑ tɑhtmɑ]
tiredness	väsimus	[ʋʲæsimus]
tired (adj)	väsinud	[ʋʲæsinud]
to get tired	väsima	[ʋʲæsimɑ]
mood (humor)	tuju	[tuy]
boredom	igavus	[igɑʋus]
to be bored	igavlema	[igɑʋlemɑ]
seclusion	üksindus	[yksindus]
to seclude oneself	üksi olema	[yksi olemɑ]
to worry (make anxious)	muret tegema	[muret tegemɑ]
to be worried	muretsema	[muretsemɑ]
worrying (n)	rahutus	[rɑhutus]
anxiety	häire	[hæjre]
preoccupied (adj)	muretsev	[muretseʋ]
to be nervous	närveerima	[nærʋeːrimɑ]
to panic (vi)	paanikasse sattuma	[pɑːnikɑsse sɑttumɑ]
hope	lootus	[loːtus]
to hope (vi, vt)	lootma	[loːtmɑ]
certainty	enesekindlus	[ənesekindlus]
certain, sure (adj)	enesekindel	[ənesekindeʌ]
uncertainty	ebakindlus	[ebɑkindlus]
uncertain (adj)	ebakindel	[ebɑkindeʌ]
drunk (adj)	purjus	[purjys]
sober (adj)	kaine	[kɑjne]
weak (adj)	nõrk	[nɪrk]
happy (adj)	õnnelik	[ɪŋelik]
to scare (vt)	ehmatama	[əhmɑtɑmɑ]
fury (madness)	märatsushoog	[mʲærɑtsushoːg]

rage (fury)	raev	[raeʊ]
depression	depressioon	[depressio:n]
discomfort	ebamugavus	[əbamugaʊus]
comfort	mugavus	[mugaʊus]
to regret (be sorry)	kahetsema	[kahetsema]
regret	kahetsus	[kahetsus]
bad luck	ebaõnnestumine	[əbaɪŋestumine]
sadness	kurvastus	[kurʋastus]

shame (remorse)	häbi	[ħæbi]
gladness	pidu	[pidu]
enthusiasm, zeal	entusiasm	[əntusiasm]
enthusiast	entusiast	[əntusiast]
to show enthusiasm	entusiasmi üles näitama	[əntusiasmi yles ɲæjtama]

62. Character. Personality

character	iseloom	[iselo:m]
character flaw	nõrkus	[nɪrkus]
mind	mõistus	[mɪjstus]
reason	aru	[aru]

conscience	südametunnistus	[sydametuŋistus]
habit (custom)	harjumus	[harjʏmus]
ability	võimed	[ʊɪjmed]
can (e.g., ~ swim)	oskama	[oskama]

patient (adj)	kannatlik	[kaŋatlik]
impatient (adj)	kannatamatu	[kaŋatamatu]
curious (inquisitive)	uudishimulik	[u:dishimulik]
curiosity	uudishimu	[u:dishimu]

modesty	tagasihoidlikkus	[tagasihojdlikkus]
modest (adj)	tagasihoidlik	[tagasihojdlik]
immodest (adj)	taktitundetu	[taktitundetu]

laziness	laiskus	[lajskus]
lazy (adj)	laisk	[lajsk]
lazy person (masc.)	laiskvorst	[lajskʊorst]

cunning (n)	kavalus	[kaʊalus]
cunning (as adj)	kaval	[kaʊal]
distrust	umbusaldus	[umbusaʎdus]
distrustful (adj)	umbusklik	[umbusklik]

generosity	heldus	[heʎdus]
generous (adj)	helde	[heʎde]
talented (adj)	andekas	[andekas]
talent	anne	[aŋe]
courageous (adj)	julge	[ylge]

68

courage	**julgus**	[ylgus]
honest (adj)	**aus**	[aus]
honesty	**ausus**	[ausus]
careful (cautious)	**ettevaatlik**	[etteʋaːtlik]
brave (courageous)	**vapper**	[ʋapper]
serious (adj)	**tõsine**	[tɪsine]
strict (severe, stern)	**range**	[raŋe]
decisive (adj)	**otsustav**	[otsustaʋ]
indecisive (adj)	**kõhklev**	[kɪhkleʋ]
shy, timid (adj)	**kartlik**	[kartlik]
shyness, timidity	**kartlikkus**	[kartlikkus]
confidence (trust)	**usaldus**	[usaʎdus]
to believe (trust)	**usaldama**	[usaʎdama]
trusting (naïve)	**usaldav**	[usaʎdaʋ]
sincerely (adv)	**siiralt**	[siːraʎt]
sincere (adj)	**siiras**	[siːras]
sincerity	**siirus**	[siːrus]
open (person)	**aval**	[aʋaʎ]
calm (adj)	**vaikne**	[ʋajkne]
frank (sincere)	**avameelne**	[aʋameːʎne]
naïve (adj)	**naiivne**	[naiːʋne]
absent-minded (adj)	**hajameelne**	[haæmeːʎne]
funny (odd)	**naljakas**	[naʎækas]
greed	**ahnus**	[ahnus]
greedy (adj)	**ahne**	[ahne]
stingy (adj)	**kitsi**	[kitsi]
evil (adj)	**kuri**	[kuri]
stubborn (adj)	**kangekaelne**	[kaŋekaʎne]
unpleasant (adj)	**ebameeldiv**	[ebameːʎdiʋ]
selfish person (masc.)	**egoist**	[egoist]
selfish (adj)	**egoistlik**	[egoistlik]
coward	**argpüks**	[argpyks]
cowardly (adj)	**arg**	[arg]

63. Sleep. Dreams

to sleep (vi)	**magama**	[magama]
sleep, sleeping	**uni**	[uni]
dream	**unenägu**	[uneɲægu]
to dream (in sleep)	**und nägema**	[und ɲægema]
sleepy (adj)	**unine**	[unine]
bed	**voodi**	[ʋoːdi]
mattress	**madrats**	[madrats]

blanket (comforter)	tekk	[tekk]
pillow	padi	[pɑdi]
sheet	voodilina	[ʋoːdilinɑ]

insomnia	unetus	[unetus]
sleepless (adj)	unetu	[unetu]
sleeping pill	unerohi	[unerohi]
to take a sleeping pill	unerohtu võtma	[unerohtu ʋɪtmɑ]

to feel sleepy	magada tahtma	[mɑgɑdɑ tɑhtmɑ]
to yawn (vi)	haigutama	[hɑjgutɑmɑ]
to go to bed	magama minema	[mɑgɑmɑ minemɑ]
to make up the bed	voodit üles tegema	[ʋoːdit yles tegemɑ]
to fall asleep	magama jääma	[mɑgɑmɑ æːmɑ]

nightmare	õudusunenägu	[ɪudusuneɲægu]
snoring	norskamine	[norskɑmine]
to snore (vi)	norskama	[norskɑmɑ]

alarm clock	äratuskell	[ərɑtuskeʎ]
to wake (vt)	äratama	[ərɑtɑmɑ]
to wake up	ärkama	[ərkɑmɑ]
to get up (vi)	üles tõusma	[yles tɪusmɑ]
to wash up (vi)	nägu pesema	[ɲægu pesemɑ]

64. Humour. Laughter. Gladness

| humor (wit, fun) | huumor | [huːmor] |
| sense of humor | huumorimeel | [huːmorimeːʎ] |

to have fun	lõbutsema	[lɪbutsemɑ]
cheerful (adj)	lõbus	[lɪbus]
merriment, fun	lust	[lust]

| smile | naeratus | [nɑerɑtus] |
| to smile (vi) | naeratama | [nɑerɑtɑmɑ] |

to start laughing	naerma hakkama	[nɑermɑ hɑkkɑmɑ]
to laugh (vi)	naerma	[nɑermɑ]
laugh, laughter	naer	[nɑer]

anecdote	anekdoot	[ɑnekdoːt]
funny (anecdote, etc.)	naljakas	[nɑʎækɑs]
funny (odd)	naljakas	[nɑʎækɑs]

to joke (vi)	nalja tegema	[nɑʎæ tegemɑ]
joke (verbal)	nali	[nɑli]
joy (emotion)	rõõm	[rɪːm]
to rejoice (vi)	rõõmustama	[rɪːmustɑmɑ]
glad, cheerful (adj)	rõõmus	[rɪːmus]

65. Discussion, conversation. Part 1

communication	**suhtlemine**	[suhtlemine]
to communicate	**suhtlema**	[suhtlema]
conversation	**vestlus**	[ʋestlus]
dialog	**dialoog**	[dialo:g]
discussion (discourse)	**diskussioon**	[diskussio:n]
debate	**vaidlus**	[ʋajdlus]
to debate (vi)	**vaidlema**	[ʋajdlema]
interlocutor	**vestluskaaslane**	[ʋestluska:slane]
topic (theme)	**teema**	[te:ma]
point of view	**seisukoht**	[sejsukoht]
opinion (viewpoint)	**arvamus**	[arʋamus]
speech (talk)	**kõne**	[kɪne]
discussion (of report, etc.)	**arutelu**	[arutelu]
to discuss (vt)	**arutama**	[arutama]
talk (conversation)	**vestlus**	[ʋestlus]
to talk (vi)	**vestlema**	[ʋestlema]
meeting	**kohtumine**	[kohtumine]
to meet (vi, vt)	**kohtuma**	[kohtuma]
proverb	**vanasõna**	[ʋanasɪna]
saying	**kõnekäänd**	[kɪnəkæ:nd]
riddle (poser)	**mõistatus**	[mɪjstatus]
to ask a riddle	**mõistatust andma**	[mɪjstatust andma]
password	**parool**	[paro:ʎ]
secret	**saladus**	[saladus]
oath (vow)	**tõotus**	[tɪotus]
to swear (an oath)	**tõotama**	[tɪotama]
promise	**lubadus**	[lubadus]
to promise (vt)	**lubama**	[lubama]
advice (counsel)	**nõu**	[nɪu]
to advise (vt)	**soovitama**	[so:ʋitama]
to listen to … (obey)	**sõna kuulma**	[sɪna ku:ʎma]
news	**uudis**	[u:dis]
sensation (news)	**sensatsioon**	[sensatsio:n]
information (data)	**andmed**	[andmed]
conclusion (decision)	**kokkuvõte**	[kokkuʋɪte]
voice	**hääl**	[hæ:ʎ]
compliment	**kompliment**	[kompliment]
kind (nice)	**armastusväärne**	[armastusʋæ:rne]
word	**sõna**	[sɪna]
phrase	**väljend**	[ʋæʎjend]
answer	**vastus**	[ʋastus]

truth	tõde	[tɪdə]
lie	vale	[ʋɑle]

thought	mõte	[mɪte]
idea (inspiration)	idee, mõte	[ide:], [mɪte]
fantasy	väljamõeldis	[ʋʲæʎæmɪːʎdis]

66. Discussion, conversation. Part 2

respected (adj)	austatud	[ɑustɑtud]
to respect (vt)	austama	[ɑustɑmɑ]
respect	austus	[ɑustus]
Dear ... (letter)	Lugupeetud ...	[lugupe:tud]

to introduce (present)	tutvustama	[tutʋustɑmɑ]
intention	kavatsus	[kɑʋɑtsus]
to intend (have in mind)	kavatsema	[kɑʋɑtsemɑ]
wish	soov	[so:ʋ]
to wish (~ good luck)	soovima	[so:ʋimɑ]

surprise (astonishment)	imestus	[imestus]
to surprise (amaze)	üllatama	[yllɑtɑmɑ]
to be surprised	imestama	[imestɑmɑ]

to give (vt)	andma	[ɑndmɑ]
to take (get hold of)	võtma	[ʋɪtmɑ]
to give back	tagastama	[tɑgɑstɑmɑ]
to return (give back)	tagasi andma	[tɑgɑsi ɑndmɑ]

to apologize (vi)	vabandama	[ʋɑbɑndɑmɑ]
apology	vabandus	[ʋɑbɑndus]
to forgive (vt)	andeks andma	[ɑndeks ɑndmɑ]

to talk (speak)	rääkima	[ræ:kimɑ]
to listen (vi)	kuulama	[ku:lɑmɑ]
to hear out	ära kuulama	[ɑrɑ ku:lɑmɑ]
to understand (vt)	mõistma	[mɪjstmɑ]

to show (display)	näitama	[næjtɑmɑ]
to look at ...	vaatama	[ʋɑ:tɑmɑ]
to call (with one's voice)	kutsuma	[kutsumɑ]
to disturb (vt)	tülitama	[tylitɑmɑ]
to pass (to hand sth)	üle andma	[yle ɑndmɑ]

demand (request)	palve	[pɑlʋe]
to request (ask)	paluma	[pɑlumɑ]
demand (firm request)	nõue	[nɪue]
to demand (request firmly)	nõudma	[nɪudmɑ]
to tease (nickname)	narrima	[nɑrrimɑ]
to mock (make fun of)	pilkama	[piʎkɑmɑ]

mockery, derision	**pilge**	[piʎge]
nickname	**hüüdnimi**	[hy:dnimi]
allusion	**vihje**	[ʋihje]
to allude (vi)	**vihjama**	[ʋihæma]
to imply (vt)	**silmas pidama**	[siʎmas pidama]
description	**kirjeldus**	[kirjeʎdus]
to describe (vt)	**kirjeldama**	[kirjeʎdama]
praise (compliments)	**kiitus**	[ki:tus]
to praise (vt)	**kiitma**	[ki:tma]
disappointment	**pettumus**	[pettumus]
to disappoint (vt)	**petma**	[petma]
to be disappointed	**pettuma**	[pettuma]
supposition	**eeldus**	[ee ʎdus]
to suppose (assume)	**eeldama**	[eeʎdama]
warning (caution)	**hoiatus**	[hojatus]
to warn (vt)	**hoiatama**	[hojatama]

67. Discussion, conversation. Part 3

to talk into (convince)	**veenma**	[ʋe:nma]
to calm down (vt)	**rahustama**	[rahustama]
silence (~ is golder)	**vaikimine**	[ʋajkimine]
to keep silent	**vaikima**	[ʋajkima]
to whisper (vi, vt)	**sosistama**	[sosistama]
whisper	**sosin**	[sosin]
frankly, sincerely (acv)	**avameelselt**	[aʋame:ʎseʎt]
in my opinion …	**minu arvates …**	[minu arʋates]
detail (of the story)	**üksikasi**	[yksikasi]
detailed (adj)	**üksikasjalik**	[yksikasʲælik]
in detail (adv)	**üksikasjalikult**	[yksikasʲælikuʎt]
hint, clue	**etteütlemine**	[etteytlemine]
to give a hint	**ette ütlema**	[ette ytlema]
look (glance)	**pilk**	[piʎk]
to have a look	**pilku heitma**	[piʎku hejtma]
fixed (look)	**liikumatu**	[li:kumatu]
to blink (vi)	**pilgutama**	[piʎgutama]
to wink (vi)	**pilgutama**	[piʎgutama]
to nod (in assent)	**noogutama**	[no:gutama]
sigh	**ohe**	[ohe]
to sigh (vi)	**ohkama**	[ohkama]

to shudder (vi)	võpatama	[ʋɪpatama]
gesture	žest	[ʒest]
to touch (one's arm, etc.)	puudutama	[puːdutama]
to seize (by the arm)	haarama	[haːrama]
to tap (on the shoulder)	patsutama	[patsutama]

Look out!	Ettevaatust!	[ǝtteʋɑːtust]
Really?	Kas tõesti?	[kɑs tɪːsti]
Are you sure?	Oled sa kindel?	[oled sɑ kindeʎ]
Good luck!	Õnn kaasa!	[ɪɲ ⁱkɑːsɑ]
I see!	Selge!	[selge]
It's a pity!	Kahju!	[kɑɦjy]

68. Agreement. Refusal

consent (agreement)	nõusolek	[nɪusolek]
to agree (say yes)	nõustuma	[nɪustuma]
approval	heakskiitmine	[heɑkskiːtmine]
to approve (vt)	heaks kiitma	[heɑks kiːtma]

| refusal | keeldumine | [keːʎdumine] |
| to refuse (vi, vt) | keelduma | [keːʎduma] |

Great!	Suurepärane!	[suːrepⁱærane]
All right!	Hästi!	[hæsti]
Okay! (I agree)	Hea küll!	[heɑ kyʎ]

| forbidden (adj) | keelatud | [keːlatud] |
| it's forbidden | ei tohi | [ǝj tohi] |

| it's impossible | võimatu | [ʋɪjmatu] |
| incorrect (adj) | vale | [ʋale] |

to reject (~ a demand)	tagasi lükkama	[tagasi lykkama]
to support (cause, idea)	toetama	[toetama]
to accept (~ an apology)	vastu võtma	[ʋastu ʋɪtma]

to confirm (vt)	kinnitama	[kiɲitama]
confirmation	kinnitus	[kiɲitus]
permission	luba	[luba]
to permit (vt)	lubama	[lubama]

| decision | otsus | [otsus] |
| to say nothing | vaikima | [ʋajkima] |

| condition (term) | tingimus | [tiɲimus] |
| excuse (pretext) | ettekääne | [ǝttekæːne] |

| praise (compliments) | kiitus | [kiːtus] |
| to praise (vt) | kiitma | [kiːtma] |

69. Success. Good luck. Failure

success	edu	[ədu]
successfully (adv)	edukalt	[ədukaʎt]
successful (adj)	edukas	[ədukɑs]
good luck	vedamine	[ʋedɑmine]
Good luck!	Õnn kaasa!	[ɪŋʲ kɑːsɑ]
lucky (e.g., ~ day)	õnnestunud	[ɪŋestunud]
lucky (fortunate)	õnneseen	[ɪŋeseːn]
failure	äpardus	[æpɑrdus]
misfortune	ebaõnn	[əbɑɪŋʲ]
bad luck	ebaõnnestumine	[əbɑɪŋestumine]
unsuccessful (adj)	ebaõnnestunud	[əbɑɪŋestunud]
catastrophe	katastroof	[kɑtɑstroːf]
pride	uhkus	[uhkus]
proud (adj)	uhke	[uhke]
to be proud	uhkust tundma	[uhkust tundmɑ]
winner	võitja	[ʋɪjtʲæ]
to win (vi)	võitma	[ʋɪjtmɑ]
to lose (not win)	kaotama	[kɑotɑmɑ]
try	katse	[kɑtse]
to try (vi)	püüdma	[pyːdmɑ]
chance (opportunity)	šanss	[ʃɑns]

70. Quarrels. Negative emotions

shout (scream)	karje	[kɑrje]
to shout (vi)	karjuma	[kɑrjumɑ]
to start to cry out	karjuma hakkama	[kɑrjumɑ hɑkkɑmɑ]
quarrel	tüli	[tyli]
to quarrel (vi)	tülitsema	[tylitsemɑ]
fight (scandal)	skandaal	[skɑndɑːl]
to have a fight	skandaali tegema	[skɑndɑːli tegemɑ]
conflict	konflikt	[konflikt]
misunderstanding	arusaamatus	[ɑrusɑːmɑtus]
insult	solvamine	[soʎʋɑmine]
to insult (vt)	solvama	[soʎʋɑmɑ]
insulted (adj)	solvatud	[soʎʋɑtud]
resentment	solvumine	[soʎʋumine]
to offend (vt)	solvama	[soʎʋɑmɑ]
to take offense	solvuma	[soʎʋumɑ]
indignation	pahameel	[pɑhɑmeːʎ]
to be indignant	pahane olema	[pɑhɑne olemɑ]

| complaint | kaebus | [kaəbus] |
| to complain (vi, vt) | kaebama | [kaəbama] |

apology	vabandus	[ʋabandus]
to apologize (vi)	vabandama	[ʋabandama]
to beg pardon	andeks paluma	[andeks paluma]

criticism	kriitika	[kriːtika]
to criticize (vt)	kritiseerima	[kritiseːrima]
accusation	süüdistus	[syːdistus]
to accuse (vt)	süüdistama	[syːdistama]

revenge	kättemaks	[kʲættemaks]
to revenge (vt)	kätte maksma	[kʲætte maksma]
to pay back	kätte maksma	[kʲætte maksma]

disdain	põlgus	[pɪʌgus]
to despise (vt)	põlgama	[pɪʌgama]
hatred, hate	viha	[ʋiha]
to hate (vt)	vihkama	[ʋihkama]

nervous (adj)	närviline	[ɲærʋiline]
to be nervous	närveerima	[ɲærʋeːrima]
angry (mad)	vihane	[ʋihane]
to make angry	vihale ajama	[ʋihale aæma]

humiliation	alandus	[alandus]
to humiliate (vt)	alandama	[alandama]
to humiliate oneself	alandust taluma	[alandust taluma]

| shock | šokk | [ʃokk] |
| to shock (vt) | šokeerima | [ʃokeːrima] |

| trouble (annoyance) | ebameeldivus | [əbameːʌdiʋus] |
| unpleasant (adj) | ebameeldiv | [əbameːʌdiʋ] |

fear (dread)	hirm	[hirm]
terrible (storm, heat)	hirmus	[hirmus]
scary (e.g., ~ story)	kole	[kole]
horror	õudus	[ɪudus]
awful (crime, news)	õudne	[ɪudne]

to cry (weep)	nutma	[nutma]
to start crying	nutma hakkama	[nutma hakkama]
tear	pisar	[pisar]

fault	süü	[syu]
guilt (feeling)	süütunne	[syːtuɲe]
dishonor (disgrace)	häbi	[hæbi]
protest	protest	[protest]
stress	stress	[stress]
to disturb (vt)	segama	[segama]

to be furious	**vihastama**	[ʋihastama]
mad, angry (adj)	**vihane**	[ʋihane]
to end (~ a relationship)	**katkestama**	[katkestama]
to swear (at sb)	**sõimama**	[sɪjmama]

to be scared	**ehmuma**	[əhmuma]
to hit (strike with hand)	**lööma**	[lø:ma]
to fight (vi)	**kaklema**	[kaklema]

to settle (a conflict)	**korda ajama**	[korda aæma]
discontented (adj)	**rahulolematu**	[rɑhuʎolematu]
furious (adj)	**raevukas**	[raəʋukas]

It's not good!	**See ei ole hea!**	[se: əj ole hea]
It's bad!	**See on halb!**	[se: on haʎb]

Medicine

71. Diseases

sickness	**haigus**	[hɑjgus]
to be sick	**haige olema**	[hɑjge olemɑ]
health	**tervis**	[teruis]
runny nose (coryza)	**nohu**	[nohu]
angina	**angiin**	[ɑŋi:n]
cold (illness)	**külmetus**	[kyʎmetus]
to catch a cold	**külmetuma**	[kyʎmetumɑ]
bronchitis	**bronhiit**	[bronhi:t]
pneumonia	**kopsupõletik**	[kopsupɪletik]
flu, influenza	**gripp**	[gripp]
near-sighted (adj)	**lühinägelik**	[lyhiɲægelik]
far-sighted (adj)	**kaugenägelik**	[kɑugeɲægelik]
strabismus (crossed eyes)	**kõõrdsilmsus**	[kɪ:rdsiʎmsus]
cross-eyed (adj)	**kõõrdsilmne**	[kɪ:rdsiʎmne]
cataract	**katarakt**	[kɑtɑrɑkt]
glaucoma	**glaukoom**	[glɑuko:m]
stroke	**insult**	[insuʎt]
heart attack	**infarkt**	[infɑrkt]
myocardial infarction	**müokardi infarkt**	[myokɑrdi infɑrkt]
paralysis	**halvatus**	[hɑʎuɑtus]
to paralyze (vt)	**halvama**	[hɑʎuɑmɑ]
allergy	**allergia**	[ɑllergiɑ]
asthma	**astma**	[ɑstmɑ]
diabetes	**diabeet**	[diɑbe:t]
toothache	**hambavalu**	[hɑmbɑuɑlu]
caries	**kaaries**	[kɑ:ries]
diarrhea	**kõhulahtisus**	[kɪhulɑhtisus]
constipation	**kõhukinnisus**	[kɪhukiɲisus]
stomach upset	**kõhulahtisus**	[kɪhulɑhtisus]
food poisoning	**mürgitus**	[myrgitus]
to have a food poisoning	**mürgitust saama**	[myrgitust sɑ:mɑ]
arthritis	**artriit**	[ɑrtri:t]
rickets	**rahhiit**	[rɑhi:t]
rheumatism	**reuma**	[reumɑ]

atherosclerosis	ateroskleroos	[atərosklero:s]
gastritis	gastriit	[gastri:t]
appendicitis	apenditsiit	[apenditsijt]
cholecystitis	koletsüstiit	[koletsysti:t]
ulcer	haavand	[ha:ʋand]

measles	leetrid	[le:trid]
German measles	punetised	[punetised]
jaundice	kollatõbi	[kollatıbi]
hepatitis	hepatiit	[hepati:t]

schizophrenia	skisofreenia	[skisofre:nia]
rabies (hydrophobia)	marutaud	[marutaud]
neurosis	neuroos	[neuro:s]
concussion	ajuvapustus	[ayʋapustus]

cancer	vähk	[ʋæhk]
sclerosis	skleroos	[sklero:s]
multiple sclerosis	hajameelne skleroos	[haæme:ʌne sklero:s]

alcoholism	alkoholism	[alkoholism]
alcoholic (n)	alkohoolik	[alkoho:lik]
syphilis	süüfilis	[sy:filis]
AIDS	AIDS	[ajds]

tumor	kasvaja	[kasʋaæ]
malignant (adj)	pahaloomuline	[pahalo:muline]
benign (adj)	healoomuline	[healo:muline]

fever	palavik	[palaʋik]
malaria	malaaria	[mala:riæ]
gangrene	gangreen	[gaŋre:n]
seasickness	merehaigus	[merehajgus]
epilepsy	epilepsia	[əpilepsia]

epidemic	epideemia	[əpide:mia]
typhus	tüüfus	[ty:fus]
tuberculosis	tuberkuloos	[tuberkulo:s]
cholera	koolera	[ko:lera]
plague (bubonic ~)	katk	[katk]

72. Symptoms. Treatments. Part 1

symptom	sümptom	[symptom]
temperature	temperatuur	[temperatu:r]
high temperature	kõrge palavik	[kırge palaʋik]
pulse	pulss	[puʌss]

| giddiness | peapööritus | [peapø:ritus] |
| hot (adj) | kuum | [ku:m] |

shivering	**vappekülm**	[ʋappekyʌm]
pale (e.g., ~ face)	**kahvatu**	[kahʋatu]

cough	**köha**	[køha]
to cough (vi)	**köhima**	[køhima]
to sneeze (vi)	**aevastama**	[aeʋastama]
faint	**minestus**	[minestus]
to faint (vi)	**teadvust kaotama**	[teadʋust kaotama]

bruise (hématome)	**sinikas**	[sinikas]
bump (lump)	**muhk**	[muhk]
to bruise oneself	**ära lööma**	[æra lø:ma]
bruise (contusion)	**haiget saanud koht**	[hajget sa:nud koht]
to get bruised	**haiget saama**	[hajget sa:ma]

to limp (vi)	**lonkama**	[loŋkama]
dislocation	**nihestus**	[nihestus]
to dislocate (vt)	**nihestama**	[nihestama]
fracture	**luumurd**	[lu:murd]
to have a fracture	**luud murdma**	[lu:d murdma]

cut (e.g., paper ~)	**lõikehaav**	[lɪjkeha:ʋ]
to cut oneself	**endale sisse lõikama**	[əndale sisse lɪjkama]
bleeding	**verejooks**	[ʋerejo:ks]

burn (injury)	**põletushaav**	[pɪletusha:ʋ]
to scald oneself	**end ära põletama**	[ənd æra pɪletama]

to prick (vt)	**torkama**	[torkama]
to prick oneself	**end torkama**	[ənd torkama]
to injure (vt)	**kergelt haavama**	[kergeʌt ha:ʋama]
injury	**vigastus**	[ʋigastus]
wound	**haav**	[ha:ʋ]
trauma	**trauma**	[trauma]

to be delirious	**sonima**	[sonima]
to stutter (vi)	**kokutama**	[kokutama]
sunstroke	**päiksepiste**	[pʲæjkesepiste]

73. Symptoms. Treatments. Part 2

pain	**valu**	[ʋalu]
splinter (in foot, etc.)	**pind**	[pind]

sweat (perspiration)	**higi**	[higi]
to sweat (perspire)	**higistama**	[higistama]
vomiting	**okse**	[okse]
convulsions	**krambid**	[krambid]
pregnant (adj)	**rase**	[rase]
to be born	**sündima**	[syndima]

delivery, labor	sünnitus	[syŋitus]
to deliver (~ a baby)	sünnitama	[syŋitama]
abortion	abort	[abort]

breathing, respiration	hingamine	[hiŋamine]
inhalation	sissehingamine	[sissehiŋamine]
exhalation	väljahingamine	[ᵘæʎæhiŋamine]
to exhale (vi)	välja hingama	[ᵘæʎæ hiŋama]
to inhale (vi)	sisse hingama	[sisse hiŋama]

disabled person	invaliid	[inʋaliːd]
cripple	vigane	[ʋigane]
drug addict	narkomaan	[narkomaːn]

deaf (adj)	kurt	[kurt]
dumb, mute	tumm	[tumm]
deaf-and-dumb (ad.)	kurttumm	[kurttumm]

mad, insane (adj)	hullumeelne	[hullumeːʎne]
madman	vaimuhaige	[ʋajmuhajge]
madwoman	vaimuhaige	[ʋajmuhajge]
to go insane	hulluks minema	[hulluks minema]

gene	geen	[geːn]
immunity	immuniteet	[immuniteːt]
hereditary (adj)	pärilik	[pʲærilik]
congenital (adj)	kaasasündinud	[kaːsasyndinud]

virus	viirus	[ʋiːrus]
microbe	mikroob	[mikroːb]
bacterium	bakter	[bakter]
infection	nakkus	[nakkus]

74. Symptoms. Treatments. Part 3

| hospital | haigla | [hajgla] |
| patient | patsient | [patsiənt] |

diagnosis	diagnoos	[diagnoːs]
cure	iseravimine	[iseraʋimine]
medical treatment	ravimine	[raʋimine]
to get treatment	ennast ravima	[əŋast raʋima]
to treat (vt)	ravima	[raʋima]
to nurse (look after)	hoolitsema	[hoːlitsema]
care (nursing ~)	hoolitsus	[hoːlitsus]

operation, surgery	operatsioon	[operatsioːn]
to bandage (head, limb)	siduma	[siduma]
bandaging	sidumine	[sidumine]
vaccination	vaktsineerimine	[ʋaktsineːrimine]

to vaccinate (vt)	vaktsineerima	[ʋaktsine:rima]
injection, shot	süst	[syst]
to give an injection	süstima	[systima]

attack	haigushoog	[hajgusho:g]
amputation	amputeerimine	[ampute:rimine]
to amputate (vt)	amputeerima	[ampute:rima]
coma	kooma	[ko:ma]
to be in a coma	koomas olema	[ko:mas olema]
intensive care	reanimatsioon	[reanimatsio:n]

to recover (~ from flu)	terveks saama	[terʋeks sa:ma]
state (patient's ~)	seisund	[sejsund]
consciousness	teadvus	[teadʋus]
memory (faculty)	mälu	[mʲælu]

to extract (tooth)	hammast välja tõmbama	[hammast ʋʲæʎæ timbama]
filling	plomm	[plomm]
to fill (a tooth)	plombeerima	[plombe:rima]

hypnosis	hüpnoos	[hypno:s]
to hypnotize (vt)	hüpnotiseerima	[hypnotise:rima]

75. Doctors

doctor	arst	[arst]
nurse	medõde	[medɪde]
private physician	isiklik arst	[isiklik arst]

dentist	hambaarst	[hamba:rst]
ophthalmologist	silmaarst	[siʎma:rst]
internist	sisearst	[sisearst]
surgeon	kirurg	[kirurg]

psychiatrist	psühhiaater	[psyhia:ter]
pediatrician	lastearst	[lastearst]
psychologist	psühholoog	[psyholo:g]
gynecologist	naistearst	[najstearst]
cardiologist	kardioloog	[kardiolo:g]

76. Medicine. Drugs. Accessories

medicine, drug	ravim	[raʋim]
remedy	vahend	[ʋahend]
to prescribe (vt)	välja kirjutama	[ʋʲæʎæ kirjytama]
prescription	retsept	[retsept]
tablet, pill	tablett	[tablett]

ointment	**salv**	[sɑʌʋ]
ampule	**ampull**	[ɑmpuʎ]
mixture	**mikstuur**	[mikstuːr]
syrup	**siirup**	[siːrup]
pill	**pill**	[piʎ]
powder	**pulber**	[puʌber]

bandage	**side**	[side]
cotton wool	**vatt**	[ʋattⁱ]
iodine	**jood**	[joːd]

Band-Aid	**plaaster**	[plɑːster]
eyedropper	**pipett**	[pipett]
thermometer	**kraadiklaas**	[krɑːdiklɑːs]
syringe	**süstal**	[systɑʌ]

| wheelchair | **invaliidikäru** | [inʋɑliːdikⁱæru] |
| crutches | **kargud** | [kɑrgud] |

painkiller	**valuvaigisti**	[ʋɑluʋɑjgisti]
laxative	**kõhulahtisti**	[kɪhulɑhtisti]
spirit (ethanol)	**piiritus**	[piːritus]
medicinal herbs	**maarohud**	[mɑːrohud]
herbal (~ tea)	**maarohtudest**	[mɑːrohtudest]

77. Smoking. Tobacco products

tobacco	**tubakas**	[tubɑkɑs]
cigarette	**sigarett**	[sigɑrett]
cigar	**sigar**	[sigɑr]
pipe	**piip**	[piːp]
pack (of cigarettes)	**suitsupakk**	[sujʦupɑkk]

matches	**tikud**	[tikud]
matchbox	**tikutoos**	[tikutoːs]
lighter	**välgumihkel**	[ʋⁱælgumihkeʌ]
ashtray	**tuhatoos**	[tuhɑtoːs]
cigarette case	**portsigar**	[porʦigɑr]

| cigarette holder | **munstükk** | [munsttykk] |
| filter (cigarette tip) | **filter** | [fiʌter] |

to smoke (vi, vt)	**suitsetama**	[sujʦetɑmɑ]
to light a cigarette	**suitsetama hakkama**	[sujʦetɑmɑ hɑkkɑmɑ]
smoking	**suitsetamine**	[sujʦetɑmine]
smoker	**suitsetaja**	[sujʦetɑæ]

stub, butt (of cigarette)	**koni**	[koni]
smoke, fumes	**suits**	[sujʦ]
ash	**tuhk**	[tuhk]

HUMAN HABITAT

City

78. City. Life in the city

city, town	linn	[liŋ]
capital city	pealinn	[pealiŋ]
village	küla	[kyla]

city map	linnaplaan	[liŋapla:n]
downtown	kesklinn	[keskliŋ]
suburb	linnalähedane asula	[iŋaʎæhedane asula]
suburban (adj)	linnalähedane	[liŋaʎæhedane]

outskirts	äärelinn	[æ:reliŋ]
environs (suburbs)	ümbrus	[ymbrus]
city block	kvartal	[kʊartal]
residential block	elamukvartal	[elamukʊartal]

traffic	liiklus	[li:klus]
traffic lights	valgusfoor	[ʊalgusfo:r]
public transportation	linnatransport	[liŋatransport]
intersection	ristmik	[ristmik]

crosswalk	ülekäik	[ylekʲæjk]
pedestrian underpass	jalakäijate tunnel	[ælakʲæjate tuŋeʎ]
to cross (vt)	üle tänava minema	[yle tʲænaʊa minema]
pedestrian	jalakäija	[ælakʲæja]
sidewalk	kõnnitee	[kɪŋite:]

bridge	sild	[siʎd]
bank (riverbank)	kaldapealne	[kaʎdapeaʎne]
fountain	purskkaev	[purskkaeʊ]

allée	allee	[alle:]
park	park	[park]
boulevard	puiestee	[pujeste:]
square	väljak	[ʊæʎæk]
avenue (wide street)	prospekt	[prospekt]
street	tänav	[tʲænaʊ]
side street	põiktänav	[pɪjktʲænaʊ]
dead end	umbtänav	[umbtʲænaʊ]
house	maja	[maæ]
building	hoone	[ho:ne]

skyscraper	**pilvelõhkuja**	[piʎʋelɪhkuæ]
facade	**fassaad**	[fɑssɑːd]
roof	**katus**	[kɑtus]
window	**aken**	[ɑken]
arch	**võlv**	[ʋɪʎʋ]
column	**sammas**	[sɑmmɑs]
corner	**nurk**	[nurk]

store window	**vaateaken**	[ʋɑːteɑken]
store sign	**silt**	[siʎt]
poster	**kuulutus**	[kuːlutus]
advertising poster	**reklaamiplakat**	[reklɑːmiplɑkɑt]
billboard	**reklaamikilp**	[reklɑːmikiʎp]

garbage, trash	**prügi**	[prygi]
garbage can	**prügiurn**	[prygiurn]
to litter (vi)	**prahti maha viskama**	[prɑhti mɑhɑ ʋiskɑmɑ]
garbage dump	**prügimägi**	[prygimʲægi]

phone booth	**telefoniputka**	[telefoniputkɑ]
lamppost	**laternapost**	[lɑternɑpostʲ]
bench (park ~)	**pink**	[piŋk]

police officer	**politseinik**	[politsejnik]
police	**politsei**	[politsej]
beggar	**kerjus**	[kerjys]
homeless, bum	**pätt**	[pʲættʲ]

79. Urban institutions

store	**kauplus**	[kɑuplus]
drugstore, pharmacy	**apteek**	[ɑpteːk]
optical store	**optika**	[optikɑ]
shopping mall	**kaubanduskeskus**	[kɑubɑnduskeskus]
supermarket	**supermarket**	[supermɑrket]

bakery	**leivapood**	[lejʋɑpoːd]
baker	**pagar**	[pɑgɑr]
candy store	**kondiitripood**	[kondiːtripoːd]
grocery store	**toidupood**	[tojdupoːd]
butcher shop	**lihakarn**	[lihɑkɑrn]

| produce store | **juurviljapood** | [yːrʋiʎæpoːd] |
| market | **turg** | [turg] |

coffee house	**kohvik**	[kohʋik]
restaurant	**restoran**	[restorɑn]
pub	**õllebaar**	[ɪlːebɑːr]
pizzeria	**pitsabaar**	[pitsɑbɑːr]
hair salon	**juuksurisalong**	[yːksurisɑloŋ]

post office	**postkontor**	[post'kontor]
dry cleaners	**keemiline puhastus**	[keːmiline puhastus]
photo studio	**fotoateljee**	[fotoateʎjeɛ]
shoe store	**kingapood**	[kiŋapoːd]
bookstore	**raamatukauplus**	[raːmatukauplus]
sporting goods store	**sporditarvete kauplus**	[sporditarʋete kauplus]
clothes repair	**riieteparandus**	[riːeteparandus]
formal wear rental	**riietelaenutus**	[riːetelaɘnutus]
movie rental store	**filmilaenutus**	[fiʎmilaɘnutus]
circus	**tsirkus**	[ʦirkus]
zoo	**loomaaed**	[loːmaːɘd]
movie theater	**kino**	[kino]
museum	**muuseum**	[muːseum]
library	**raamatukogu**	[raːmatukogu]
theater	**teater**	[teater]
opera	**ooper**	[oːper]
nightclub	**ööklubi**	[øːklubi]
casino	**kasiino**	[kasiːno]
mosque	**mošee**	[moʃeː]
synagogue	**sünagoog**	[synagoːg]
cathedral	**katedraal**	[katedraːl]
temple	**pühakoda**	[pyhakoda]
church	**kirik**	[kirik]
college	**instituut**	[instituːt]
university	**ülikool**	[ylikoːʎ]
school	**kool**	[koːʎ]
prefecture	**linnaosa valitsus**	[liŋaosa ʋalitsus]
city hall	**linnavalitsus**	[liŋaʋalitsus]
hotel	**hotell**	[hoteʎ]
bank	**pank**	[paŋk]
embassy	**suursaatkond**	[suːrsaːtkond]
travel agency	**reisibüroo**	[rejsibyroː]
information office	**teadete büroo**	[teadete byroː]
money exchange	**rahavahetus**	[rahaʋahetus]
subway	**metroo**	[metroː]
hospital	**haigla**	[hajgla]
gas station	**tankla**	[taŋkla]
parking lot	**parkla**	[parkla]

80. Signs

store sign	**silt**	[siʌt]
notice (written text)	**pealkiri**	[peaʌkiri]
poster	**plakat**	[plɑkɑt]
direction sign	**teeviit**	[teːʋiːt]
arrow (sign)	**nool**	[noːʌ]
caution	**hoiatus**	[hojɑtus]
warning sign	**hoiatus**	[hojɑtus]
to warn (vt)	**hoiatama**	[hojɑtɑmɑ]
day off	**puhkepäev**	[puhkepæːʋ]
timetable (schedule)	**sõiduplaan**	[sɪjduplɑːn]
opening hours	**töötunnid**	[tøːtuŋid]
WELCOME!	**TERE TULEMAST!**	[tere tulemɑst]
ENTRANCE	**SISSEPÄÄS**	[sissepæːs]
EXIT	**VÄLJAPÄÄS**	[ʋʲæʌʌæpæːs]
PUSH	**LÜKKA**	[lykkɑ]
PULL	**TÕMBA**	[tɪmbɑ]
OPEN	**AVATUD**	[ɑʋɑtud]
CLOSED	**SULETUD**	[suletud]
WOMEN	**NAISTELE**	[nɑjstele]
MEN	**MEESTELE**	[meːstele]
DISCOUNTS	**SOODUSTUSED**	[soːdustused]
SALE	**VÄLJAMÜÜK**	[ʋʲæʌʌæmyːk]
NEW!	**UUS KAUP!**	[uːskɑup]
FREE	**TASUTA**	[tɑsutɑ]
ATTENTION!	**ETTEVAATUST!**	[ətteʋɑːtust]
NO VACANCIES	**TÄIELIKULT BRONEERITUD**	[tʲæjelikuʌt broneːritud]
RESERVED	**RESERVEERITUD**	[reserʋeːritud]
ADMINISTRATION	**JUHTKOND**	[yhtkond]
STAFF ONLY	**AINULT PERSONALILE**	[ɑjnuʌt personɑlile]
BEWARE OF THE DOG!	**KURI KOER**	[kuri koər]
NO SMOKING	**MITTE SUITSETADA!**	[mitte sujtsetɑdɑ]
DO NOT TOUCH!	**MITTE PUUTUDA!**	[mitte puːtudɑ]
DANGEROUS	**OHTLIK**	[ohtlik]
DANGER	**OHT**	[oht]
HIGH TENSION	**KÕRGEPINGE**	[kɪrgepiŋe]
NO SWIMMING!	**UJUMINE KEELATUD!**	[ujumine keːlɑtud]
OUT OF ORDER	**EI TÖÖTA**	[əj tøːtɑ]
FLAMMABLE	**TULEOHTLIK**	[tuleohtlik]

FORBIDDEN	**KEELATUD**	[keːlɑtud]
NO TRESPASSING!	**LÄBIKÄIK KEELATUD**	[ʎæbikʲæjk keːlɑtud]
WET PAINT	**VÄRSKE VÄRV**	[ʊʲærske ʊʲærʊ]

81. Urban transportation

bus	**buss**	[bussʲ]
streetcar	**tramm**	[trɑmm]
trolley	**troll**	[troʎ]
route (of bus)	**marsruut**	[mɑrsruːt]
number (e.g., bus ~)	**number**	[number]
to go by ...	**... sõitma**	[sʲɪjtmɑ]
to get on (~ the bus)	**sisenema**	[sisenemɑ]
to get off ...	**maha minema**	[mɑhɑ minemɑ]
stop (e.g., bus ~)	**peatus**	[peɑtus]
next stop	**järgmine peatus**	[ærgmine peɑtus]
terminus	**lõpp-peatus**	[lɪpp peɑtus]
schedule	**sõiduplaan**	[sʲɪjduplɑːn]
to wait (vt)	**ootama**	[oːtɑmɑ]
ticket	**pilet**	[pilet]
fare	**pileti hind**	[piletihind]
cashier (ticket seller)	**kassiir**	[kɑssiːr]
ticket inspection	**piletikontroll**	[piletikontroʎ]
conductor	**kontrolör**	[kontrolør]
to be late (for ...)	**hilinema**	[hilinemɑ]
to miss (~ the train, etc.)	**hiljaks jääma**	[hiʎæks æːmɑ]
to be in a hurry	**ruttama**	[ruttɑmɑ]
taxi, cab	**takso**	[tɑkso]
taxi driver	**taksojuht**	[tɑksoyht]
by taxi	**taksoga**	[tɑksogɑ]
taxi stand	**taksopeatus**	[tɑksopeɑtus]
to call a taxi	**taksot välja kutsuma**	[tɑksot ʊʲæʎæ kutsumɑ]
to take a taxi	**taksot võtma**	[tɑksot ʊɪtmɑ]
traffic	**tänavaliiklus**	[tʲænɑʋɑliːklus]
traffic jam	**liiklusummik**	[liːklusummik]
rush hour	**tipptund**	[tipptuɲd]
to park (vi)	**parkima**	[pɑrkimɑ]
to park (vt)	**parkima**	[pɑrkimɑ]
parking lot	**parkla**	[pɑrklɑ]
subway	**metroo**	[metroː]
station	**jaam**	[æːm]
to take the subway	**metrooga sõitma**	[metroːgɑ sʲɪjtmɑ]

| train | **rong** | [roŋ] |
| train station | **raudteejaam** | [raudte:æ:m] |

82. Sightseeing

monument	**mälestussammas**	[mʲælestussammas]
fortress	**kindlus**	[kindlus]
palace	**loss**	[lossʲ]
castle	**loss**	[lossʲ]
tower	**torn**	[torn]
mausoleum	**mausoleum**	[mausoleum]

architecture	**arhitektuur**	[arhitektu:r]
medieval (adj)	**keskaegne**	[keskaəgne]
ancient (adj)	**vanaaegne**	[vana:əgne]
national (adj)	**rahvuslik**	[rahuuslik]
well-known (adj)	**tuntud**	[tuntud]

tourist	**turist**	[turist]
guide (person)	**giid**	[gi:d]
excursion, guided tour	**ekskursioon**	[ekskursio:n]
to show (vt)	**näitama**	[næjtama]
to tell (vt)	**jutustama**	[ytustama]

to find (vt)	**leidma**	[lejdma]
to get lost (lose one's way)	**ära kaduma**	[əra kaduma]
map (e.g., subway ~)	**skeem**	[ske:m]
map (e.g., city ~)	**plaan**	[pla:n]

souvenir, gift	**suveniir**	[suveni:r]
gift shop	**suveniirikauplus**	[suveni:rikauplus]
to take pictures	**pildistama**	[piʎdistama]
to be photographed	**laskma pildistada**	[laskma piʎdistada]

83. Shopping

to buy (purchase)	**ostma**	[ostma]
purchase	**ost**	[ost]
to go shopping	**oste tegema**	[oste tegema]
shopping	**šoppamine**	[ʃoppamine]

| to be open (ab. store) | **lahti olema** | [lahti olema] |
| to be closed | **kinni olema** | [kiɲi olema] |

footwear	**jalatsid**	[ælatsid]
clothes, clothing	**riided**	[ri:ded]
cosmetics	**kosmeetika**	[kosme:tika]
food products	**toiduained**	[tojduajned]

gift, present	**kingitus**	[kiŋitus]
salesman	**müüja**	[myːæ]
saleswoman	**müüja**	[myːæ]
check out, cash desk	**kassa**	[kɑssɑ]
mirror	**peegel**	[peːgeʎ]
counter (in shop)	**lett**	[lettʲ]
fitting room	**proovikabiin**	[proːʋikɑbiːn]
to try on	**selga proovima**	[seʎgɑ proːʋimɑ]
to fit (ab. dress, etc.)	**paras olema**	[pɑrɑs olemɑ]
to like (I like ...)	**meeldima**	[meːʎdimɑ]
price	**hind**	[hind]
price tag	**hinnalipik**	[hiŋɑlipik]
to cost (vt)	**maksma**	[mɑksmɑ]
How much?	**Kui palju?**	[kuj pɑʎjy]
discount	**allahindlus**	[ɑllɑhindlus]
inexpensive (adj)	**odav**	[odɑʊ]
cheap (adj)	**odav**	[odɑʊ]
expensive (adj)	**kallis**	[kɑllis]
It's expensive	**See on kallis.**	[seː on kɑllis]
rental (n)	**laenutus**	[lɑenutus]
to rent (~ a tuxedo)	**laenutama**	[lɑenutɑmɑ]
credit	**pangalaen**	[pɑŋɑlɑen]
on credit (adv)	**krediiti võtma**	[krediːti ʊɪtmɑ]

84. Money

money	**raha**	[rɑhɑ]
currency exchange	**vahetus**	[ʋɑhetus]
exchange rate	**kurss**	[kurss]
ATM	**pangaautomaat**	[pɑŋɑːutomɑːt]
coin	**münt**	[mynt]
dollar	**dollar**	[dollɑr]
euro	**euro**	[əuro]
lira	**liir**	[liːr]
Deutschmark	**mark**	[mɑrk]
franc	**frank**	[frɑŋk]
pound sterling	**naelsterling**	[nɑeʎsterliŋ]
yen	**jeen**	[jeːn]
debt	**võlg**	[ʊɪʎg]
debtor	**võlgnik**	[ʊɪʎgnik]
to lend (money)	**võlgu andma**	[ʊɪʎgu ɑndmɑ]
to borrow (vi, vt)	**võlgu võtma**	[ʊɪʎgu ʊɪtmɑ]

bank	pank	[paŋk]
account	pangakonto	[paŋakonto]
to deposit into the account	arvele panema	[arʋele panema]
to withdraw (vt)	arvelt võtma	[arʋeʌt ʋɪtma]

credit card	krediidikaart	[kredi:dika:rt]
cash	sularaha	[sularaha]
check	tšekk	[tʃek]
to write a check	tšekki välja kirjutama	[tʃekki ʋæʌæ kirjytama]
checkbook	tšekiraamat	[tʃekira:mat]

wallet	rahatasku	[rahatasku]
change purse	rahakott	[rahakottʲ]
billfold	rahatasku	[rahatasku]
safe	seif	[sejf]

heir	pärija	[pʲæriæ]
inheritance	pärandus	[pʲærandus]
fortune (wealth)	varandus	[ʋarandus]

lease, rent	rent	[rent]
rent money	korteriüür	[korteriy:r]
to rent (sth from sb)	üürima	[y:rima]

price	hind	[hind]
cost	maksumus	[maksumus]
sum	summa	[summa]

to spend (vt)	raiskama	[rajskama]
expenses	kulutused	[kulutused]
to economize (vi, vt)	kokku hoidma	[kokku hojdma]
economical	kokkuhoidlik	[kokkuhojdlik]

to pay (vi, vt)	tasuma	[tasuma]
payment	maksmine	[maksmine]
change (give the ~)	raha tagasi	[raha tagasi]

tax	maks	[maks]
fine	trahv	[trahʋ]
to fine (vt)	trahvima	[trahʋima]

85. Post. Postal service

post office	postkontor	[postʲkontor]
mail (letters, etc.)	post	[postʲ]
mailman	postiljon	[postiʎon]
opening hours	töötunnid	[tø:tuɲid]

| letter | kiri | [kiri] |
| registered letter | tähitud kiri | [tʲæhitud kiri] |

postcard	postkaart	[post'kɑ:rt]
telegram	telegramm	[telegrɑmm]
parcel	pakk	[pɑkk]
money transfer	rahaülekanne	[rɑhɑylekɑŋe]

to receive (vt)	kätte saama	[k'ætte sɑ:mɑ]
to send (vt)	saatma	[sɑ:tmɑ]
sending	saatmine	[sɑ:tmine]

address	aadress	[ɑ:dress]
ZIP code	indeks	[indeks]
sender	saatja	[sɑ:t'æ]
receiver, addressee	saaja	[sɑ:æ]

| name | eesnimi | [əesnimi] |
| family name | perekonnanimi | [perekoŋanimi] |

rate (of postage)	tariif	[tɑri:f]
standard (adj)	harilik	[hɑrilik]
economical (adj)	soodustariif	[so:dustɑri:f]

weight	kaal	[kɑ:l]
to weigh up (vt)	kaaluma	[kɑ:lumɑ]
envelope	ümbrik	[ymbrik]
postage stamp	mark	[mɑrk]

Dwelling. House. Home

86. House. Dwelling

house	**maja**	[mɑæ]
at home (adv)	**kodus**	[kodus]
courtyard	**õu**	[ɪu]
fence	**tara**	[tɑrɑ]
brick (n)	**telliskivi**	[təlliskivi]
brick (as adj)	**telliskivist**	[telliskivist]
stone (n)	**kivi**	[kivi]
stone (as adj)	**kivist**	[kivist]
concrete (n)	**betoon**	[beto:n]
concrete (as adj)	**betoonist**	[beto:nist]
new (new-built)	**uus**	[u:s]
old (adj)	**vana**	[vɑnɑ]
decrepit (house)	**kõdunenud**	[kɪdunenud]
modern (adj)	**kaasaegne**	[kɑ:sɑegne]
multistory (adj)	**mitmekorruseline**	[mitmekorruseline]
high (adj)	**kõrge**	[kɪrge]
floor, story	**korrus**	[korrus]
single-story (adj)	**ühekorruseline**	[yhekorruseline]
ground floor	**alumine korrus**	[ɑlumine korrus]
top floor	**ülemine korrus**	[ylemine korrus]
roof	**katus**	[kɑtus]
chimney (stack)	**korsten**	[korsten]
roof tiles	**katusekivi**	[kɑtusekivi]
tiled (adj)	**katusekivist**	[kɑtusekivist]
loft (attic)	**pööning**	[pø:niŋ]
window	**aken**	[ɑken]
glass	**klaas**	[klɑ:s]
window ledge	**aknalaud**	[ɑknɑlaud]
shutters	**aknaluugid**	[ɑknɑlu:gid]
wall	**sein**	[sejn]
balcony	**rõdu**	[rɪdu]
downspout	**vihmaveetoru**	[vihmɑve:toru]
upstairs (to be ~)	**üleval**	[ylevɑʎ]
to go upstairs	**trepist üles minema**	[trepist yles minemɑ]
to come down	**laskuma**	[lɑskumɑ]
to move (to new premises)	**kolima**	[kolimɑ]

87. House. Entrance. Lift

entrance	**trepikoda**	[trepikoda]
stairs (stairway)	**trepp**	[trepp]
steps	**astmed**	[astmed]
banisters	**käsipuu**	[kʲæsipu:]
lobby (hotel ~)	**hall**	[haʎ]
mailbox	**postkast**	[postʲkastʲ]
trash container	**prügikonteiner**	[prygikontejner]
trash chute	**prügišaht**	[prygiʃaht]
elevator	**lift**	[lift]
freight elevator	**veolift**	[ʋeolift]
elevator cage	**kabiin**	[kabi:n]
to take the elevator	**liftiga sõitma**	[liftiga sɪjtma]
apartment	**korter**	[korter]
residents, inhabitants	**elanikud**	[əlanikud]
neighbor (masc.)	**naaber**	[na:ber]
neighbor (fem.)	**naabrinaine**	[na:brinajne]
neighbors	**naabrid**	[na:brid]

88. House. Electricity

electricity	**elekter**	[əlekter]
light bulb	**elektripirn**	[əlektripirn]
switch	**lüliti**	[lyliti]
fuse	**kork**	[kork]
cable, wire (electric ~)	**juhe**	[yhe]
wiring	**juhtmestik**	[yhtmestik]
electricity meter	**arvesti**	[arʋesti]
readings	**näit**	[ɲæjt]

89. House. Doors. Locks

door	**uks**	[uks]
vehicle gate	**värav**	[ʋʲærɑʋ]
handle, doorknob	**ukselink**	[ukseliŋk]
to unlock (unbolt)	**lukust lahti keerama**	[lukust lɑnti ke:rama]
to open (vt)	**avama**	[aʋama]
to close (vt)	**sulgema**	[sulgema]
key	**võti**	[ʋɪti]
bunch (of keys)	**võtmekimp**	[ʋɪtʲmekimp]
to creak (door hinge)	**kriuksuma**	[kriuksuma]

creak	**kriuks**	[kriuks]
hinge (of door)	**uksehing**	[uksehiŋ]
doormat	**uksematt**	[uksemattʲ]

door lock	**lukk**	[lukk]
keyhole	**lukuauk**	[lukuauk]
bolt (sliding bar)	**riiv**	[riːʋ]
door latch	**riiv**	[riːʋ]
padlock	**tabalukk**	[tabalukk]

to ring (~ the door bell)	**helistama**	[helistama]
ringing (sound)	**uksekella helin**	[uksekella helin]
doorbell	**uksekell**	[uksekeʎ]
doorbell button	**kellanupp**	[kellanupp]
knock (at the door)	**koputus**	[koputus]
to knock (vi)	**koputama**	[koputama]

code	**kood**	[koːd]
code lock	**koodlukk**	[koːdlukk]
door phone	**sisetelefon**	[sisetelefon]
number (on the door)	**number**	[number]
doorplate	**tabel**	[tabeʎ]
peephole	**uksesilm**	[uksesiʎm]

90. Country house

village	**küla**	[kyla]
vegetable garden	**aiamaa**	[ajamaː]
fence	**tara**	[tara]

| picket fence | **hekk** | [hekk] |
| wicket gate | **aiavärav** | [ajaʋʲæraʋ] |

| granary | **ait** | [ajt] |
| cellar | **kelder** | [keʎder] |

| shed (in garden) | **kuur** | [kuːr] |
| well (water) | **kaev** | [kaəʋ] |

| stove (wood-fired ~) | **ahi** | [ahi] |
| to stoke the stove | **kütma** | [kytma] |

| firewood | **ahjupuud** | [aɦjypuːd] |
| log (firewood) | **puuhalg** | [puːhalg] |

| veranda, stoop | **veranda** | [ʋeranda] |
| terrace (patio) | **terrass** | [terrassʲ] |

| front steps | **välistrepp** | [ʋʲælistrepp] |
| swing (hanging seat) | **kiik** | [kiːk] |

91. Villa. Mansion

country house	maamaja	[mɑːmɑæ]
villa (by sea)	villa	[ʋillɑ]
wing (of building)	välistrepp	[ʋʲælistrepp]

garden	aed	[ɑed]
park	park	[pɑrk]
tropical greenhouse	kasvuhoone	[kɑsʋuhoːne]
to look after (garden, etc.)	hoolitsema	[hoːlitsema]

swimming pool	bassein	[bɑssejn]
gym	spordisaal	[spordisɑːʎ]
tennis court	tenniseväljak	[tenʲiseʋʲæʎæk]
home theater room	kino	[kino]
garage	garaaž	[gɑrɑːʒ]

private property	eraomand	[erɑomɑnd]
private land	eravaldus	[erɑʋɑʎdus]

warning (caution)	hoiatus	[hojɑtus]
warning sign	kirjalik hoiatus	[kirʲælik hojɑtus]

security	valve	[ʋɑʎʋe]
security guard	turvamees	[turʋɑmeːs]
burglar alarm	signalisatsioon	[signɑlisɑtsioːn]

92. Castle. Palace

castle	loss	[lossʲ]
palace	loss	[lossʲ]
fortress	kindlus	[kindlus]

wall (round castle)	kindlusemüür	[kindlusemyːr]
tower	torn	[torn]
keep, donjon	peatorn	[peɑtorn]

portcullis	tõstetav värav	[tɨstetɑʋ ʋʲærɑʋ]
underground passage	maa-alune käik	[mɑː ɑlune kʲæjk]
moat	vallikraav	[ʋɑllikrɑːʋ]

chain	kett	[kettʲ]
arrow loop	laskeava	[lɑskeɑʋɑ]

magnificent (adj)	suurepärane	[suːrepʲ ærɑne]
majestic (adj)	suursugune	[suːrsugune]

impregnable (adj)	juurdepääsmatu	[yurdepæːsmɑtu]
medieval (adj)	keskaegne	[keskɑəgne]

93. Apartment

apartment	korter	[korter]
room	tuba	[tubɑ]
bedroom	magamistuba	[mɑgɑmistubɑ]
dining room	söögituba	[søːgitubɑ]
living room	külalistuba	[kylɑlistubɑ]
study (home office)	kabinet	[kɑbinet]

entry room	esik	[əsik]
bathroom	vannituba	[ʋɑŋitubɑ]
half bath	tualett	[tuɑlet]

ceiling	lagi	[lɑgi]
floor	põrand	[pɪrɑnd]
corner	nurk	[nurk]

94. Apartment. Cleaning

to clean (vi, vt)	korda tegema	[kordɑ tegemɑ]
to put away (to stcw)	ära koristama	[ərɑ koristɑmɑ]
dust	tolm	[toʎm]
dusty (adj)	tolmune	[toʎmune]
to dust (vt)	tolmu pühkima	[toʎmu pyhkimɑ]
vacuum cleaner	tolmuimeja	[toʎmuimeæ]
to vacuum (vt)	tolmuimejaga koristama	[toʎmuimeæga koristɑmɑ]

to sweep (vi, vt)	pühkima	[pyhkimɑ]
sweepings	prügi	[prygi]
order	kord	[kord]
disorder, mess	korralagedus	[korrɑlɑgedus]

mop	hari	[hɑri]
dust cloth	lapp	[lɑpp]
broom	luud	[luːd]
dustpan	prügikühvel	[prygikyhʋeʎ]

95. Furniture. Interior

furniture	mööbel	[møːbəʎ]
table	laud	[lɑud]
chair	tool	[toːʎ]
bed	voodi	[ʋoːdi]
couch, sofa	diivan	[diːʋɑn]
armchair	tugitool	[tugitoːʎ]
bookcase	raamatukapp	[rɑːmɑtukɑpp]
shelf	raamaturiiul	[rɑːmɑturiːuʎ]

set of shelves	riiul	[riːuʎ]
wardrobe	riidekapp	[riːdekɑpp]
coat rack	varn	[ʋɑrn]
coat stand	nagi	[nɑgi]

| dresser | kummut | [kummut] |
| coffee table | diivanilaud | [diːʋɑnilɑud] |

mirror	peegel	[peːgeʎ]
carpet	vaip	[ʋɑjp]
rug, small carpet	uksematt	[uksemɑttʲ]

fireplace	kamin	[kɑmin]
candle	küünal	[kyːnɑʎ]
candlestick	küünlajalg	[kyːnlɑælg]

drapes	külgkardinad	[kyʎgkardinɑd]
wallpaper	tapeet	[tɑpeːt]
blinds (jalousie)	ribakardinad	[ribɑkardinɑd]

table lamp	laualamp	[lɑuɑlɑmp]
wall lamp (sconce)	valgusti	[ʋɑlgusti]
floor lamp	põrandalamp	[pɪrɑndɑlɑmp]
chandelier	lühter	[lyhter]

leg (of chair, table)	jalg	[ælg]
armrest	käetugi	[kæːtugi]
back (backrest)	seljatugi	[seʎætugi]
drawer	sahtel	[sɑhteʎ]

96. Bedding

bedclothes	voodipesu	[ʋoːdipesu]
pillow	padi	[pɑdi]
pillowcase	padjapüür	[pɑdʲæpyːr]
blanket (comforter)	tekk	[tekk]
sheet	voodilina	[ʋoːdilinɑ]
bedspread	voodikate	[ʋoːdikɑte]

97. Kitchen

kitchen	köök	[køːk]
gas	gaas	[gɑːs]
gas cooker	gaasipliit	[gɑːsipliːt]
electric cooker	elektripliit	[əlektripliːt]
oven	praeahi	[prɑeɑhi]
microwave oven	mikrolaineahi	[mikrolɑjnəɑhi]
refrigerator	külmkapp	[kyʎmkɑpp]

| freezer | jääkapp | [æːkɑpp] |
| dishwasher | nõudepesumasin | [nɪudepesumɑsin] |

meat grinder	hakklihamasin	[hɑkklihɑmɑsin]
juicer	mahlapress	[mɑhlɑpress]
toaster	röster	[røstər]
mixer	mikser	[mikser]

coffee maker	kohvikeetja	[kohʋikeːtʲæ]
coffee pot	kohvikann	[kohʋikɑŋʲ]
coffee grinder	kohviveski	[kohʋiʋeski]

kettle	veekeetja	[ʋeːkeːtʲæ]
teapot	teekann	[teːkɑŋʲ]
lid	kaas	[kɑːs]
tea strainer	teesõel	[teːsɪʎ]

spoon	lusikas	[lusikɑs]
teaspoon	teelusikas	[teːlusikɑs]
tablespoon	supilusikas	[supilusikɑs]
fork	kahvel	[kɑhʋeʎ]
knife	nuga	[nugɑ]
tableware (dishes)	toidunõud	[tojdunɪud]
plate (dinner ~)	taldrik	[tɑldrik]
saucer	alustass	[ɑlustɑssʲ]

shot glass	napsiklaas	[nɑpsiklɑːs]
glass (~ of water)	klaas	[klɑːs]
cup	tass	[tɑssʲ]

sugar bowl	suhkrutoos	[suhkrutoːs]
salt shaker	soolatoos	[soːlɑtoːs]
pepper shaker	pipratops	[piprɑtops]
butter dish	võitoos	[ʋɪjtoːs]

saucepan	pott	[pottʲ]
frying pan	pann	[pɑŋʲ]
ladle	supikulp	[supikuʎp]
colander	kurnkopsik	[kurŋkopsik]
tray	kandik	[kɑndik]

bottle	pudel	[pudeʎ]
jar (glass)	purk	[purk]
can	purk	[purk]

bottle opener	pudeliavaja	[pudeliɑʋɑæ]
can opener	konserviavaja	[konserʋiɑʋɑæ]
corkscrew	korgitser	[korgitʲser]
filter	filter	[fiʎter]
to filter (vt)	filtreerima	[fiʎtreːrimɑ]
trash	prügi	[prygi]
trash can	prügiämber	[prygiəmber]

98. Bathroom

bathroom	vannituba	[ʋɑŋitubɑ]
water	vesi	[ʋesi]
tap, faucet	kraan	[krɑːn]
hot water	soe vesi	[soə ʋesi]
cold water	külm vesi	[kyʌm ʋesi]
toothpaste	hambapasta	[hɑmbɑpɑstɑ]
to brush one's teeth	hambaid pesema	[hɑmbɑjd pesəmɑ]
to shave (vi)	habet ajama	[hɑbet ɑæmɑ]
shaving foam	habemeajamiskreem	[hɑbemeɑæmiskreːm]
razor	pardel	[pɑrdəʌ]
to wash (one's hands, etc.)	pesema	[pesemɑ]
to take a bath	ennast pesema	[əŋɑst pesemɑ]
shower	dušš	[duʃ]
to take a shower	duši all käima	[duʃi ɑʌ kʲæjmɑ]
bathtub	vann	[ʋɑŋʲ]
toilet (toilet bowl)	WC-pott	[ʋeːtse: pottʲ]
sink (washbasin)	kraanikauss	[krɑːnikɑussʲ]
soap	seep	[seːp]
soap dish	seebikarp	[seːbikɑrp]
sponge	nuustik	[nuːstik]
shampoo	šampoon	[ʃɑmpoːn]
towel	käterätik	[kʲæterʲætik]
bathrobe	hommikumantel	[hommikumɑnteʌ]
laundry (process)	pesupesemine	[pesupesemine]
washing machine	pesumasin	[pesumɑsin]
to do the laundry	pesu pesema	[pesu pesemɑ]
laundry detergent	pesupulber	[pesupuʌber]

99. Household appliances

TV set	televiisor	[teleʋiːsor]
tape recorder	magnetofon	[mɑgnetofon]
video, VCR	videomagnetofon	[ʋideomɑgnetofon]
radio	raadio	[rɑːdio]
player (CD, MP3, etc.)	pleier	[plejer]
video projector	videoprojektor	[ʋideoproektor]
home movie theater	kodukino	[kodukino]
DVD player	DVD-mängija	[deːʋeːdeː mʲæŋiæ]
amplifier	võimendi	[ʋɪjmendi]

video game console	mängukonsool	[mˈæŋukonsoːʎ]
video camera	videokaamera	[ʋideokaːmera]
camera (photo)	fotoaparaat	[fotoɑpɑrɑːt]
digital camera	fotokaamera	[fotokɑːmera]

vacuum cleaner	tolmuimeja	[toʎmuimeæ]
iron (e.g., steam ~)	triikraud	[triːkrɑud]
ironing board	triikimislaud	[triːkimislɑud]

telephone	telefon	[telefon]
mobile phone	mobiiltelefon	[mobiːʎtelefon]
typewriter	kirjutusmasin	[kirjytusmɑsin]
sewing machine	õmblusmasin	[ɪmblusmɑsin]

microphone	mikrofon	[mikrofon]
headphones	kõrvaklapid	[kɪrʋɑklɑpid]
remote control (TV)	pult	[puʎt]

CD, compact disc	CD-plaat	[tseːdeː plɑːt]
cassette	kassett	[kɑssett]
vinyl record	heliplaat	[heliplɑːt]

100. Repairs. Renovation

renovations	remont	[remont]
to renovate (vt)	remonti tegema	[remonti tegemɑ]
to repair (vt)	remontima	[remontimɑ]
to put in order	korda tegema	[kordɑ tegemɑ]
to redo (do again)	ümber tegema	[ymber tegemɑ]

paint	värv	[ʋˈæru]
to paint (~ a wall)	värvima	[ʋˈæruimɑ]
house painter	maaler	[mɑːler]
paintbrush	pintsel	[pintseʎ]

| whitewash | lubivärv | [lubiʋˈæru] |
| to whitewash (vt) | valgendama | [ʋɑlgendɑmɑ] |

wallpaper	tapeet	[tɑpeːt]
to wallpaper (vt)	tapeeti panema	[tɑpeːti pɑnemɑ]
varnish	lakk	[lɑkk]
to varnish (vt)	lakkima	[lɑkkimɑ]

101. Plumbing

water	vesi	[ʋesi]
hot water	soe vesi	[soə ʋesi]
cold water	külm vesi	[kyʎm ʋesi]

tap, faucet	kraan	[krɑːn]
drop (of water)	tilk	[tiʌk]
to drip (vi)	tilkuma	[tiʌkuma]
to leak (ab. pipe)	läbi jooksma	[ʌæbi joːksma]
leak (pipe ~)	leke	[leke]
puddle	loik	[lojk]

pipe	toru	[toru]
stop valve	ventiil	[ʋentiːʌ]
to be clogged up	umbe minema	[umbe minema]

tools	tööriistad	[tøːriːstɑd]
adjustable wrench	mutrivõti	[mutriʋiti]
to unscrew, untwist (vt)	lahti keerama	[lɑhti keːrɑmɑ]
to screw (tighten)	kinni keerama	[kiɲi keːrɑmɑ]

to unclog (vt)	puhastama	[puhɑstɑmɑ]
plumber	torulukksepp	[torulukksepp]
basement	kelder	[keʌder]
sewerage (system)	kanalisatsioon	[kɑnɑlisɑtsioːn]

102. Fire. Conflagration

fire (to catch ~)	tuli	[tuli]
flame	leek	[leːk]
spark	säde	[sʲæde]
smoke (from fire)	suits	[sujts]
torch (flaming stick)	tõrvik	[tɪrʋik]
campfire	lõke	[lɪke]

gas, gasoline	bensiin	[bensiːn]
kerosene (for aircraft)	petrooleum	[petroːleum]
flammable (adj)	põlevaine	[pileʋɑjne]
explosive (adj)	plahvatusohtlik	[plɑhʋɑtusohtlik]
NO SMOKING	MITTE SUITSETADA!	[mitte sujtsetɑdɑ]

safety	tuleohutus	[tuleohutus]
danger	oht	[oht]
dangerous (adj)	ohtlik	[ohtlik]

to catch fire	põlema minema	[pilemɑ minemɑ]
explosion	plahvatus	[plɑhʋɑtus]
to set fire	süütama	[syːtɑmɑ]
incendiary (arsonist)	süütaja	[syːtɑæ]
arson	süütamine	[syːtɑmine]

to blaze (vi)	leegitsema	[leːgitsemɑ]
to burn (be on fire)	põlema	[pilemɑ]
to burn down	maha põlema	[mɑhɑ pilemɑ]
fireman	tuletõrjuja	[tuletɪrjyæ]

fire truck	tuletõrjeauto	[tuletɪrjeauto]
fire department	tuletõrjemeeskond	[tuletɪrjeme:skond]
fire truck ladder	redel	[redeʎ]

fire hose	voolik	[ʋo:lik]
fire extinguisher	tulekustuti	[tulekustuti]
helmet	kiiver	[ki:ʋer]
siren	sireen	[sire:n]

to call out	karjuma	[karjyma]
to call for help	appi kutsuma	[appi kutsuma]
rescuer	päästja	[pæ:stʲæ]
to rescue (vt)	päästma	[pæ:stma]

to arrive (vi)	kohale sõitma	[kohale sɪjtma]
to extinguish (vt)	kustutama	[kustutama]
water	vesi	[ʋesi]
sand	liiv	[li:ʋ]

ruins (destruction)	varemed	[ʋaremed]
to collapse (building, etc.)	kokku kukkuma	[kokku kukkuma]
to fall down (vi)	kokku langema	[kokku laŋema]
to cave in (ceiling, floor)	kokku varisema	[kokku ʋarisema]

| piece of wreckage | tükk | [tykk] |
| ash | tuhk | [tuhk] |

| to suffocate (die) | lämbuma | [ʎæmbuma] |
| to be killed (perish) | hukkuma | [hukkuma] |

HUMAN ACTIVITIES

Job. Business. Part 1

103. Office. Working in the office

office (of firm)	**kontor**	[kontor]
office (of director, etc.)	**kabinet**	[kabinet]
secretary	**sekretär**	[sekretʲær]
director	**direktor**	[direktor]
manager	**juht**	[yht]
accountant	**raamatupidaja**	[rɑːmɑtupidɑæ]
employee	**töötaja**	[tøːtɑæ]
furniture	**mööbel**	[møːbeʌ]
desk	**laud**	[laud]
desk chair	**tugitool**	[tugitoːʌ]
chest of drawers	**kapp**	[kɑpp]
coat stand	**nagi**	[nɑgi]
computer	**arvuti**	[ɑrʋuti]
printer	**printer**	[printer]
fax machine	**faks**	[fɑks]
photocopier	**koopiamasin**	[koːpiɑmɑsin]
paper	**paber**	[pɑber]
office supplies	**kantseleikaubad**	[kɑntselejkɑubɑd]
mouse pad	**hiirevaip**	[hiːreʋɑjp]
sheet (of paper)	**leht**	[leht]
folder, binder	**mapp**	[mɑpp]
catalog	**kataloog**	[kɑtɑloːg]
phone book (directory)	**teatmik**	[teɑtmik]
documentation	**dokumendid**	[dokumendid]
brochure	**brošüür**	[broʃyːr]
(e.g., 12 pages ~)		
leaflet	**lendleht**	[lendleht]
sample	**näidis**	[næjdis]
training meeting	**treening**	[treːniŋ]
meeting (of managers)	**nõupidamine**	[nɪupidɑmine]
lunch time	**lõunavaheaeg**	[lɪunɑʋɑheɑeg]
to make a copy	**koopiat tegema**	[koːpiɑt tegemɑ]
to make copies	**paljundama**	[pɑʌjyndɑmɑ]

to receive a fax	**faksi saama**	[fɑksi sɑːmɑ]
to send a fax	**faksi saatma**	[fɑksi sɑːtmɑ]
to call (by phone)	**helistama**	[helistɑmɑ]
to answer (vt)	**vastama**	[ʋɑstɑmɑ]
to put through	**ühendama**	[yhendɑmɑ]
to arrange, to set up	**määrama**	[mæːrɑmɑ]
to demonstrate (vt)	**demonstreerima**	[demonstreːrimɑ]
to be absent	**puuduma**	[puːdumɑ]
absence	**vahelejätmine**	[ʋɑheleætmine]

104. Business processes. Part 1

occupation	**asi**	[ɑsi]
firm	**firma**	[firmɑ]
company	**kompanii**	[kompɑniː]
corporation	**korporatsioon**	[korporɑtsioːn]
enterprise	**ettevõte**	[etteʋɪte]
agency	**agentuur**	[ɑgentuːr]
agreement (contract)	**leping**	[lepiŋ]
contract	**kontraht**	[kontrɑht]
deal	**tehing**	[tehiŋ]
order (to place an ~)	**tellimus**	[tellimus]
term (of contract)	**tingimus**	[tiŋimus]
wholesale (adv)	**hulgi**	[huʎgi]
wholesale (adj)	**hulgi-**	[huʎgi]
wholesale (n)	**hulgimüük**	[huʎgimyːk]
retail (adj)	**jae**	[æe]
retail (n)	**jaemüük**	[æːmyːk]
competitor	**konkurent**	[koŋkurent]
competition	**konkurents**	[koŋkurents]
to compete (vi)	**konkureerima**	[koŋkureːrimɑ]
partner (associate)	**partner**	[pɑrtner]
partnership	**partnerlus**	[pɑrtnerlus]
crisis	**kriis**	[kriːs]
bankruptcy	**pankrot**	[pɑŋkrot]
to go bankrupt	**pankrotistuma**	[pɑŋkrotistumɑ]
difficulty	**raskus**	[rɑskus]
problem	**probleem**	[probleːm]
catastrophe	**katastroof**	[kɑtɑstroːf]
economy	**majandus**	[mɑændus]
economic (~ growth)	**majanduslik**	[mɑænduslik]
economic recession	**majanduslangus**	[mɑænduslɑŋus]

| goal (aim) | eesmärk | [eesmʲærk] |
| task | ülesanne | [ylesɑŋe] |

to trade (vi)	kauplema	[kɑuplemɑ]
network (distribution ~)	võrk	[ʋɪrk]
inventory (stock)	ladu	[lɑdu]
assortment	valik	[ʋɑlik]

leader (leading company)	liider	[liːder]
large (~ company)	suur	[suːr]
monopoly	monopol	[monopoʎ]

theory	teooria	[teoːriæ]
practice	praktika	[prɑktikɑ]
experience (in my ~)	kogemus	[kogemus]
trend (tendency)	trend	[trend]
development	areng	[ɑrəŋ]

105. Business processes. Part 2

| benefit, profit | kasu | [kɑsu] |
| profitable (adj) | kasulik | [kɑsulik] |

delegation (group)	delegatsioon	[delegɑtsioːn]
salary	töötasu	[tøːtɑsu]
to correct (an error)	parandama	[pɑrɑndɑmɑ]
business trip	lähetus	[ʎæhetus]
commission	komisjon	[komisʲon]

to control (vt)	kontrollima	[kontrollimɑ]
conference	konverents	[konʋerents]
license	litsents	[litsents]
reliable (~ partner)	usaldusväärne	[usɑʎdusʋæːrne]

initiative (undertaking)	algatus	[ɑʎgɑtus]
norm (standard)	norm	[norm]
circumstance	asjaolu	[asʲæolu]
duty (of employee)	kohustus	[kohustus]

organization (company)	organisatsioon	[orgɑnisɑtsioːn]
organization (process)	korraldamine	[korrɑʎdamine]
organized (adj)	organiseeritud	[orgɑniseːritud]
cancellation	ärajätmine	[ærɑætmine]
to cancel (call off)	ära jätma	[ærɑ ætmɑ]
report (official ~)	aruanne	[ɑruɑŋe]

patent	patent	[pɑtent]
to patent (obtain patent)	patenti saama	[pɑtenti sɑːmɑ]
to plan (vt)	planeerima	[plɑneːrimɑ]
bonus (money)	preemia	[preːmiɑ]

| professional (adj) | professionaalne | [professionɑːʎne] |
| procedure | protseduur | [protseduːr] |

to examine (contract, etc.)	läbi vaatama	[ʎæbi ʋɑːtɑmɑ]
calculation	arvestus	[ɑrʋestus]
reputation	reputatsioon	[reputɑtsioːn]
risk	risk	[risk]

to manage, to run	juhtima	[yhtimɑ]
information	andmed	[ɑndmed]
property	omand	[omɑnd]
union	liit	[liːt]

life insurance	elukindlustus	[əlukindlustus]
to insure (vt)	kindlustama	[kindlustɑmɑ]
insurance	kindlustus	[kindlustus]

auction (~ sale)	oksjon	[oksʲon]
to notify (inform)	teavitama	[teɑʋitɑmɑ]
management (process)	juhtimine	[yhtimine]
service (~ industry)	teenus	[teːnus]

forum	foorum	[foːrum]
to function (vi)	funktsioneerima	[fuŋktsioneːrimɑ]
stage (phase)	etapp	[ətɑpp]
legal (~ services)	juriidiline	[yriːdiline]
lawyer (legal expert)	jurist	[yrist]

106. Production. Works

plant	tehas	[tehɑs]
factory	vabrik	[ʋɑbrik]
workshop	tsehh	[tseh]
works, production site	tootmine	[toːtmine]

industry	tööstus	[tøːstus]
industrial (adj)	tööstuslik	[tøːstuslik]
heavy industry	rasketööstus	[rɑsketøːstus]
light industry	kergetööstus	[kergetøːstus]

products	toodang	[toːdɑŋ]
to produce (vt)	tootma	[toːtmɑ]
raw materials	tooraine	[toːrɑjne]

foreman	brigadir	[brigɑdir]
workers team	brigaad	[brigɑːd]
worker	tööline	[tøːline]

| working day | tööpäev | [tøːpæːʋ] |
| pause | seisak | [sejsɑk] |

| meeting | koosolek | [ko:solek] |
| to discuss (vt) | arutama | [arutama] |

plan	plaan	[pla:n]
to fulfill the plan	plaani täitma	[pla:ni tʲæjtma]
rate of output	norm	[norm]
quality	kvaliteet	[kʋalite:t]
checking (control)	kontroll	[kontroʎ]
quality control	kvaliteedikontroll	[kʋalite:dikontroʎ]

work safety	tööohutus	[tø:ohutus]
discipline	distsipliin	[distʲsipli:n]
violation	rikkumine	[rikkumine]
(of safety rules, etc.)		
to violate (rules)	rikkuma	[rikkuma]

| strike | streik | [strejk] |
| striker | streikija | [strejkiæ] |

| to be on strike | streikima | [strejkima] |
| labor union | ametiühing | [ametiyhiŋ] |

to invent (machine, etc.)	leiutama	[lejutama]
invention	leiutis	[lejutis]
research	uurimine	[u:rimine]
to improve (make better)	parendama	[parendama]

| technology | tehnoloogia | [tehnolo:gia] |
| technical drawing | joonis | [jo:nis] |

load, cargo	koorem	[ko:rem]
loader (person)	laadija	[la:diæ]
to load (vehicle, etc.)	laadima	[la:dima]
loading (process)	laadimine	[la:dimine]

| to unload (vi, vt) | maha laadima | [maha la:dima] |
| unloading | mahalaadimine | [mahala:dimine] |

transportation	transport	[transport]
transportation company	transpordikompanii	[transpordikompani:]
to transport (vt)	transportima	[transportima]

freight car	vagun	[ʋagun]
cistern	tsistern	[tʲsistern]
truck	veoauto	[ʋeoauto]

| machine tool | tööpink | [tø:piŋk] |
| mechanism | mehhanism | [mehanism] |

industrial waste	jäätmed	[æ:tmed]
packing (process)	pakkimine	[pakkimine]
to pack (vt)	pakkima	[pakkima]

107. Contract. Agreement

contract	kontraht	[kontrɑht]
agreement	kokkulepe	[kokkulepe]
addendum	lisa	[lisɑ]
to sign a contract	kontrahti sõlmima	[kontrɑhti sɪʎmimɑ]
signature	allkiri	[ɑʎkiri]
to sign (vt)	allkirjastama	[ɑʎkirʲæstɑmɑ]
stamp (seal)	pitsat	[pitsɑt]
subject of contract	lepingu objekt	[lepiŋu objekt]
clause	punkt	[puŋkt]
parties (in contract)	osapooled	[osɑpoːled]
legal address	juriidiline aadress	[yriːdiline ɑːdres]
to break the contract	kontrahti rikkuma	[kontrɑhti rikkumɑ]
commitment	kohustus	[kohustus]
responsibility	vastutus	[ʋɑstutus]
force majeure	vääramatu jõud	[ʋæːrɑmɑtu jɪud]
dispute	vaidlus	[ʋɑjdlus]
penalties	karistusmeetmed	[kɑristusmeːtmed]

108. Import & Export

import	sissevedu	[sisseʋedu]
importer	sissevedaja	[sisseʋedɑæ]
to import (vt)	sisse vedama	[sisse ʋedɑmɑ]
import (e.g., ~ goods)	sissevedu	[sisseʋedu]
exporter	väljavedaja	[ʋʲæʎæʋedɑæ]
to export (vi, vt)	välja vedama	[ʋʲæʎæ ʋedɑmɑ]
goods	kaup	[kɑup]
consignment, lot	partii	[pɑrtiː]
weight	kaal	[kɑːl]
volume	maht	[mɑht]
cubic meter	kuupmeeter	[kuːpmeːter]
manufacturer	tootja	[toːtʲæ]
transportation company	transpordikompanii	[trɑnspordikompɑniː]
container	konteiner	[kontejner]
border	riigipiir	[riːgipiːr]
customs	toll	[toʎ]
customs duty	tollilõiv	[tolliljʲu]
customs officer	tolliametnik	[tolliɑmetnik]
smuggling	salakaubandus	[sɑlɑkɑubɑndus]
contraband (goods)	salakaup	[sɑlɑkɑup]

109. Finances

stock (share)	**aktsia**	[aktsia]
bond (certificate)	**obligatsioon**	[obligatsio:n]
bill of exchange	**veksel**	[ʋekseʎ]
stock exchange	**börs**	[børs]
stock price	**aktsiate kurss**	[aktsiate kurs]
to go down	**odavnema**	[odaʋnema]
to go up	**kallinema**	[kallinema]
controlling interest	**kontrollpakk**	[kontroʎpakk]
investment	**investeeringud**	[inʋeste:riŋud]
to invest (vt)	**investeerima**	[inʋeste:rima]
percent	**protsent**	[protsent]
interest (on investment)	**protsendid**	[protsendid]
profit	**kasum**	[kasum]
profitable (adj)	**kasumiga**	[kasumiga]
tax	**maks**	[maks]
currency (foreign ~)	**valuuta**	[ʋalu:ta]
national (adj)	**rahvuslik**	[rahʋuslik]
exchange (currency ~)	**vahetus**	[ʋahetus]
accountant	**raamatupidaja**	[ra:matupidaæ]
accounting	**raamatupidamine**	[ra:matupidamine]
bankruptcy	**pankrot**	[paŋkrot]
collapse, crash	**nurjumine**	[nurjymine]
ruin	**laostumine**	[laostumine]
to be ruined	**laostuma**	[laostuma]
inflation	**inflatsioon**	[inflatsio:n]
devaluation	**devalvatsioon**	[deʋaʎʋatsio:n]
capital	**kapital**	[kapital]
income	**tulu**	[tulu]
turnover	**käive**	[kʲæjʋe]
resources	**ressursid**	[resursid]
monetary resources	**rahalised vahendid**	[rahalised ʋahendid]
to reduce (expenses)	**vähendama**	[ʋʲæhendama]

110. Marketing

marketing	**turu-uurimine**	[turu u:rimine]
market	**turg**	[turg]
market segment	**turuosa**	[turuosa]
product	**toode**	[to:de]

goods	kaup	[kɑup]
trademark	kaubamärk	[kɑubɑmʲærk]
logotype	firmamärk	[firmɑmʲærk]
logo	logotüüp	[logoty:p]

demand	nõudmine	[nıudmine]
supply	pakkumine	[pɑkkumine]
need	vajadus	[ʋɑædus]
consumer	tarbija	[tɑrbiæ]

analysis	analüüs	[ɑnɑly:s]
to analyze (vt)	analüüsima	[ɑnɑly:simɑ]
positioning	positsioneerimine	[positsone:rimine]
to position (vt)	positsioneerima	[positsone:rimɑ]

price	hind	[hind]
pricing policy	hinnapoliitika	[hiŋɑpoli:tikɑ]
formation of price	hinnakujundamine	[hiŋɑkuyndɑmine]

111. Advertising

advertising	reklaam	[reklɑ:m]
to advertise (vt)	reklaamima	[reklɑ:mimɑ]
budget	eelarve	[ee人ærʋe]

ad, advertisement	reklaam	[reklɑ:m]
TV advertising	telereklaam	[telereklɑ:m]
radio advertising	raadioreklaam	[rɑ:dioreklɑ:m]
outdoor advertising	välisreklaam	[ʋʲælisreklɑ:m]

mass media	massiteabevahendid	[mɑssiteɑbeʋɑhendid]
periodical (n)	perioodilised väljaanded	[perio:dilised ʋʲæ人ʲæɑnded]
image (public appearance)	imago	[imɑgo]
slogan	loosung	[lo:suŋ]
motto (maxim)	juhtlause	[yhtlɑuse]

campaign	kampaania	[kɑmpɑ:niɑ]
advertising campaign	reklaamikampaania	[reklɑ:mikɑmpɑ:niɑ]
target group	huvirühm	[huʋiryhm]

business card	visiitkaart	[ʋisi:tkɑ:rt]
leaflet	lendleht	[lendleht]
brochure (e.g., 12 pages ~)	brošüür	[broʃy:r]
pamphlet	buklett	[buklet]
newsletter	bülletään	[bylletæ:n]

store sign	silt	[si人t]
poster	plakat	[plɑkɑt]
billboard	reklaamtahvel	[reklɑ:mtɑhʋe人]

112. Banking

bank	pank	[paŋk]
branch (of bank, etc.)	osakond	[osakond]

bank clerk, consultant	konsultant	[konsuʌtant]
manager (director)	juhataja	[yhataæ]

banking account	pangakonto	[paŋakonto]
account number	arve number	[arʋe number]
checking account	jooksev arve	[joːkseʋ arʋe]
savings account	kogumisarve	[kogumisarʋe]

to open an account	arvet avama	[arʋet aʋama]
to close the account	arvet lõpetama	[arʋet lɪpetama]
to deposit into the account	arvele panema	[arʋele panema]
to withdraw (vt)	arvelt võtma	[arʋeʌt ʋɪtma]

deposit	hoius	[hojus]
to make a deposit	hoiust tegema	[hojust tegema]
wire transfer	ülekanne	[ylekaŋe]
to wire, to transfer	üle kandma	[yle kandma]

sum	summa	[summa]
How much?	Kui palju?	[kuj paʌjy]

signature	allkiri	[aʌkiri]
to sign (vt)	allkirjastama	[aʌkirʲæstama]

credit card	krediidikaart	[krediːdikaːrt]
code	kood	[koːd]
credit card number	krediidikaardi number	[krediːdikaːrdi number]
ATM	pangaautomaat	[paŋaːutomaːt]

check	tšekk	[tʃek]
to write a check	tšekki välja kirjutama	[tʃekki ʋʲæʌæ kirjytama]
checkbook	tšekiraamat	[tʃekiraːmat]

loan (bank ~)	pangalaen	[paŋalaen]
to apply for a loan	laenu taotlema	[laenu taotlema]
to get a loan	laenu võtma	[laenu ʋɪtma]
to give a loan	laenu andma	[laenu andma]
guarantee	tagatis	[tagatis]

113. Telephone. Phone conversation

telephone	telefon	[telefon]
mobile phone	mobiiltelefon	[mobiːʌtelefon]
answering machine	automaatvastaja	[automaːtʋastaæ]

| to call (telephone) | helistama | [helistama] |
| phone call | telefonihelin | [telefonihelin] |

to dial a number	numbrit valima	[numbrit valima]
Hello!	hallo!	[hallo]
to ask (vt)	küsima	[kysima]
to answer (vi, vt)	vastama	[vastama]

to hear (vt)	kuulma	[kuːʎma]
well (adv)	hästi	[hæsti]
not well (adv)	halvasti	[haʎvasti]
noises (interference)	häired	[hæjred]

receiver	telefonitoru	[telefonitoru]
to pick up (~ the phone)	toru hargilt võtma	[toru hargiʎt vitma]
to hang up (~ the phone)	toru hargile panema	[toru hargile panema]

busy (adj)	liin on kinni	[liːn on kiŋi]
to ring (ab. phone)	telefon heliseb	[telefon heliseb]
telephone book	telefoniraamat	[telefoniraːmat]

local (adj)	kohalik kõne	[kohalik kɪne]
long distance (~ call)	kaugekõne	[kaugekɪne]
international (adj)	rahvusvaheline	[rahvusvaheline]

114. Mobile telephone

mobile phone	mobiiltelefon	[mobiːʎtelefon]
display	kuvar	[kuvar]
button	nupp	[nupp]
SIM card	SIM-kaart	[sim kaːrt]

battery	patarei	[patarej]
to be dead (battery)	tühjaks minema	[tyhæks minema]
charger	laadimisseade	[laːdimisseade]

| menu | menüü | [menyu] |
| settings | häälestused | [hæːlestused] |

| tune (melody) | viis | [viːs] |
| to select (vt) | valima | [valima] |

| calculator | kalkulaator | [kalkulaːtor] |
| voice mail | automaatvastaja | [automaːtvastaæ] |

| alarm clock | äratuskell | [əratuskeʎ] |
| contacts | telefoniraamat | [telefoniraːmat] |

| SMS (text message) | SMS-sõnum | [əsəməs sɪnum] |
| subscriber | abonent | [abonent] |

115. Stationery

| ballpoint pen | pastakas | [pɑstɑkɑs] |
| fountain pen | sulepea | [sulepeɑ] |

pencil	pliiats	[pli:ɑts]
highlighter	marker	[mɑrker]
felt-tip pen	viltpliiats	[ʋiʌtpli:ɑts]

| notepad | klade | [klɑde] |
| agenda (diary) | päevik | [pæ:ʋik] |

ruler	joonlaud	[jo:nlɑud]
calculator	kalkulaator	[kɑlkulɑ:tor]
eraser	kustutuskumm	[kustutuskumm]
thumbtack	rõhknael	[rɪhknɑəʌ]
paper clip	kirjaklamber	[kirʲæklɑmber]

glue	liim	[li:m]
stapler	stepler	[stepler]
hole punch	auguraud	[ɑugurɑud]
pencil sharpener	pliiatsiteritaja	[pli:ɑtsiteritɑæ]

116. Various kinds of documents

account (report)	aruanne	[ɑruɑŋe]
agreement	kokkulepe	[kokkulepe]
application form	tellimusavaldus	[tellimusɑʋɑʌdus]
authentic (adj)	originaaldokument	[originɑ:ʌdokument]
badge (identity tag)	nimesilt	[nimesiʌt]
business card	visiitkaart	[ʋisi:tkɑ:rt]

certificate (~ of quality)	sertifikaat	[sertifikɑ:t]
check (e.g., draw a ~)	pangatšekk	[pɑŋɑtʃek]
check (in restaurant)	arve	[ɑrʋe]
constitution	konstitutsioon	[konstitutsio:n]

contract	leping	[lepiŋ]
copy	ärakiri	[ærakiri]
copy (of contract, etc.)	eksemplar	[eksemplɑr]

customs declaration	deklaratsioon	[deklɑrɑtsio:n]
document	dokument	[dokument]
driver's license	juhiload	[yhilɑad]
addendum	lisa	[lisɑ]
form	ankeet	[ɑŋke:t]

| identity card, ID | tõend | [tɪ:nd] |
| inquiry (request) | järelepärimine | [ærelepʲærimine] |

| invitation card | **kutse** | [kutse] |
| invoice | **arve** | [arʋe] |

law	**seadus**	[seadus]
letter (mail)	**kiri**	[kiri]
letterhead	**plank**	[plaŋk]
list (of names, etc.)	**nimekiri**	[nimekiri]
manuscript	**käsikiri**	[kʲæsikiri]
newsletter	**bülletään**	[bylletæːn]
note (short message)	**sedel**	[sedeʎ]

pass (for worker, visitor)	**sissepääsuluba**	[sissepæːsuluba]
passport	**pass**	[passʲ]
permit	**luba**	[luba]
résumé	**elulookirjeldus**	[əluloːkirjeldus]
debt note, IOU	**vastuvõtmist tõendav allkiri**	[ʋastuʋɪtmist tɪːndaʋ aʎkiri]
receipt (for purchase)	**kviitung**	[kʋiːtuŋ]
sales slip, receipt	**kassatšekk**	[kassatʃek]
report	**raport**	[raport]

to show (ID, etc.)	**esitama**	[əsitama]
to sign (vt)	**allkirjastama**	[aʎkirʲæstama]
signature	**allkiri**	[aʎkiri]
stamp (seal)	**pitsat**	[pitsat]
text	**tekst**	[tekst]
ticket (for entry)	**pilet**	[pilet]

| to cross out | **maha tõmbama** | [maha tɪmbama] |
| to fill out (~ a form) | **täitma** | [tʲæjtma] |

| waybill | **saateleht** | [saːteleht] |
| will (testament) | **testament** | [testament] |

117. Kinds of business

advertising	**reklaam**	[reklaːm]
advertising agency	**reklaamiagentuur**	[reklaːmiagentuːr]
air-conditioners	**konditsioneerid**	[konditsioneːrid]
airline	**lennukompanii**	[leŋukompaniː]

alcoholic drinks	**alkohoolsed joogid**	[alkohoːʎsed joːgid]
antiquities	**antikvariaat**	[antikʋariaːt]
art gallery	**galerii**	[galeriː]
audit services	**audititeenused**	[audititeːnused]

banks	**pangandus**	[paŋandus]
bar	**baar**	[baːr]
beauty parlor	**ilusalong**	[ilusaloŋ]
bookstore	**raamatukauplus**	[raːmatukauplus]

brewery	õlletehas	[ɪlletehɑs]
business center	ärikeskus	[ærikeskus]
business school	majanduskool	[mɑændusko:ʎ]

casino	kasiino	[kɑsi:no]
construction	ehitus	[əhitus]
consulting	konsulteerimine	[konsuʎte:rimine]

dental clinic	stomatoloogia	[stomɑtolo:giɑ]
design	disain	[disɑjn]
drugstore, pharmacy	apteek	[ɑpte:k]
dry cleaners	keemiline puhastus	[ke:miline puhɑstus]
employment agency	kaadriagentuur	[kɑ:driɑgentu:r]

financial services	finantsteenused	[finɑnʦte:nused]
food products	toiduained	[tojduɑjned]
funeral home	matusebüroo	[mɑtusebyro:]
furniture (e.g., house ~)	mööbel	[mø:bəʎ]
garment	riided	[ri:ded]
hotel	hotell	[hoteʎ]

ice-cream	jäätis	[æ:tis]
industry	tööstus	[tø:stus]
insurance	kindlustus	[kindlustus]
Internet	internet	[internet]
investment	investeeringud	[inʋeste:riŋud]

jeweler	juveliir	[yʋeli:r]
jewelry	juveelikaubad	[yʋe:likɑubɑd]
laundry (shop)	pesumaja	[pesumɑæ]
legal advisor	õigusabi	[ɪjgusɑbi]
light industry	kergetööstus	[kergetø:stus]

| magazine | ajakiri | [ɑæki

ri] |
mail-order selling	kataloogikaubandus	[kɑtɑlo:gikɑubɑndus]
medicine	meditsiin	[meditsijn]
movie theater	kino	[kino]
museum	muuseum	[mu:seum]

news agency	teadete agentuur	[teɑdete ɑgentu:r]
newspaper	ajaleht	[ɑæleht]
nightclub	ööklubi	[ø:klubi]

oil (petroleum)	nafta	[nɑftɑ]
parcels service	kulleriteenistus	[kullerite:nistus]
pharmaceuticals	farmaatsia	[fɑrmɑ:ʦiæ]
printing (industry)	polügraafia	[poligrɑ:fiæ]
publishing house	kirjastus	[kirˈæstus]

radio (~ station)	raadio	[rɑ:dio]
real estate	kinnisvara	[kiŋisʋɑrɑ]
restaurant	restoran	[restorɑn]

security agency	**turvafirma**	[turʋafirmɑ]
sports	**sport**	[sport]
stock exchange	**börs**	[børs]
store	**kauplus**	[kɑuplus]
supermarket	**supermarket**	[supermɑrket]
swimming pool	**bassein**	[bɑssejn]
tailors	**ateljee**	[ateʎjeə]
television	**televisioon**	[teleʋisio:n]
theater	**teater**	[teɑter]
trade	**kaubandus**	[kɑubɑndus]
transportation	**kaubavedu**	[kɑubɑʋedu]
travel	**turism**	[turism]
veterinarian	**loomaarst**	[lo:mɑ:rst]
warehouse	**ladu**	[lɑdu]
waste collection	**prügivedu**	[prygiʋedu]

Job. Business. Part 2

118. Show. Exhibition

exhibition, show	näitus	[ɲæjtus]
trade show	kaubandusnäitus	[kɑubɑndusɲæjtus]
participation	osavõtt	[osɑuɪtt]
to participate (vi)	osa võtma	[osɑ uɪtmɑ]
participant (exhibitor)	osavõtja	[osɑuɪtʲæ]
director	direktor	[direktor]
organizer	organisaator	[orgɑnisɑːtor]
to organize (vt)	korraldama	[korrɑʎdɑmɑ]
participation form	osavõtuavaldus	[osɑuɪtuɑuɑʎdus]
to fill out (vt)	täitma	[tʲæjtmɑ]
details	üksikasjad	[yksikɑsʲæd]
information	teave	[teɑue]
price	hind	[hind]
including	kaasa arvatud	[kɑːsɑ ɑruɑtud]
to include (vt)	sisaldama	[sisɑʎdɑmɑ]
to pay (vi, vt)	maksma	[mɑksmɑ]
registration fee	registreerimistasu	[registreːrimistɑsu]
entrance	sissepääs	[sissepæːs]
pavilion, hall	paviljon	[pɑuiʎon]
to register (vt)	registreerima	[registreːrimɑ]
badge (identity tag)	nimesilt	[nimesiʎt]
booth, stand	stend	[stend]
to reserve, to book	reserveerima	[reserue:rimɑ]
display case	vitriin	[uitri:n]
spotlight	lamp	[lɑmp]
design	disain	[disɑjn]
to place (put, set)	paigutama	[pɑjgutɑmɑ]
distributor	maaletooja	[mɑːleto:æ]
supplier	tarnija	[tɑrniæ]
country	riik	[ri:k]
foreign (adj)	välismaine	[uʲælismɑjne]
product	toode	[to:de]
association	assotsiatsioon	[ɑssotsiɑtsio:n]
conference hall	konverentsisaal	[konuerentsisɑ:ʎ]

congress	kongress	[koŋress]
contest (competition)	konkurss	[koŋkurss]

visitor	külastaja	[kylɑstɑæ]
to visit (attend)	külastama	[kylɑstɑmɑ]
customer	tellija	[telliæ]

119. Mass Media

newspaper	ajaleht	[ɑæleht]
magazine	ajakiri	[ɑækiri]
press (printed media)	press	[press]
radio	raadio	[rɑːdio]
radio station	raadiojaam	[rɑːdioæɑm]
television	televisioon	[teleʋisioːn]

presenter, host	saatejuht	[sɑːteyht]
newscaster	diktor	[diktor]
commentator	kommentaator	[kommentɑːtor]

journalist	ajakirjanik	[ɑækirʲænik]
correspondent (reporter)	korrespondent	[korrespondent]
press photographer	fotokorrespondent	[fotokorrespondent]
reporter	reporter	[reporter]

editor	toimetaja	[tojmetɑæ]
editor-in-chief	peatoimetaja	[peɑtojmetɑæ]

to subscribe (to ...)	tellima	[tellimɑ]
subscription	tellimine	[tellimine]
subscriber	tellija	[telliæ]
to read (vi, vt)	lugema	[lugemɑ]
reader	lugeja	[lugeæ]

circulation (of newspaper)	tiraaž	[tirɑːʒ]
monthly (adj)	igakuine	[igɑkujne]
weekly (adj)	iganädalane	[igɑɲædɑlɑne]
issue (edition)	number	[number]
new (~ issue)	värske	[ʋʲærske]

headline	pealkiri	[peɑʎkiri]
short article	sõnum	[sınum]
column (regular article)	rubriik	[rubriːk]
article	artikkel	[ɑrtikkeʎ]
page	lehekülg	[lehekyʎg]

reportage, report	reportaaž	[reportɑːʒ]
event (happening)	sündmus	[syndmus]
sensation (news)	sensatsioon	[sensɑtsioːn]
scandal	skandaal	[skɑndɑːl]

| scandalous (adj) | skandaalne | [skɑndɑːʎne] |
| great (~ scandal) | kõmuline | [kɪmuline] |

program	saade	[sɑːde]
interview	intervjuu	[interʋjy]
live broadcast	otseülekanne	[otseylekɑŋe]
channel	kanal	[kɑnɑl]

120. Agriculture

agriculture	põllumajandus	[pɪllumɑændus]
peasant (masc.)	talumees	[tɑlumeːs]
peasant (fem.)	talunaine	[tɑlunɑjne]
farmer	talunik	[tɑlunik]

| tractor | traktor | [trɑktor] |
| combine, harvester | kombain | [kombɑjn] |

plow	sahk	[sɑhk]
to plow (vi, vt)	kündma	[kyndmɑ]
plowland	künnimaa	[kyŋimɑː]
furrow (in field)	vagu	[ʋɑgu]

to sow (vi, vt)	külvama	[kyʎʋɑmɑ]
seeder	külvik	[kyʎʋik]
sowing (process)	külv	[kyʎʋ]

| scythe | vikat | [ʋikɑt] |
| to mow, to scythe | niitma | [niːtmɑ] |

| spade (tool) | labidas | [lɑbidɑs] |
| to dig (to till) | kaevama | [kɑeʋɑmɑ] |

hoe	kõbla	[kɪblɑ]
to hoe, to weed	rohima	[rohimɑ]
weed (plant)	umbrohi	[umbrohi]

watering can	kastekann	[kɑstekɑŋʲ]
to water (plants)	kastma	[kɑstmɑ]
watering (act)	kastmine	[kɑstmine]

| pitchfork | vigla | [ʋiglɑ] |
| rake | reha | [rehɑ] |

fertilizer	väetis	[ʋæːtis]
to fertilize (vt)	väetama	[ʋæːtɑmɑ]
manure (fertilizer)	sõnnik	[sɪŋik]

| field | põld | [pɪʎd] |
| meadow | luht | [luht] |

vegetable garden	**aiamaa**	[ajamɑː]
orchard (e.g., apple ~)	**aed**	[aed]
to pasture (vt)	**karjatama**	[karˈætama]
herdsman	**karjus**	[karjys]
pastureland	**karjamaa**	[karˈæmɑː]
cattle breeding	**loomakasvatus**	[loːmakasʋatus]
sheep farming	**lambakasvatus**	[lambakasʋatus]
plantation	**istandus**	[istandus]
row (garden bed ~s)	**peenar**	[peːnar]
hothouse	**kasvuhoone**	[kasʋuhoːne]
drought (lack of rain)	**põud**	[pɪud]
dry (~ summer)	**põuane**	[pɪuane]
cereal crops	**viljad**	[ʋiʎæd]
to harvest, to gather	**koristama**	[koristama]
miller (person)	**mölder**	[møʎdər]
mill (e.g., gristmill)	**veski**	[ʋeski]
to grind (grain)	**vilja jahvatama**	[ʋiʎæ æhʋatama]
flour	**jahu**	[æhu]
straw	**õled**	[ɪled]

121. Building. Building process

construction site	**ehitus**	[əhitus]
to build (vt)	**ehitama**	[əhitama]
construction worker	**ehitaja**	[əhitaæ]
project	**projekt**	[proekt]
architect	**arhitekt**	[arhitekt]
worker	**tööline**	[tøːline]
foundation (of building)	**vundament**	[ʋundament]
roof	**katus**	[katus]
foundation pile	**vai**	[ʋaj]
wall	**sein**	[sejn]
reinforcing bars	**armatuur**	[armatuːr]
scaffolding	**tellingud**	[telliŋud]
concrete	**betoon**	[betoːn]
granite	**graniit**	[graniːt]
stone	**kivi**	[kiʋi]
brick	**telliskivi**	[telliskiʋi]
sand	**liiv**	[liːʋ]
cement	**tsement**	[ʦement]

plaster (for walls)	krohv	[krohʊ]
to plaster (vt)	krohvima	[krohʊimɑ]
paint	värv	[ʋˈæaerʊ]
to paint (~ a wall)	värvima	[ʋˈæaerʊimɑ]
barrel	tünn	[tyŋ']

crane	kraana	[krɑ:nɑ]
to lift (vt)	tõstma	[tɪstmɑ]
to lower (vt)	alla laskma	[ɑllɑ lɑskmɑ]

bulldozer	buldooser	[buʌdo:ser]
excavator	ekskavaator	[ekskɑʊɑ:tor]
scoop, bucket	kopp	[kopp]
to dig (excavate)	kaevama	[kɑeʊɑmɑ]
hard hat	kiiver	[ki:ʋer]

122. Science. Research. Scientists

science	teadus	[teɑdus]
scientific (adj)	teaduslik	[teɑduslik]
scientist	teadlane	[teɑdlɑne]
theory	teooria	[teo:riæ]

axiom	aksioom	[ɑksio:m]
analysis	analüüs	[ɑnɑly:s]
to analyze (vt)	analüüsima	[ɑnɑly:simɑ]
argument (strong ~)	argument	[ɑrgument]
substance (matter)	aine	[ɑjne]

hypothesis	hüpotees	[hypote:s]
dilemma	dilemma	[dilemmɑ]
dissertation	väitekiri	[ʋˈæjtekiri]
dogma	dogma	[dogmɑ]

doctrine	doktriin	[doktri:n]
research	uurimine	[u:rimine]
to do research	uurima	[u:rimɑ]
testing	katse	[kɑtse]
laboratory	labor	[lɑbor]

method	meetod	[me:tod]
molecule	molekul	[molekul]
monitoring	seire	[sejre]
discovery (act, event)	avastus	[ɑʊastus]

postulate	postulaat	[postulɑ:t]
principle	põhimõte	[pɪhimɪte]
forecast	prognoos	[progno:s]
prognosticate (vt)	prognoosima	[progno:simɑ]
synthesis	süntees	[synte:s]

trend (tendency)	**trend**	[trend]
theorem	**teoreem**	[teore:m]
teachings	**õpetus**	[ɪpetus]
fact	**tõsiasi**	[tɪsiɑsi]
expedition	**ekspeditsioon**	[əkspeditsio:n]
experiment	**eksperiment**	[əksperiment]
academician	**akadeemik**	[ɑkɑde:mik]
bachelor (e.g., ~ of Arts)	**bakalaureus**	[bɑkɑlɑureus]
doctor (PhD)	**doktor**	[doktor]
Associate Professor	**dotsent**	[dotsent]
Master (e.g., ~ of Arts)	**magister**	[mɑgister]
professor	**professor**	[professor]

Professions and occupations

123. Job search. Dismissal

job	töö	[tø:]
staff (work force)	koosseis	[ko:ssejs]
career	karjäär	[karʲæər]
prospects	perspektiiv	[perspekti:ʋ]
skills (mastery)	meisterlikkus	[mejsterlikkus]
selection (screening)	valik	[ʋɑlik]
employment agency	kaadriagentuur	[ka:driɑgentu:r]
résumé	elulookirjeldus	[əlulo:kirjeldus]
interview (for job)	tööintervjuu	[tø:interʋjyu]
vacancy, opening	vakants	[ʋɑkɑnts]
salary, pay	töötasu	[tø:tɑsu]
fixed salary	palk	[pɑʎk]
pay, compensation	maksmine	[mɑksmine]
position (job)	töökoht	[tø:koht]
duty (of employee)	kohustus	[kohustus]
range of duties	kohustuste ring	[kohustuste riŋ]
busy (I'm ~)	hõivatud	[hijʋɑtud]
to fire (dismiss)	vallandama	[ʋɑllɑndɑmɑ]
dismissal	vallandamine	[ʋɑllɑndɑmine]
unemployment	tööpuudus	[tø:pu:dus]
unemployed (n)	töötu	[tø:tu]
retirement	pension	[pensʲon]
to retire (from job)	pensionile minema	[pensʲonile minemɑ]

124. Business people

director	direktor	[direktor]
manager (director)	juhataja	[yhɑtɑæ]
boss	juhataja	[yhɑtɑæ]
superior	ülemus	[ylemus]
superiors	juhtkond	[yhtkond]
president	president	[president]
chairman	esimees	[əsime:s]

deputy (substitute)	asetäitja	[ɑset'æjt'æ]
assistant	abi	[ɑbi]
secretary	sekretär	[sekret'ær]
personal assistant	isiklik sekretär	[isiklik sekret'ær]

businessman	ärimees	[ærime:s]
entrepreneur	ettevõtja	[ətteʋɪt'æ]
founder	rajaja	[rɑæ:]
to found (vt)	rajama	[rɑæmɑ]

incorporator	asutaja	[ɑsutɑæ]
partner	partner	[pɑrtner]
stockholder	aktsionär	[ɑktsioɲær]

| millionaire | miljonär | [miʌ'oɲær] |
| billionaire | miljardär | [miʌærd'ær] |

| owner, proprietor | omanik | [omɑnik] |
| landowner | maavaldaja | [mɑ:ʋɑldɑæ] |

client	klient	[klient]
regular client	püsiklient	[pysiklient]
buyer (customer)	ostja	[ost'æ]
visitor	külastaja	[kylɑstɑæ]

professional (n)	professionaal	[professionɑ:l]
expert	ekspert	[əkspert]
specialist	spetsialist	[spetsiɑlist]

| banker | pankur | [pɑŋkur] |
| broker | vahendaja | [ʋɑhendɑæ] |

cashier, teller	kassiir	[kɑssi:r]
accountant	raamatupidaja	[rɑ:mɑtupidɑæ]
security guard	turvamees	[turʋɑme:s]

investor	investeerija	[inʋeste:riæ]
debtor	võlgnik	[ʋɪʌgnik]
creditor	võlausaldaja	[ʋɪlausɑʌdɑæ]
borrower	laenaja	[lɑenɑæ]

| importer | sissevedaja | [sisseʋedɑæ] |
| exporter | väljavedaja | [ʋ'æʌæʋedɑæ] |

manufacturer	tootja	[to:t'æ]
distributor	maaletooja	[mɑ:leto:æ]
middleman	vahendaja	[ʋɑhendɑæ]

consultant	konsultant	[konsuʌtɑnt]
sales representative	esindaja	[əsindɑæ]
agent	agent	[ɑgent]
insurance agent	kindlustusagent	[kindlustusɑgent]

125. Service professions

cook	kokk	[kokk]
chef (kitchen chef)	peakokk	[peakokk]
baker	pagar	[pagar]

bartender	baarimees	[bɑːrimeːs]
waiter	kelner	[keʌner]
waitress	ettekandja	[ettekandʲæ]

lawyer, attorney	advokaat	[aduokaːt]
lawyer (legal expert)	jurist	[yrist]
notary	notar	[notar]

electrician	elektrik	[əlektrik]
plumber	torulukksepp	[torulukksepp]
carpenter	puussepp	[puːssepp]

masseur	massöör	[massøːr]
masseuse	massöör	[massøːr]
doctor	arst	[arst]

taxi driver	taksojuht	[taksoyht]
driver	autojuht	[autoyht]
delivery man	käskjalg	[kʲæskʰælg]

chambermaid	toatüdruk	[toatydruk]
security guard	turvamees	[turuameːs]
flight attendant	stjuardess	[styardess]

teacher (in primary school)	õpetaja	[ɪpetaæ]
librarian	raamatukoguhoidja	[raːmatukoguhojdʲæ]
translator	tõlk	[tɪʌk]
interpreter	tõlk	[tɪʌk]
guide	giid	[giːd]

hairdresser	juuksur	[yːksur]
mailman	postiljon	[postiʌʲon]
salesman (store staff)	müüja	[myːæ]

gardener	aednik	[aədnik]
domestic servant	teener	[teːner]
maid	teenija	[teːniæ]
cleaner (cleaning lady)	koristaja	[koristaæ]

126. Military professions and ranks

private	reamees	[reameːs]
sergeant	seersant	[seːrsant]

| lieutenant | leitnant | [lejtnɑnt] |
| captain | kapten | [kɑpten] |

major	major	[mɑør]
colonel	kolonel	[kolonel]
general	kindral	[kindrɑl]
marshal	marssal	[mɑrsɑl]
admiral	admiral	[ɑdmirɑl]

military man	sõjaväelane	[sıæʋæːlɑne]
soldier	sõdur	[sıdur]
officer	ohvitser	[ohʋitsər]
commander	komandör	[komɑndør]

border guard	piirivalvur	[piːriʋɑʎuur]
radio operator	radist	[rɑdist]
scout (searcher)	luuraja	[luːrɑæ]
pioneer (sapper)	sapöör	[sɑpøːr]
marksman	laskur	[lɑskur]
navigator	tüürimees	[tyːrimeːs]

127. Officials. Priests

| king | kuningas | [kuniŋɑs] |
| queen | kuninganna | [kuniŋɑŋɑ] |

| prince | prints | [prints] |
| princess | printsess | [printsess] |

| tsar, czar | tsaar | [tsɑːr] |
| czarina | tsaarinna | [tsɑːriŋɑ] |

president	president	[president]
Secretary (~ of State)	minister	[minister]
prime minister	peaminister	[peɑminister]
senator	senaator	[senɑːtor]

diplomat	diplomaat	[diplomɑːt]
consul	konsul	[konsul]
ambassador	suursaadik	[suːrsɑːdik]
advisor (military ~)	nõunik	[nıunik]

official (civil servant)	ametnik	[ɑmetnik]
prefect	prefekt	[prefekt]
mayor	linnapea	[liŋɑpeɑ]

judge	kohtunik	[kohtunik]
district attorney (prosecutor)	prokurör	[prokurør]
missionary	misjonär	[misʲoɲær]

monk	munk	[muŋk]
abbot	abee	[abe:]
rabbi	rabi	[rabi]

vizier	vesiir	[ʋesi:r]
shah	šahh	[ʃah]
sheikh	šeih	[ʃəjh]

128. Agricultural professions

beekeeper	mesinik	[mesinik]
herder, shepherd	karjus	[karjys]
agronomist	agronoom	[agrono:m]
cattle breeder	loomakasvataja	[lo:makasʋataæ]
veterinarian	loomaarst	[lo:ma:rst]

farmer	talunik	[talunik]
winemaker	veinimeister	[ʋejnimejster]
zoologist	zooloog	[zo:lo:g]
cowboy	kauboi	[kauboj]

129. Art professions

| actor | näitleja | [ɲæjtleæ] |
| actress | näitlejanna | [ɲæjtleæŋa] |

| singer (masc.) | laulja | [lauʎæ] |
| singer (fem.) | lauljanna | [lauʎæŋa] |

| dancer (masc.) | tantsija | [tantsiæ] |
| dancer (fem.) | tantsijanna | [tantsiæŋa] |

| performing artist (masc.) | näitleja | [ɲæjtleæ] |
| performing artist (fem.) | näitlejanna | [ɲæjtleæŋa] |

musician	muusik	[mu:sik]
pianist	pianist	[pianist]
guitar player	kitarrist	[kitarrist]

conductor (orchestra ~)	dirigent	[dirigent]
composer	helilooja	[helilo:æ]
impresario	impressaario	[imressa:rio]

movie director	lavastaja	[laʋastaæ]
producer	produtsent	[produtsent]
scriptwriter	stsenarist	[stsenarist]
critic	kriitik	[kri:tik]
writer	kirjanik	[kirˈænik]

poet	luuletaja	[luːletɑæ]
sculptor	skulptor	[skuʌptor]
artist (painter)	kunstnik	[kunstnik]

juggler	žonglöör	[ʒoŋløːr]
clown	kloun	[kloun]
acrobat	akrobaat	[ɑkrobɑːt]
magician	mustkunstnik	[mustkunstnik]

130. Various professions

doctor	arst	[ɑrst]
nurse	medõde	[medɪde]
psychiatrist	psühhiaater	[psyhiɑːter]
dentist	stomatoloog	[stomɑtoloːg]
surgeon	kirurg	[kirurg]

| astronaut | astronaut | [ɑstronɑut] |
| astronomer | astronoom | [ɑstronoːm] |

driver (of taxi, etc.)	autojuht	[ɑutoyht]
engineer (train driver)	vedurijuht	[ʋeduriyht]
mechanic	mehaanik	[mehɑːnik]

miner	kaevur	[kɑəʋur]
worker	tööline	[tøːline]
metalworker	lukksepp	[lukksepp]
joiner (carpenter)	tisler	[tisler]
turner	treial	[trejɑʌ]
construction worker	ehitaja	[əhitɑæ]
welder	keevitaja	[keːʋitɑæ]

professor (title)	professor	[professor]
architect	arhitekt	[ɑrhitekt]
historian	ajaloolane	[ɑæloːlɑne]
scientist	teadlane	[teɑdlɑne]
physicist	füüsik	[fyːsik]
chemist (scientist)	keemik	[keːmik]

archeologist	arheoloog	[ɑrheoloːg]
geologist	geoloog	[geoloːg]
researcher	uurija	[uːriæ]

| babysitter | lapsehoidja | [lɑpsehojdʲæ] |
| teacher, educator | pedagoog | [pedɑgoːg] |

editor	toimetaja	[tojmetɑæ]
editor-in-chief	peatoimetaja	[peɑtojmetɑæ]
correspondent	korrespondent	[korrespondent]
typist (fem.)	masinakirjutaja	[mɑsinɑkirjytɑæ]

designer	disainer	[disɑjner]
computer expert	arvutispetsialist	[ɑrʋutispetsiɑlist]
programmer	programmeerija	[progrɑmme:riæ]
engineer (designer)	insener	[insener]

sailor	meremees	[mereme:s]
seaman	madrus	[mɑdrus]
rescuer	päästja	[pæ:stʲæ]

fireman	tuletõrjuja	[tuletɪrjyæ]
policeman	politseinik	[politsejnik]
watchman	valvur	[ʋɑʎʋur]
detective	detektiiv	[detekti:ʋ]

customs officer	tolliametnik	[tolliɑmetnik]
bodyguard	ihukaitsja	[ihukɑjtsʲæ]
prison guard	järelvaataja	[æreʎʋɑ:tɑæ]
inspector	inspektor	[inspektor]

sportsman	sportlane	[sportlɑne]
trainer, coach	treener	[tre:ner]
butcher	lihunik	[lihunik]
cobbler	kingsepp	[kiŋsepp]
merchant	kaubareisija	[kaubɑrejsiæ]
loader (person)	laadija	[lɑ:diæ]

| fashion designer | moekunstnik | [moekunstnik] |
| model (fam.) | modell | [modeʎ] |

131. Occupations. Social status

| schoolboy | kooliõpilane | [ko:liɪpilɑne] |
| student (college ~) | üliõpilane | [yliɪpilɑne] |

philosopher	filosoof	[filoso:f]
economist	majandusteadlane	[mɑændusteɑdlɑne]
inventor	leiutaja	[lejutɑæ]

unemployed (n)	töötu	[tø:tu]
retiree	pensionär	[pensʲoɳær]
spy, secret agent	spioon	[spio:n]

prisoner	vang	[ʋɑŋ]
striker	streikija	[strejkiæ]
bureaucrat	bürokraat	[byrokrɑ:t]
traveler	rändur	[rʲændur]

homosexual	homoseksualist	[homoseksuɑlist]
hacker	häkker	[hækker]
bandit	bandiit	[bɑndi:t]

hit man, killer	**palgamõrvar**	[paʎgamɪrʋar]
drug addict	**narkomaan**	[narkomɑ:n]
drug dealer	**narkokaupmees**	[narkokaupme:s]
prostitute (fem.)	**prostituut**	[prostitu:t]
pimp	**sutenöör**	[sutenø:r]
sorcerer	**nõid**	[nɪjd]
sorceress	**nõiamoor**	[nɪjamo:r]
pirate	**piraat**	[pirɑ:t]
slave	**ori**	[ori]
samurai	**samurai**	[samuraj]
savage (primitive)	**metslane**	[metslane]

Sports

132. Kinds of sports. Sportspersons

sportsman	sportlane	[sportlɑne]
kind of sports	spordiala	[spordiɑlɑ]
basketball	korvpall	[korʊpɑʎ]
basketball player	korvpallur	[korʊpɑllur]
baseball	pesapall	[pesɑpɑʎ]
baseball player	pesapallur	[resɑpɑllur]
soccer	jalgpall	[ælgpɑʎ]
soccer player	jalgpallur	[ælgpɑllur]
goalkeeper	väravavaht	[ʊ'ærɑʊɑʊɑht]
hockey	hoki	[hoki]
hockey player	hokimängija	[hokimʲæŋiæ]
volleyball	võrkpall	[ʊɪrkpɑʎ]
volleyball player	võrkpallur	[ʊɪrkpɑllur]
boxing	poks	[poks]
boxer	poksija	[poksiæ]
wrestling	maadlus	[mɑːdlus]
wrestler	maadleja	[mɑːdleæ]
karate	karate	[kɑrɑtə]
karate fighter	karatist	[kɑrɑtist]
judo	judo	[ydo]
judo athlete	džuudomaadleja	[dʒydo mɑːdleæ]
tennis	tennis	[təŋis]
tennis player	tennisemängija	[təŋisemʲæŋiæ]
swimming	ujumine	[uymine]
swimmer	ujuja	[uyæ]
fencing	vehklemine	[ʊehklemine]
fencer	vehkleja	[ʊehkleæ]
chess	male	[mɑle]
chess player	maletaja	[mɑletɑæ]

| alpinism | alpinism | [aʌpinism] |
| alpinist | alpinist | [aʌpinist] |

| running | jooks | [joːks] |
| runner | jooksja | [joːksʲæ] |

| athletics | kergejõustik | [kergejʉstik] |
| athlete | atleet | [atleːt] |

| horseback riding | ratsasport | [ratsasport] |
| horse rider | ratsutaja | [ratsutaæ] |

figure skating	iluuisutamine	[iluːjsutamine]
figure skater (masc.)	iluuisutaja	[iluːjsutaæ]
figure skater (fem.)	iluuisutaja	[iluːjsutaæ]

weightlifting	raskejõustik	[raskejʉstik]
car racing	autovõidusõit	[autoʋijdusijt]
racing driver	võidusõitja	[ʋijdusijtʲæ]

| cycling | jalgrattasport | [ælgrattasijt] |
| cyclist | jalgrattur | [ælgrattur] |

broad jump	kaugushüpe	[kaugushype]
pole vault	teivashüpe	[tejʋashype]
jumper	hüppaja	[hyppaæ]

133. Kinds of sports. Miscellaneous

football	ameerika jalgpall	[ameːrika ælgpaʌ]
badminton	sulgpall	[suʌgpaʌ]
biathlon	laskesuusatamine	[laskesuːsatamine]
billiards	piljard	[piʌærd]

bobsled	bobisõit	[bobisijt]
bodybuilding	bodybilding	[bodibildiŋ]
water polo	veepall	[ʋeːpaʌ]
handball	väravpall	[ʋʲæraʋpaʌ]
golf	golf	[goʌf]

rowing	sõudmine	[sijudmine]
scuba diving	allveeujumine	[aʌʋeːujumine]
cross-country skiing	murdmaasuusatamine	[murdmaːsuːsatamine]
ping-pong	lauatennis	[lauateŋis]

sailing	purjesport	[purjesport]
rally racing	ralli	[ralli]
rugby	rägbi	[rʲægbi]
snowboarding	lumelauasõit	[lumelauasport]
archery	vibulaskmine	[ʋibulaskmine]

134. Gym

barbell	**kang**	[kɑŋ]
dumbbells	**hantlid**	[hɑntlid]
training machine	**trenazöör**	[trenaʒøːr]
bicycle trainer	**velotrenazöör**	[velotrenaʒøːr]
treadmill	**jooksurada**	[joːksurɑdɑ]
horizontal bar	**võimlemiskang**	[vɪjmlemiskɑŋ]
parallel bars	**rööbaspuud**	[røːbɑspuːd]
vaulting horse	**hobune**	[hobune]
mat (in gym)	**matt**	[mɑttʲ]
aerobics	**aeroobika**	[ɑeroːbikɑ]
yoga	**jooga**	[joːgɑ]

135. Hockey

hockey	**hoki**	[hoki]
hockey player	**hokimängija**	[hokimʲæŋiæ]
to play hockey	**jäähokit mängima**	[æːhokit mʲæŋimɑ]
ice	**jää**	[æː]
puck	**litter**	[litter]
hockey stick	**hokikepp**	[hokikepp]
ice skates	**uisud**	[ujsud]
board	**poord**	[poːrd]
shot	**vise**	[vise]
goaltender	**väravavaht**	[vʲæravauɑht]
goal (score)	**värav**	[vʲærav]
to score a goal	**väravat lööma**	[vʲæravat løːma]
period	**periood**	[perioːd]
substitutes bench	**varumängijate pink**	[varumʲæŋiæte piŋk]

136. Football

soccer	**jalgpall**	[ælgpaʎ]
soccer player	**jalgpallur**	[ælgpallur]
to play soccer	**jalgpalli mängima**	[ælgpalli mʲæŋima]
major league	**kõrgliiga**	[kɪrgliːga]
soccer club	**jalgpalliklubi**	[ælgpalliklubi]
coach	**treener**	[treːner]

owner, proprietor	**omanik**	[omanik]
team	**meeskond**	[meːskond]
team captain	**meeskonna kapten**	[meːskoŋa kapten]
player	**mängija**	[mʲæŋiæ]
substitute	**varumängija**	[ʋarumʲæŋiæ]

forward	**ründemängija**	[ryndemʲæŋiæ]
center forward	**keskründemängija**	[keskryndemʲæŋiæ]
striker, scorer	**väravakütt**	[ʋʲæraʋakyttʲ]
defender, back	**kaitsja**	[kajtsʲæ]
halfback	**poolkaitsja**	[poːʎkajtsʲæ]

match	**mäng**	[mʲæŋ]
to meet (vi, vt)	**kohtuma**	[kohtuma]
final	**finaal**	[finaːʎ]
semi-final	**poolfinaal**	[poːʎfinaːʎ]
championship	**meistrivõistlused**	[mejstriʋɪjstlusəd]

period, half	**poolaeg**	[poːlæːg]
first period	**esimene poolaeg**	[əsimene poːʎʲaeg]
half-time	**vaheaeg**	[ʋaheaeg]

goal	**värav**	[ʋʲæraʋ]
goalkeeper	**väravavaht**	[ʋʲæraʋaʋaht]
goalpost	**väravapost**	[ʋʲæraʋapostʲ]
crossbar	**värava põikpuu**	[ʋʲæraʋa pɪjkpuː]
net	**väravavõrk**	[ʋʲæraʋaʋɪrk]
to concede a goal	**palli väravasse laskma**	[palli ʋʲæraʋasse laskma]

ball	**pall**	[paʎ]
pass	**sööt**	[søːt]
kick	**löök**	[løːk]
to kick (~ the ball)	**lööma**	[løːma]
free kick	**trahvilöök**	[trahʋiløːk]
corner kick	**nurgalöök**	[nurgaløːk]

attack	**rünnak**	[ryŋak]
counterattack	**vasturünnak**	[ʋasturyŋak]
combination	**kombinatsioon**	[kombinatsioːn]

referee	**kohtunik**	[kohtunik]
to whistle (vi)	**vilistama**	[ʋilistama]
whistle (sound)	**vile**	[ʋile]
foul, misconduct	**rikkumine**	[rikkumine]
to commit a foul	**rikkuma**	[rikkuma]
to send off	**väljakult eemaldama**	[ʋʲæʎækuʎt əemaʎdama]

yellow card	**kollane kaart**	[kollane kaːrt]
red card	**punane kaart**	[punane kaːrt]
disqualification	**diskvalifitseerimine**	[diskʋalifitseerimine]
to disqualify (vt)	**diskvalifitseerima**	[diskʋalifitseerima]
penalty kick	**penalti**	[penaʎti]

wall	sein	[sejn]
to score (vi, vt)	lööma	[lø:ma]
goal (score)	värav	[ʋʲærɑʋ]
to score a goal	väravat lööma	[ʋʲærɑʋɑt lø:ma]

substitution	vahetus	[ʋɑhetus]
to replace (vt)	vahetama	[ʋɑhetɑmɑ]
rules	reeglid	[re:glid]
tactics	taktika	[tɑktikɑ]

stadium	staadion	[stɑ:dion]
stand (bleachers)	tribüün	[triby:n]
fan, supporter	fänn, poolehoidja	[fʲæŋ], [po:lehojdʲæ]
to shout (vi)	karjuma	[kɑrjymɑ]

| scoreboard | tabloo | [tɑblo:] |
| score | seis | [sejs] |

defeat	kaotus	[kɑotus]
to lose (not win)	kaotama	[kɑotɑmɑ]
draw	viik	[ʋi:k]
to draw (vi)	viiki mängima	[ʋi:ki mʲæŋimɑ]

victory	võit	[ʋɯjt]
to win (vi, vt)	võitma	[ʋɯjtmɑ]
champion	tšempion	[t͡ʃempion]
best (adj)	parim	[pɑrim]
to congratulate (vt)	õnnitlema	[ɯŋitlemɑ]

commentator	kommentaator	[kommentɑ:tor]
to commentate (vt)	kommenteerima	[kommente:rimɑ]
broadcast	saade	[sɑ:de]

137. Alpine skiing

skis	suusad	[su:sɑd]
to ski (vi)	suusatama	[su:sɑtɑmɑ]
mountain-ski resort	mäesuusatamiskuurort	[mʲæesu:sɑtɑmisku:rort]
ski lift	tõstuk	[tɪstuk]

ski poles	suusakepid	[su:sɑkepid]
slope	nõlv	[nɪʎʊ]
slalom	slaalom	[slɑ:lom]

138. Tennis. Golf

| golf | golf | [goʎf] |
| golf club | golfiklubi | [goʎfiklubi] |

golfer	golfimängija	[goʌfimˈæŋiæ]
hole	auk	[ɑuk]
club	golfikepp	[goʌfikepp]
golf trolley	käru	[kˈæru]

tennis	tennis	[teŋis]
tennis court	tenniseväljak	[teŋiseʊˈæʎæk]
serve	serv	[serʊ]
to serve (vt)	servima	[serʊimɑ]
racket	reket	[rəket]
net	võrk	[ʊɪrk]
ball	pall	[pɑʎ]

139. Chess

chess	male	[mɑle]
chessmen	malendid	[mɑlendid]
chess player	maletaja	[mɑletɑæ]
chessboard	malelaud	[mɑlelɑud]
chessman	malend	[mɑlend]

| White (white pieces) | valged | [ʊɑlged] |
| Black (black pieces) | mustad | [mustɑd] |

pawn	ettur	[əttur]
bishop	oda	[odɑ]
knight	ratsu	[rɑtsu]
rook (castle)	vanker	[ʊɑŋker]
queen	lipp	[lipp]
king	kuningas	[kuniŋɑs]

move	käik	[kˈæjk]
to move (vi, vt)	käima	[kˈæjmɑ]
to sacrifice (vt)	ohverdama	[ohʊerdɑmɑ]
castling	vangerdus	[ʊɑŋerdus]
check	tuli	[tuli]
checkmate	matt	[mɑttˈ]

chess tournament	maleturniir	[mɑleturni:r]
Grand Master	suurmeister	[su:rmejster]
combination	kombinatsioon	[kombinɑtsio:n]
game (in chess)	partii	[pɑrti:]
checkers	kabe	[kɑbe]

140. Boxing

| boxing | poks | [poks] |
| fight (bout) | võistlus | [ʊɪjstlus] |

boxing match	kahevõitlus	[kɑheʋɪjstlus]
round (in boxing)	raund	[rɑund]

ring	ring	[riŋ]
gong	gong	[goŋ]

punch	löök	[løːk]
knock-down	nokdaun	[nokdɑun]
knockout	nokaut	[nokɑut]
to knock out	nokauti lööma	[nokɑuti løːmɑ]

boxing glove	poksikinnas	[poksikiŋɑs]
referee	vahekohtunik	[ʋɑhekohtunik]

lightweight	kergekaal	[kergekɑːʎ]
middleweight	keskkaal	[keskkɑːʎ]
heavyweight	raskekaal	[rɑskekɑːʎ]

141. Sports. Miscellaneous

Olympic Games	Olümpiamängud	[olympiamʲæŋud]
winner	võitja	[ʋɪjtʲæ]
to be winning	võitma	[ʋɪjtmɑ]
to win (vi)	võitma	[ʋɪjtmɑ]

leader	liider	[liːder]
to lead (vi)	liidriks olema	[liːdriks olemɑ]

first place	esimene koht	[əsimene koht]
second place	teine koht	[tejne koht]
third place	kolmas koht	[koʎmɑs koht]

medal	medal	[medɑʎ]
trophy	trofee	[trofeː]
prize cup (trophy)	karikas	[kɑrikɑs]
prize (in game)	auhind	[ɑuhind]
main prize	peaauhind	[peɑːuhind]

record	rekord	[rekord]
to set a record	rekordit püstitama	[rekordit pystitɑmɑ]

final	finaal	[finɑːʎ]
final (adj)	finaal-	[finɑːʎ]

champion	tšempion	[tʃempion]
championship	meistrivõistlused	[mejstriʋɪjstlusəd]

stadium	staadion	[stɑːdion]
stand (bleachers)	tribüün	[tribyːn]
fan, supporter	poolehoidja	[poːlehojdʲæ]

opponent, rival	**vastane**	[ʋastane]
start	**start**	[start]
finish line	**finiš**	[finiʃ]
defeat	**kaotus**	[kaotus]
to lose (not win)	**kaotama**	[kaotama]
referee	**kohtunik**	[kohtunik]
jury	**žürii**	[ʒyriː]
score	**seis**	[sejs]
draw	**viik**	[ʋiːk]
to draw (vi)	**viiki mängima**	[ʋiːki mʲæŋima]
point	**punkt**	[puŋkt]
result (final score)	**tulemus**	[tulemus]
half-time	**vaheaeg**	[ʋaheaeg]
doping	**doping**	[dopiŋ]
to penalize (vt)	**karistama**	[karistama]
to disqualify (vt)	**diskvalifitseerima**	[diskʋalifitseerima]
apparatus	**vahend**	[ʋahend]
javelin	**oda**	[oda]
shot put ball	**kuul**	[kuːʎ]
ball (snooker, etc.)	**kuul**	[kuːʎ]
aim (target)	**sihtmärk**	[sihtmʲærk]
target	**märklaud**	[mʲærklaud]
to shoot (vi)	**tulistama**	[tulistama]
precise (~ shot)	**tabamine**	[tabamine]
trainer, coach	**treener**	[treːner]
to train (sb)	**treenima**	[treːnima]
to train (vi)	**treenima**	[treːnima]
training	**trenn**	[trenʲ]
gym	**spordisaal**	[spordisaːʎ]
exercise (physical)	**harjutus**	[harjytus]
warm-up (of athlete)	**soojendus**	[soːjendus]

Education

142. School

school	kool	[koːʎ]
headmaster	koolidirektor	[koːlidirektor]
pupil (boy)	õpilane	[ɪpilɑne]
pupil (girl)	õpilane	[ɪpilɑne]
schoolboy	kooliõpilane	[koːliɪpilɑne]
schoolgirl	koolitüdruk	[koːlitydruk]
to teach (sb)	õpetama	[ɪpetɑmɑ]
to learn (language, etc.)	õppima	[ɪppimɑ]
to learn by heart	pähe õppima	[pʲæhe ɪppimɑ]
to study (work to learn)	õppima	[ɪppimɑ]
to be in school	koolis käima	[koːlis kʲæɛjmɑ]
to go to school	kooli minema	[koːli minemɑ]
alphabet	tähestik	[tʲæhestik]
subject (at school)	õppeaine	[ɪppeɑjne]
classroom	klass	[klɑssʲ]
lesson	tund	[tuɲd]
recess	vahetund	[ʋɑhəuɲd]
school bell	kell	[keʎ]
school desk	koolipink	[koːlipiŋk]
chalkboard	tahvel	[tɑhʋeʎ]
grade	hinne	[hiŋe]
good grade	hea hinne	[heɑ hiŋe]
bad grade	halb hinne	[hɑʎb hiŋe]
to give a grade	hinnet panema	[hiŋet pɑnemɑ]
mistake, error	viga	[ʋigɑ]
to make mistakes	vigu tegema	[ʋigu tegemɑ]
to correct (an error)	parandama	[pɑrɑndɑmɑ]
cheat sheet	spikker	[spikker]
homework	kodune ülesanne	[kodune ylesɑŋe]
exercise (in education)	harjutus	[hɑrjytus]
to be present	kohal olema	[kohɑʎ olemɑ]
to be absent	puuduma	[puːdumɑ]
to punish (vt)	karistama	[kɑristɑmɑ]

punishment	**karistus**	[kɑristus]
conduct (behavior)	**käitumine**	[kʲæjtumine]
report card	**päevik**	[pæːʋik]
pencil	**pliiats**	[pliːɑts]
eraser	**kustutuskumm**	[kustutuskumm]
chalk	**kriit**	[kriːt]
pencil case	**pinal**	[pinɑl]
schoolbag	**portfell**	[portfeʎ]
pen	**sulepea**	[sulepeɑ]
school notebook	**vihik**	[ʋihik]
textbook	**õpik**	[ɪpik]
compasses	**sirkel**	[sirkeʎ]
to draw (a blueprint, etc.)	**joonestama**	[joːnestɑmɑ]
technical drawing	**joonis**	[joːnis]
poem	**luuletus**	[luːletus]
by heart (adv)	**peas olema**	[peɑs olemɑ]
to learn by heart	**pähe õppima**	[pʲæhe ɪppimɑ]
school vacation	**koolivaheaeg**	[koːliʋɑheɑeg]
to be on vacation	**koolivaheajal olema**	[koːliʋɑheɑæʎ olemɑ]
test (written math ~)	**kontrolltöö**	[kontroʎtøː]
essay (composition)	**kirjand**	[kirʲænd]
dictation	**etteütlus**	[ətteytlus]
exam	**eksam**	[əksɑm]
to take an exam	**eksamit sooritama**	[əksɑmit soːritɑmɑ]
experiment (chemical ~)	**katse**	[kɑtse]

143. College. University

academy	**akadeemia**	[ɑkɑdeːmiɑ]
university	**ülikool**	[ylikoːʎ]
faculty (section)	**teaduskond**	[teɑduskond]
student (masc.)	**üliõpilane**	[yliɪpilɑne]
student (fem.)	**üliõpilane**	[yliɪpilɑne]
lecturer (teacher)	**õppejõud**	[ɪppejɪud]
lecture hall, room	**auditoorium**	[ɑuditoːrium]
graduate	**ülikoolilõpetaja**	[ylikoːliliɪpetɑæ]
diploma	**diplom**	[diplom]
dissertation	**väitekiri**	[ʋʲæjtəkiri]
study (report)	**teaduslik töö**	[teɑduslik tøː]
laboratory	**labor**	[lɑbor]
lecture	**loeng**	[loəŋ]

course mate	kursusekaaslane	[kursuseka:slane]
scholarship	stipendium	[stipendium]
academic degree	teaduslik kraad	[teaduslik kra:d]

144. Sciences. Disciplines

mathematics	matemaatika	[matema:tika]
algebra	algebra	[algebra]
geometry	geomeetria	[geome:triæ]

astronomy	astronoomia	[astrono:mia]
biology	bioloogia	[biolo:gia]
geography	geograafia	[geogra:fia]
geology	geoloogia	[geolo:gia]
history	ajalugu	[aælugu]

medicine	meditsiin	[meditsijn]
pedagogy	pedagoogika	[pedago:gika]
law	õigus	[ijgus]

physics	füüsika	[fy:sika]
chemistry	keemia	[ke:mia]
philosophy	filosoofia	[filoso:fia]
psychology	psühholoogia	[psyholo:gia]

145. Writing system. Orthography

grammar	grammatika	[grammatika]
vocabulary	sõnavara	[sinavara]
phonetics	foneetika	[fone:tika]

noun	nimisõnad	[nimisinad]
adjective	omadussõnad	[omadussinad]
verb	tegusõna	[tegusina]
adverb	määrsõna	[mæ:rsina]

pronoun	asesõna	[asesina]
interjection	hüüdsõna	[hy:dsina]
preposition	eessõna	[eessina]

root	sõna tüvi	[sina tyui]
ending	lõpp	[lipp]
prefix	eesliide	[eesli:de]

syllable	silp	[siʌp]
suffix	järelliide	[æreʌi:de]
stress mark	rõhk	[rihk]
apostrophe	apostroof	[apostro:f]

period, dot	**punkt**	[puŋkt]
comma	**koma**	[koma]
semicolon	**semikoolon**	[semiko:lon]
colon	**koolon**	[ko:lon]
ellipsis	**kolmpunkt**	[koʌmpuŋkt]
question mark	**küsimärk**	[kysimʲærk]
exclamation point	**hüüumärk**	[hy:ymʲærk]
quotation marks	**jutumärgid**	[ytumʲærgid]
in quotation marks	**jutumärkides**	[ytumʲærkides]
parenthesis	**sulud**	[sulud]
in parenthesis	**sulgudes**	[suʌgudes]
hyphen	**sidekriips**	[sidekri:ps]
dash	**mõttekriips**	[mɪttekri:ps]
space (between words)	**sõnavahe**	[sɪnɑʋɑhe]
letter	**täht**	[tʲæht]
capital letter	**suur algustäht**	[su:r ɑʌgustʲæht]
vowel (n)	**täishäälik**	[tʲæjshæ:lik]
consonant (n)	**kaashäälik**	[kɑ:shæ:lik]
sentence	**pakkumine**	[pɑkkumine]
subject	**alus**	[ɑlus]
predicate	**öeldis**	[ø:ldis]
line	**rida**	[ridɑ]
on a new line	**uuelt realt**	[u:əʌt reaʌt]
paragraph	**lõik**	[lɪjk]
word	**sõna**	[sɪnɑ]
group of words	**sõnaühend**	[sɪnɑyhend]
expression	**väljend**	[ʋʲæʌjend]
synonym	**sünonüüm**	[synony:m]
antonym	**antonüüm**	[antony:m]
rule	**reegel**	[re:geʌ]
exception	**erand**	[ərand]
correct (adj)	**õige**	[ɪjge]
conjugation	**pööramine**	[pø:ramine]
declension	**käänamine**	[kæ:namine]
nominal case	**kääne**	[kæ:ne]
question	**küsimus**	[kysimus]
to underline (vt)	**alla kriipsutama**	[ɑllɑ kri:psutamɑ]
dotted line	**punktiir**	[puŋkti:r]

146. Foreign languages

language	keel	[ke:ʎ]
foreign language	võõrkeel	[ʋɪːrke:ʎ]
to study (vt)	uurima	[uːrima]
to learn (language, etc.)	õppima	[ɪppima]
to read (vi, vt)	lugema	[lugema]
to speak (vi, vt)	rääkima	[ræːkima]
to understand (vt)	aru saama	[aru saːma]
to write (vt)	kirjutama	[kirjytama]
fast (adv)	kiiresti	[kiːresti]
slowly (adv)	aeglaselt	[aeglaseʎt]
fluently (adv)	vabalt	[ʋabaʎt]
rules	reeglid	[reːglid]
grammar	grammatika	[grammatika]
vocabulary	sõnavara	[sɪnaʋara]
phonetics	foneetika	[foneːtika]
textbook	õpik	[ɪpik]
dictionary	sõnaraamat	[sɪnaraːmat]
teach-yourself book	õpik iseõppijaile	[ɪpik iseɪppiæjle]
phrasebook	vestmik	[ʋestmik]
cassette	kassett	[kassett]
videotape	videokassett	[ʋideokassett]
CD, compact disc	CD-plaat	[tse:de: plaːt]
DVD	DVD	[de: ʋe: de:]
alphabet	tähestik	[tʲæhestik]
to spell (vt)	veerima	[ʋeːrima]
pronunciation	hääldamine	[hæːʎdamine]
accent	aktsent	[aktsent]
with an accent	aktsendiga	[aktsendiga]
without an accent	ilma aktsendita	[iʎma aktsendita]
word	sõna	[sɪna]
meaning	mõiste	[mɪjste]
course (e.g., a French ~)	kursused	[kursused]
to sign up	kirja panema	[kirʲæ panema]
teacher	õppejõud	[ɪppejɪud]
translation (process)	tõlkimine	[tɪʎkimine]
translation (text, etc.)	tõlge	[tɪʎge]
translator	tõlk	[tɪʎk]
interpreter	tõlk	[tɪʎk]
polyglot	polüglott	[polyglott]
memory	mälu	[mʲælu]

147. Fairy tale characters

Santa Claus	**Jõuluvana**	[jɪuluʋɑnɑ]
mermaid	**Näkineid**	[ɲækinejd]
magician, wizard	**võlur**	[ʋɪlur]
fairy	**võlur**	[ʋɪlur]
magic (adj)	**võlu-**	[ʋɪlu]
magic wand	**võlukepike**	[ʋɪlukepike]
fairy tale	**muinasjutt**	[mujnɑsʰytt]
miracle	**ime**	[ime]
dwarf	**päkapikk**	[pʲækɑpikk]
to turn into …	**… muutuda**	[mu:tudɑ]
ghost	**kummitus**	[kummitus]
phantom	**viirastus**	[ʋi:rɑstus]
monster	**koletis**	[koletis]
dragon	**draakon**	[drɑ:kon]
giant	**hiiglane**	[hi:glɑne]

148. Zodiac Signs

Aries	**Jäär**	[æ:r]
Taurus	**Sõnn**	[sɪɲ]
Gemini	**Kaksikud**	[kɑksikud]
Cancer	**Vähk**	[ʋʲæhk]
Leo	**Lõvi**	[lɪʋi]
Virgo	**Neitsi**	[nejtsi]
Libra	**Kaalud**	[kɑ:lud]
Scorpio	**Skorpion**	[skorpion]
Sagittarius	**Ambur**	[ɑmbur]
Capricorn	**Kaljukits**	[kɑʎjykits]
Aquarius	**Veevalaja**	[ʋe:ʋɑlɑæ]
Pisces	**Kalad**	[kɑlɑd]
character	**iseloom**	[iselo:m]
features of character	**iseloomujooned**	[iselo:mujo:ned]
behavior	**käitumine**	[kʲæjtumine]
to tell fortunes	**ennustama**	[əɲustɑmɑ]
fortune-teller	**ennustaja**	[əɲustɑæ]
horoscope	**horoskoop**	[horosko:p]

Arts

149. Theater

theater	teater	[teater]
opera	ooper	[o:per]
operetta	operett	[operet]
ballet	ballett	[ballet]

theater poster	kuulutus	[ku:lutus]
theatrical company	trupp	[trupp]
tour	külalisetendus	[kylalisetendus]
to be on tour	gastroleerima	[gastrole:rima]
to rehearse (vi, vt)	proovi tegema	[pro:ʋi tegema]
rehearsal	proov	[pro:ʋ]
repertoire	repertuaar	[repertua:r]

performance	etendus	[ətendus]
theatrical show	etendus	[ətendus]
play	näidend	[nææjdend]

ticket	pilet	[pilet]
Box office	piletikassa	[piletikassa]
lobby, foyer	hall	[haʎ]
coat check	riietehoid	[ri:ətehojd]
coat check tag	riidehoiunumber	[ri:dehojunumber]
binoculars	binokkel	[binokkeʎ]
usher	kontrolör	[kontrolør]

orchestra seats	parter	[parter]
balcony	rõdu	[rɪdu]
dress circle	esindusrõdu	[esindusrɪdu]
box	loož	[lo:ʒ]
row	rida	[rida]
seat	koht	[koht]

audience	publik	[publik]
spectator	vaataja	[ʋa:taæ]
to clap (vi, vt)	aplodeerima	[aplode:rima]
applause	aplaus	[aplaus]
ovation	ovatsioon	[oʋatsio:n]

stage	lava	[laʋa]
curtain	eesriie	[əesri:e]
scenery	dekoratsioonid	[dekoratsio:nid]
backstage	kulissid	[kulissid]

scene (e.g., the last ~)	**stseen**	[stseən]
act	**akt**	[akt]
intermission	**vaheaeg**	[ʋaheaəg]

150. Cinema

| actor | **näitleja** | [ɲæjtleæ] |
| actress | **näitlejanna** | [ɲæjtleæŋa] |

movies (industry)	**kino**	[kino]
movie	**kino**	[kino]
episode	**seeria**	[se:ria]

detective	**kriminaalfilm**	[krimina:ʎfiʎm]
action movie	**löökfilm**	[lø:kfiʎm]
adventure movie	**põnevusfilm**	[pɪneʋusfiʎm]
science fiction movie	**aimefilm**	[ajmefiʎm]
horror movie	**õudusfilm**	[ɪudusfiʎm]

comedy movie	**komöödiafilm**	[komø:diafiʎm]
melodrama	**melodraama**	[melodra:ma]
drama	**draama**	[dra:ma]

fictional movie	**mängufilm**	[mʲæŋufiʎm]
documentary	**tõsielufilm**	[tɪsɪelufiʎm]
cartoon	**animafilm**	[animafiʎm]
silent movies	**tummfilm**	[tummfiʎm]

role (part)	**osa**	[osa]
leading role	**peaosa**	[peaosa]
to play (vi, vt)	**mängima**	[mʲæŋima]

movie star	**filmitäht**	[fiʎmitʲæht]
well-known (adj)	**tuntud**	[tuntud]
famous (adj)	**kuulus**	[ku:lus]
popular (adj)	**populaarne**	[popula:rne]

script (screenplay)	**stsenaarium**	[stsena:rium]
scriptwriter	**stsenarist**	[stsenarist]
movie director	**lavastaja**	[laʋastaæ]
producer	**produtsent**	[produtsent]
assistant	**assistent**	[assistent]
cameraman	**operaator**	[opera:tor]
stuntman	**kaskadöör**	[kaskadø:r]

to shoot a movie	**filmi võtma**	[fiʎmi ʋɪtma]
audition, screen test	**proovid**	[pro:ʋid]
shooting	**filmivõtted**	[fiʎmiʋɪtted]
movie crew	**võttegrupp**	[ʋɪttegrupp]
movie set	**võtteplats**	[ʋɪtteplats]

camera	kinokaamera	[kinokɑ:merɑ]
movie theater	kino	[kino]
screen (e.g., big ~)	ekraan	[əkrɑ:n]
to show a movie	filmi näitama	[fiʎmi ɲæjtɑmɑ]

soundtrack	heliriba	[heliribɑ]
special effects	trikid	[trikid]
subtitles	subtiitrid	[subti:trid]
credits	tiitrid	[ti:trid]
translation	tõlge	[tɪʎge]

151. Painting

art	kunst	[kunst]
fine arts	kaunid kunstid	[kɑunid kunstid]
art gallery	galerii	[gɑleri:]
art exhibition	maalinäitus	[mɑ:liɲæjtus]

painting (art)	maalikunst	[mɑ:likunst]
graphic art	graafika	[grɑ:fikɑ]
abstract art	abstraktsionism	[ɑbstrɑktsionism]
impressionism	impressionism	[imressionism]

picture (painting)	maal	[mɑ:ʎ]
drawing	joonistus	[jo:nistus]
poster	plakat	[plɑkɑt]

illustration (picture)	illustratsioon	[illustrɑtsio:n]
miniature	miniatuur	[miniɑtu:r]
copy (of painting, etc.)	ärakiri	[ærɑkiri]
reproduction	repro	[repro]

mosaic	mosaiik	[mosɑi:k]
stained glass	vitraaž	[ʋitrɑ:ʒ]
fresco	fresko	[fresko]
engraving	gravüür	[grɑʋy:r]

bust (sculpture)	rinnakuju	[riɳɑkuy]
sculpture	skulptuur	[skuʎptu:r]
statue	raidkuju	[rɑjdkuy]
plaster of Paris	kips	[kips]
plaster (as adj)	kipsist	[kipsist]

portrait	portree	[portre:]
self-portrait	autoportree	[ɑutoportre:]
landscape painting	maastikumaal	[mɑ:stikumɑ:ʎ]
still life	natüürmort	[nɑty:rmort]
caricature	karikatuur	[kɑrikɑtu:r]
sketch	visand	[ʋisɑnd]
paint	värv	[ʋʲæru]

watercolor	**akvarell**	[akʋɑreʎ]
oil (paint)	**õli**	[ɪli]
pencil	**pliiats**	[pli:ɑts]
Indian ink	**tušš**	[tuʃ]
charcoal	**süsi**	[sysi]
to draw (vi, vt)	**joonistama**	[jo:nistɑmɑ]
to paint (vi, vt)	**joonistama**	[jo:nistɑmɑ]
to pose (vi)	**poseerima**	[pose:rimɑ]
artist's model (masc.)	**modell**	[modeʎ]
artist's model (fem.)	**modell**	[modeʎ]
artist (painter)	**kunstnik**	[kunstnik]
work of art	**teos**	[təos]
masterpiece	**meistriteos**	[mejstriteos]
artist's workshop	**ateljee**	[ateʎjeə]
canvas (cloth)	**lõuend**	[lɪuənd]
easel	**molbert**	[moʎbert]
palette	**palett**	[palett]
frame (of picture, etc.)	**raam**	[rɑ:m]
restoration	**ennistamine**	[əŋistɑmine]
to restore (vt)	**ennistama**	[əŋistɑmɑ]

152. Literature & Poetry

literature	**kirjandus**	[kirˈændus]
author (writer)	**autor**	[autor]
pseudonym	**pseudonüüm**	[pseudony:m]
book	**raamat**	[rɑ:mɑt]
volume	**köide**	[køjde]
table of contents	**sisukord**	[sisukord]
page	**lehekülg**	[lehekyʎg]
main character	**peategelane**	[peɑtegelɑne]
autograph	**autogramm**	[autogrɑmm]
short story	**jutt**	[ytt]
story (novella)	**jutustus**	[ytustus]
novel	**romaan**	[romɑ:n]
work (writing)	**teos**	[təos]
fable	**valm**	[ʋaʎm]
detective novel	**kriminull**	[kriminuʎ]
poem (verse)	**luuletus**	[lu:letus]
poetry	**luule**	[lu:le]
poem (epic, ballad)	**poeem**	[poəem]
poet	**luuletaja**	[lu:letɑæ]
fiction	**ilukirjandus**	[ilukirˈændus]

science fiction	aimekirjandus	[ɑjmekirʲændus]
adventures	seiklused	[sejklused]
educational literature	õppekirjandus	[ɪppekirʲændus]
children's literature	lastekirjandus	[lɑstekirʲændus]

153. Circus

circus	tsirkus	[ʦirkus]
chapiteau circus	rändtsirkus	[rʲændʦirkus]
program	programm	[programm]
performance	etendus	[ətendus]

| act (circus ~) | number | [number] |
| circus ring | areen | [ɑre:n] |

| pantomime (act) | pantomiim | [pɑntomy:m] |
| clown | kloun | [kloun] |

acrobat	akrobaat	[ɑkrobɑ:t]
acrobatics	akrobaatika	[ɑkrobɑ:tikɑ]
gymnast	võimleja	[ʊijmleæ]
gymnastics	võimlemine	[ʊijmlemine]
somersault	salto	[sɑʎto]

athlete (strongman)	atleet	[ɑtle:t]
animal-tamer	taltsutaja	[tɑʎʦutɑæ]
equestrian	ratsutaja	[rɑʦutɑæ]
assistant	assistent	[ɑssistent]

stunt	trikk	[trikk]
magic trick	fookus	[fo:kus]
conjurer, magician	mustkunstnik	[mustkunstnik]

juggler	žonglöör	[ʒoŋlø:r]
to juggle (vi, vt)	žongleerima	[ʒoŋle:rimɑ]
animal trainer	dresseerija	[dresse:riɑ]
animal training	dresseerimine	[dresse:rimine]
to train (animals)	dresseerima	[dresse:rimɑ]

154. Music. Pop music

music	muusika	[mu:sikɑ]
musician	muusik	[mu:sik]
musical instrument	muusikariist	[mu:sikɑri:st]
to play ...	... mängima	[mʲæŋimɑ]

| guitar | kitarr | [kitɑrr] |
| violin | viiul | [ʊi:uʎ] |

cello	tšello	[tʃello]
double bass	kontrabass	[kontrabassʲ]
harp	harf	[harf]

piano	klaver	[klaʋer]
grand piano	tiibklaver	[tiːbklaʋer]
organ	orel	[orəʎ]

wind instruments	puhkpillid	[puhkpillid]
oboe	oboe	[oboə]
saxophone	saksofon	[saksofon]
clarinet	klarnet	[klarnet]
flute	flööt	[fløːt]
trumpet	trompet	[trompet]

| accordion | akordion | [akordion] |
| drum | trumm | [trumm] |

duo	duett	[duətt]
trio	trio	[trio]
quartet	kvartett	[kʋartett]
choir	koor	[koːr]
orchestra	orkester	[orkester]

pop music	popmuusika	[popmuːsika]
rock music	rokkmuusika	[rokkmuːsika]
rock group	rokkansambel	[rokkansambeʎ]
jazz	džäss	[dʒʲæss]

| idol | ebajumal | [əbaymaʎ] |
| admirer, fan | austaja | [austaæ] |

concert	kontsert	[kontsertʲ]
symphony	sümfoonia	[symfoːnia]
composition	teos	[təos]
to compose (write)	looma	[loːma]

singing	laulmine	[lauʎmine]
song	laul	[lauʎ]
tune (melody)	viis	[ʋiːs]
rhythm	rütm	[rytm]
blues	bluus	[bluːs]

sheet music	noodid	[noːdid]
baton	kepp	[kepp]
bow	poogen	[poːgen]
string	keel	[keːʎ]
case (e.g., guitar ~)	vutlar	[ʋutlar]

Rest. Entertainment. Travel

155. Trip. Travel

tourism	**turism**	[turism]
tourist	**turist**	[turist]
trip, voyage	**reis**	[rejs]
adventure	**seiklus**	[sejklus]
trip, journey	**sõit**	[sɪjt]
vacation	**puhkus**	[puhkus]
to be on vacation	**puhkusel olema**	[puhkuseʎ olema]
rest	**puhkus**	[puhkus]
train	**rong**	[roŋ]
by train	**rongiga**	[roŋiga]
airplane	**lennuk**	[leŋuk]
by airplane	**lennukiga**	[leŋukiga]
by car	**autoga**	[autoga]
by ship	**laevaga**	[laeʋaga]
luggage	**pagas**	[pagas]
suitcase, luggage	**kohver**	[kohʋer]
luggage cart	**pagasikäru**	[pagasikʲæru]
passport	**pass**	[passʲ]
visa	**viisa**	[ʋi:sa]
ticket	**pilet**	[pilet]
air ticket	**lennukipilet**	[leŋukipilet]
guidebook	**teejuht**	[te:yht]
map	**kaart**	[ka:rt]
area (rural ~)	**ala**	[ala]
place, site	**koht**	[koht]
exotic (n)	**eksootika**	[əkso:tika]
exotic (adj)	**eksootiline**	[əkso:tiline]
amazing (adj)	**üllatav**	[yllataʋ]
group	**grupp**	[grupp]
excursion	**ekskursioon**	[əkskursio:n]
guide (person)	**ekskursioonijuht**	[əkskursio:niyht]

156. Hotel

hotel	hotell	[hoteʎ]
motel	motell	[moteʎ]
three-star	kolm tärni	[koʎm tˈærni]
five-star	viis tärni	[ʋiːs tˈærni]
to stay (in hotel, etc.)	peatuma	[peɑtumɑ]
room	number	[number]
single room	üheinimesetuba	[yheinimesetubɑ]
double room	kaheinimesetuba	[kɑheinimesetubɑ]
to book a room	tuba kinni panema	[tubɑ kiɲi pɑnemɑ]
with bath	vannitoaga	[ʋɑɲitoɑgɑ]
with shower	dušiga	[duʃigɑ]
satellite television	satelliittelevisioon	[sɑtelliːtteleʋisioːn]
air-conditioner	konditsioneer	[konditsioneːr]
towel	käterätik	[kˈæterˈætik]
key	võti	[ʋɪti]
administrator	administraator	[ɑdministrɑːtor]
chambermaid	toatüdruk	[toɑtydruk]
porter, bellboy	pakikandja	[pɑkikɑndˈæ]
doorman	uksehoidja	[uksehojdˈæ]
restaurant	restoran	[restorɑn]
pub, bar	baar	[bɑːr]
breakfast	hommikusöök	[hommikusø:k]
dinner	õhtusöök	[ɪhtusø:k]
buffet	rootsi laud	[ro:tsi lɑud]
lobby	vestibüül	[ʋestibyːʎ]
elevator	lift	[lift]
DO NOT DISTURB	MITTE SEGADA	[mitte segɑdɑ]
NO SMOKING	MITTE SUITSETADA!	[mitte sujtsetɑdɑ]

157. Books. Reading

book	raamat	[rɑːmɑt]
author	autor	[ɑutor]
writer	kirjanik	[kirˈænik]
to write (~ a book)	kirjutama	[kirjytɑmɑ]
reader	lugeja	[lugeæ]
to read (vi, vt)	lugema	[lugemɑ]
reading (activity)	lugemine	[lugemine]
silently (to oneself)	omaette	[omɑette]

aloud (adv)	valjusti	[ʋɑʎjysti]
to publish (vt)	välja andma	[ʋʲæʎæ ɑndmɑ]
publishing (process)	trükk	[trykk]
publisher	kirjastaja	[kirʲæstɑæ]
publishing house	kirjastus	[kirʲæstus]

to come out (be released)	ilmuma	[iʎmumɑ]
release (of a book)	ilmumine	[iʎmumine]
print run	tiraaž	[tirɑ:ʒ]

| bookstore | raamatukauplus | [rɑ:mɑtukɑuplus] |
| library | raamatukogu | [rɑ:mɑtukogu] |

story (novella)	jutustus	[ytustus]
short story	jutt	[ytt]
novel	romaan	[romɑ:n]
detective novel	kriminull	[kriminuʎ]

memoirs	memuaarid	[memuɑ:rid]
legend	legend	[legend]
myth	müüt	[my:t]

poetry, poems	luuletused	[lu:letused]
autobiography	elulugu	[əlulugu]
selected works	valitud teosed	[ʋalitud teosed]
science fiction	aimekirjandus	[ɑjmekirʲændus]

title	nimetus	[nimetus]
introduction	sissejuhatus	[sisseyhatus]
title page	tiitelleht	[ti:teʎeht]

chapter	peatükk	[peɑtykk]
extract	katkend	[kɑtkend]
episode	episood	[əpiso:d]

plot (storyline)	süžee	[syʒe:]
contents	sisu	[sisu]
table of contents	sisukord	[sisukord]
main character	peategelane	[peɑtegelɑne]

volume	köide	[køjde]
cover	kaas	[kɑ:s]
binding	köide	[køjde]
bookmark	järjehoidja	[ærjehojdʲæ]

page	lehekülg	[lehekyʎg]
to flick through	lehitsema	[lehitsema]
margins	ääred	[æ:red]
annotation	märge	[mʲærge]
footnote	märkus	[mʲærkus]
text	tekst	[tekst]
type, font	kiri	[kiri]

misprint, typo	**trükiviga**	[trykiʋiga]
translation	**tõlge**	[tɪʌge]
to translate (vt)	**tõlkima**	[tɪʌkima]
original (n)	**originaal**	[origina:ʌ]

famous (adj)	**kuulus**	[ku:lus]
unknown (adj)	**tundmatu**	[tundmatu]
interesting (adj)	**huvitav**	[huʋitaʋ]
bestseller	**menuraamat**	[menura:mat]

dictionary	**sõnaraamat**	[sɪnara:mat]
textbook	**õpik**	[ɪpik]
encyclopedia	**entsüklopeedia**	[əntsyklope:dia]

158. Hunting. Fishing

hunting	**küttimine**	[kyttimine]
to hunt (vi, vt)	**jahil käima**	[æhiʌ kʲæjma]
hunter	**jahimees**	[æhime:s]

to shoot (vi)	**tulistama**	[tulistama]
rifle	**püss**	[pyssʲ]
bullet (shell)	**padrun**	[padrun]
shot (lead balls)	**haavlid**	[ha:ʋlid]

trap (e.g., bear ~)	**püünis**	[py:nis]
snare (for birds, etc.)	**lõks**	[lɪks]
to lay a trap	**püüniseid üles panema**	[py:nisejd yles panema]

poacher	**salakütt**	[salakyttʲ]
game (in hunting)	**metslinnud**	[metsliɲud]
hound dog	**jahikoer**	[æhikoər]
safari	**safari**	[safari]
mounted animal	**topis**	[topis]

fisherman	**kalamees**	[kalame:s]
fishing	**kalapüük**	[kalapy:k]
to fish (vi)	**kala püüdma**	[kala py:dma]

fishing rod	**õng**	[ɪŋ]
fishing line	**õngenöör**	[ɪŋenø:r]
hook	**õngekonks**	[ɪŋekoŋks]
float	**õngekork**	[ɪŋəkork]
bait	**sööt**	[sø:t]

to cast a line	**õnge vette viskama**	[ɪŋe ʋette ʋiskama]
to bite (ab. fish)	**näkkima**	[ɲækkima]
catch (of fish)	**kalasaak**	[kalasa:k]
ice-hole	**jääauk**	[æ:auk]
fishing net	**võrk**	[ʋɪrk]

boat	**paat**	[pɑːt]
to net (catch with net)	**võrguga püüdma**	[ʊɪrgugɑ pyːdmɑ]
to cast the net	**võrku vette heitma**	[ʊɪrku ʋette hejtmɑ]
to haul in the net	**võrku välja tõmbama**	[ʊɪrku ʊʲæʎæ tɪmbɑmɑ]

whaler (person)	**vaalapüük**	[ʋɑːlɑpyːk]
whaleboat	**vaalapüügilaev**	[ʋɑːlɑpyːgilɑeʋ]
harpoon	**harpuun**	[hɑrpuːn]

159. Games. Billiards

billiards	**piljard**	[piʎærd]
billiard room, hall	**piljardiruum**	[piʎærdiruːm]
ball	**piljardikuul**	[piʎærdikuːʎ]

to pocket a ball	**kuuli ajama**	[kuːli ɑæmɑ]
cue	**kii**	[kiː]
pocket	**piljardiauk**	[piʎærdiɑuk]

160. Games. Playing cards

diamonds	**ruutu**	[ruːtu]
spades	**poti**	[poti]
hearts	**ärtu**	[ərtu]
clubs	**risti**	[risti]

ace	**äss**	[əss]
king	**kuningas**	[kuniŋɑs]
queen	**daam**	[dɑːm]
jack, knave	**soldat**	[soldɑt]

playing card	**kaart**	[kɑːrt]
cards	**kaardid**	[kɑːrdid]
trump	**trump**	[trump]
deck of cards	**kaardipakk**	[kɑːrdipɑkk]

to deal (vi, vt)	**kaarte välja jagama**	[kɑːrte ʊʲæʎæ æægɑmɑ]
to shuffle (cards)	**kaarte segama**	[kɑːrte segɑmɑ]
lead, turn (n)	**käik**	[kʲæjk]
cardsharp	**suli**	[suli]

161. Casino. Roulette

casino	**kasiino**	[kɑsiːno]
roulette (game)	**rulett**	[rulett]
bet, stake	**panus**	[pɑnus]

to place bets	panust tegema	[panust tegema]
red	punane	[punane]
black	must	[must]
to bet on red	panust punasele panema	[panust punasele panema]
to bet on black	panust mustale panema	[panust mustale panema]

croupier (dealer)	krupjee	[krupjee]
to turn the wheel	trumlit keerutama	[trumlit ke:rutama]
rules (of game)	mängureeglid	[mⁱæŋure:glid]
chip	täring	[tⁱæriŋ]

| to win (vi, vt) | võitma | [ʊijtma] |
| winnings | võit | [ʊijt] |

| to lose (~ 100 dollars) | kaotama | [kaotama] |
| loss | kaotus | [kaotus] |

player	mängija	[mⁱæŋiæ]
blackjack (card game)	Must Jack	[must dʒⁱæk]
craps (dice game)	täringumäng	[tⁱæriŋumⁱæŋ]
slot machine	mänguautomaat	[mⁱæŋuautoma:t]

162. Rest. Games. Miscellaneous

to walk, to stroll (vi)	jalutama	[ælutama]
walk, stroll	jalutuskäik	[ælutuskⁱæjk]
road trip	lõbusõit	[lɪbusɪjt]
adventure	seiklus	[sejklus]
picnic	piknik	[piknik]

game (chess, etc.)	mäng	[mⁱæŋ]
player	mängija	[mⁱæŋiæ]
game (one ~ of chess)	partii	[parti:]

collector (e.g., philatelist)	kollektsionäär	[kollektsionæ:r]
to collect (vt)	koguma	[koguma]
collection	kollektsioon	[kollektsio:n]

crossword puzzle	ristsõna	[ristsɪna]
racetrack (hippodrome)	hipodroom	[hipodro:m]
discotheque	disko	[disko]

| sauna | saun | [saun] |
| lottery | loterii | [loteri:] |

camping trip	matk	[matk]
camp	laager	[la:ger]
tent (for camping)	telk	[teʎk]
compass	kompass	[kompass]
camper	matkaja	[matkaæ]

to watch (movie, etc.)	vaatama	[uɑ:tɑmɑ]
viewer	televaataja	[teleuɑ:tɑæ]
TV show	telesaade	[telesɑ:de]

163. Photography

| camera (photo) | fotoaparaat | [fotoɑpɑrɑ:t] |
| photo, picture | foto | [foto] |

photographer	fotograaf	[fotogrɑ:f]
photo studio	fotostuudio	[fotostu:dio]
photo album	fotoalbum	[fotoɑʎbum]

camera lens	objektiiv	[obʰekti:u]
telephoto lens	teleobjektiiv	[teleobʰekti:u]
filter	filter	[fiʎter]
lens	lääts	[læ:ts]

optics (high-quality ~)	optika	[optikɑ]
diaphragm (aperture)	diafragma	[diɑfrɑgmɑ]
exposure time	säriaeg	[sʲæriɑeg]
viewfinder	näidik	[ɲæjdik]

digital camera	videokaamera	[uideokɑ:merɑ]
tripod	statiiv	[stɑti:u]
flash	välkvalgus	[uʲæʎkuɑlgus]
to photograph (vt)	pildistama	[piʎdistɑmɑ]
to take pictures	üles võtma	[yles uɪtmɑ]
to be photographed	pildistama	[piʎdistɑmɑ]

focus	teravus	[terɑuus]
to adjust the focus	teravust reguleerima	[terɑuust regule:rimɑ]
sharp, in focus (adj)	terav	[terɑu]
sharpness	teravus	[terɑuus]

| contrast | kontrast | [kontrɑst] |
| contrasty (adj) | kontrastne | [kontrɑstne] |

picture (photo)	foto	[foto]
negative (n)	negatiiv	[negɑti:u]
film (a roll of ~)	filmilint	[fiʎmilint]
frame (still)	kaader	[kɑ:der]
to print (photos)	trükkima	[trykkimɑ]

164. Beach. Swimming

| beach | supelrand | [supeʎrɑnd] |
| sand | liiv | [li:u] |

deserted (beach)	inimtühi	[inimtyhi]
suntan	päevitus	[pæːʋitus]
to get a tan	päevitama	[pæːʋitama]
tan (adj)	päevitunud	[pæːʋitunud]
sunscreen	päevituskreem	[pæːʋituskreːm]

bikini	bikiinid	[bikiːnid]
bathing suit	trikoo	[trikoː]
swim briefs	supelpüksid	[supeʎpyksid]

swimming pool	bassein	[bassejn]
to swim (vi)	ujuma	[uyma]
shower	dušš	[duʃ]
to change (one's clothes)	ümber riietuma	[ymber riːetuma]
towel	käterätik	[kʲæterʲætik]

| boat | paat | [pɑːt] |
| motorboat | kaater | [kɑːter] |

water ski	veesuusad	[ʋeːsuːsad]
paddle boat	vesivelo	[ʋesiʋelo]
surfing	purjelaud	[purjelaud]
surfer	purjelaudur	[purjelaudur]

scuba set	akvalang	[akʋalaŋ]
flippers (swimfins)	lestad	[lestad]
mask	mask	[masʲk]
diver	sukelduja	[sukeʎduæ]
to dive (vi)	sukelduma	[sukeʎduma]
underwater (adv)	vee all	[ʋeː aʎ]

| beach umbrella | päevavari | [pæːʋaʋari] |
| beach chair | lamamistool | [lamamistoːʎ] |

| sunglasses | päikeseprillid | [pʲæjkeseprillid] |
| air mattress | ujumismadrats | [uymismadrats] |

| to play (amuse oneself) | mängima | [mʲæŋima] |
| to go for a swim | suplema | [suplema] |

beach ball	pall	[paʎ]
to inflate (vt)	täis puhuma	[tʲæjs puhuma]
inflatable, air- (adj)	täispuhutav	[tʲæjspuhutaʋ]

wave	laine	[lajne]
buoy	poi	[poj]
to drown (ab. person)	uppuma	[uppuma]

to save, to rescue	päästma	[pæːstma]
life vest	päästevest	[pæːsteʋest]
to observe, to watch	jälgima	[æʎgima]
lifeguard	päästja	[pæːstʲæ]

TECHNICAL EQUIPMENT. TRANSPORTATION

Technical equipment

165. Computer

computer	arvuti	[aruuti]
notebook, laptop	sülearvuti	[sylearuuti]
to turn on	sisse lülitama	[sisse lylitama]
to turn off	välja lülitama	[uˈæʎæ lylitama]
keyboard	klaviatuur	[klauiatuːr]
key	klahv	[klahu]
mouse	hiir	[hiːr]
mouse pad	hiirevaip	[hiːreuajp]
button	nupp	[nupp]
cursor	kursor	[kursor]
monitor	kuvar	[kuuar]
screen	ekraan	[əkraːn]
hard disk	kõvaketas	[kiuaketas]
hard disk volume	kõvaketta mälumaht	[kiuaketta mˈælumaht]
memory	mälu	[mˈælu]
random access memory	operatiivmälu	[operatiːumˈælu]
file	fail	[fajʎ]
folder	kataloog	[kataloːg]
to open (vt)	avama	[auama]
to close (vt)	sulgema	[sulgema]
to save (vt)	salvestama	[saʎuestama]
to delete (vt)	eemaldama	[eemaʎdama]
to copy (vt)	kopeerima	[kopeːrima]
to sort (vt)	sorteerima	[sorteːrima]
to transfer (copy)	ümber kirjutama	[ymber kirjytama]
program	programm	[programm]
software	tarkvara	[tarkuara]
programmer	programmeerija	[programmeːriæ]
to program (vt)	programmeerima	[programeːrima]
hacker	häkker	[hækker]
password	parool	[paroːʎ]

virus	**viirus**	[ʋi:rus]
to find, to detect	**avastama**	[aʋastama]
byte	**bait**	[bajt]
megabyte	**megabait**	[megabajt]
data	**andmed**	[andmed]
database	**andmebaas**	[andmeba:s]
cable (USB, etc.)	**kaabel**	[ka:beʎ]
to disconnect (vt)	**välja lülitama**	[ʋʲæʎæ lylitama]
to connect (sth to sth)	**ühendama**	[yhendama]

<h2>166. Internet. E-mail</h2>

Internet	**internet**	[internet]
browser	**brauser**	[brauser]
search engine	**otsimisressurss**	[otsimisressurs]
provider	**provaider**	[proʋajder]
web master	**veebimeister**	[ʋe:bimejster]
website	**veebilehekülg**	[ʋe:bilehekyʎg]
web page	**veebilehekülg**	[ʋe:bilehekyʎg]
address	**aadress**	[a:dress]
address book	**aadressiraamat**	[a:dressira:mat]
mailbox	**postkast**	[postʲkastʲ]
mail	**post**	[postʲ]
message	**teade**	[teade]
sender	**saatja**	[sa:tʲæ]
to send (vt)	**saatma**	[sa:tma]
sending (of mail)	**saatmine**	[sa:tmine]
receiver	**saaja**	[sa:æ]
to receive (vt)	**kätte saama**	[kʲætte sa:ma]
correspondence	**kirjavahetus**	[kirʲæʋahetus]
to correspond (vi)	**kirjavahetuses olema**	[kirʲæʋahetuses olema]
file	**fail**	[fajʎ]
to download (vt)	**allalaadimine**	[allala:dimine]
to create (vt)	**tegema**	[tegema]
to delete (vt)	**eemaldama**	[əemaʎdama]
deleted (adj)	**eemaldatud**	[əemaʎdatud]
connection (ADSL, etc.)	**side**	[side]
speed	**kiirus**	[ki:rus]
modem	**modem**	[modem]

| access | juurdepääs | [y:rdepæ:s] |
| port (e.g., input ~) | port | [port] |

| connection (make a ~) | lülitus | [lylitus] |
| to connect to ... (vi) | sisse lülitama | [sisse lylitama] |

| to select (vt) | valima | [ʋalima] |
| to search (for ...) | otsima | [otsima] |

167. Electricity

electricity	elekter	[əlekter]
electrical (adj)	elektri-	[əlektri]
electric power station	elektrijaam	[əlektriæ:m]
energy	energia	[ənərgia]
electric power	elektrienergia	[əlektrienergia]

light bulb	elektripirn	[əlektripirn]
flashlight	taskulamp	[taskulamp]
street light	tänavalatern	[tʲænaʋalatern]

light	elekter	[əlekter]
to turn on	sisse lülitama	[sisse lylitama]
to turn off	välja lülitama	[ʋʲæʎæ lylitama]
to turn off the light	tuld kustutama	[tuʎd kustutama]

to burn out (vi)	läbi põlema	[ʎæbi pɪlema]
short circuit	lühiühendus	[lyhiyhendus]
broken wire	katke	[katke]
contact	kontakt	[kontakt]

light switch	lüliti	[lyliti]
wall socket	pistikupesa	[pistikupesa]
plug	pistik	[pistik]
extension cord	pikendusjuhe	[pikendusyhe]

fuse	kaitse	[kajtse]
cable, wire	juhe	[yhe]
wiring	juhtmed	[yhtmed]

ampere	amper	[amper]
amperage	voolutugevus	[ʋo:lutugeʋus]
volt	volt	[ʋoʎt]
voltage	pinge	[piŋe]

| electrical device | elektririist | [əlektriri:st] |
| indicator | indikaator | [indika:tor] |

| electrician | elektrik | [əlektrik] |
| to solder (vt) | jootma | [jo:tma] |

| soldering iron | **jootekolb** | [jo:tekoʎb] |
| electric current | **vool** | [ʋoːʎ] |

168. Tools

tool, instrument	**tööriist**	[tø:ri:st]
tools	**tööriistad**	[tø:ri:stɑd]
equipment (factory ~)	**seadmed**	[seɑdmed]

hammer	**haamer**	[hɑ:mer]
screwdriver	**kruvikeeraja**	[kruʋike:rɑæ]
ax	**kirves**	[kirʋes]

saw	**saag**	[sɑ:g]
to saw (vt)	**saagima**	[sɑ:gimɑ]
plane (tool)	**höövel**	[hø:ʋeʎ]
to plane (vt)	**hööveldama**	[hø:ʋeʎdɑmɑ]
soldering iron	**jootekolb**	[jo:tekoʎb]
to solder (vt)	**jootma**	[jo:tmɑ]

file (for metal)	**viil**	[ʋi:ʎ]
carpenter pincers	**tangid**	[tɑŋid]
lineman's pliers	**näpitstangid**	[ɲæpitstɑŋid]
chisel	**peitel**	[pejteʎ]

drill bit	**puur**	[pu:r]
electric drill	**trellpuur**	[treʎpu:r]
to drill (vi, vt)	**puurima**	[pu:rimɑ]

knife	**nuga**	[nugɑ]
pocket knife	**taskunuga**	[tɑskunugɑ]
folding (~ knife)	**liigendnuga**	[li:gendnugɑ]
blade	**noatera**	[noɑterɑ]

sharp (blade, etc.)	**terav**	[terɑʋ]
blunt (adj)	**nüri**	[nyri]
to become blunt	**nüriks minema**	[nyriks minemɑ]
to sharpen (vt)	**teritama**	[teritɑmɑ]

bolt	**polt**	[poʎt]
nut	**mutter**	[mutter]
thread (of a screw)	**vint**	[ʋint]
wood screw	**kruvi**	[kruʋi]

| nail | **nael** | [nɑəʎ] |
| nailhead | **naelapea** | [nɑəlɑpeɑ] |

ruler (for measuring)	**joonlaud**	[jo:nlɑud]
tape measure	**mõõdulint**	[mɪ:dulint]
spirit level	**vaaderpass**	[ʋɑ:derpɑssʲ]

magnifying glass	**luup**	[lu:p]
measuring instrument	**mõõteriist**	[mɪ:teri:st]
to measure (vt)	**mõõtma**	[mɪ:tma]
scale	**skaala**	[ska:la]
(of thermometer, etc.)		
readings	**näit**	[ɲæjt]
compressor	**kompressor**	[kompressor]
microscope	**mikroskoop**	[mikrosko:p]

pump (e.g., water ~)	**pump**	[pump]
robot	**robot**	[robot]
laser	**laser**	[laser]

wrench	**mutrivõti**	[mutriʋti]
adhesive tape	**kleeplint**	[kle:plint]
glue	**liim**	[li:m]

emery paper	**liivapaber**	[li:ʋapaber]
spring	**vedru**	[ʋedru]
magnet	**magnet**	[magnet]
gloves	**kindad**	[kindad]

rope	**nöör**	[nø:r]
cord	**nöör**	[nø:r]
wire (e.g., telephone ~)	**juhe**	[yhe]
cable	**kaabel**	[ka:beʎ]

sledgehammer	**sepavasar**	[sepaʋasar]
crowbar	**kang**	[kaŋ]
ladder	**redel**	[redeʎ]
stepladder	**treppredel**	[treppredeʎ]

to screw (tighten)	**kinni keerama**	[kiɲi ke:rama]
to unscrew, untwist (vt)	**lahti keerama**	[lahti ke:rama]
to tighten (vt)	**kinni suruma**	[kiɲi suruma]
to glue, to stick	**kleepima**	[kle:pima]
to cut (vt)	**lõikama**	[lɪjkama]

malfunction (fault)	**rike**	[rike]
repair (mending)	**parandamine**	[parandamine]
to repair, to mend (vt)	**remontima**	[remontima]
to adjust (machine, etc.)	**reguleerima**	[regule:rima]

to check (to examine)	**kontrollima**	[kontrollima]
checking	**kontrollimine**	[kontrollimine]
readings	**näit**	[ɲæjt]

reliable (machine)	**töökindel**	[tø:kindeʎ]
complicated (adj)	**keeruline**	[ke:ruline]
to rust (get rusted)	**roostetama**	[ro:stetama]
rusty, rusted (adj)	**roostetanud**	[ro:stetanud]
rust	**rooste**	[ro:ste]

Transportation

169. Airplane

airplane	lennuk	[leŋuk]
air ticket	lennukipilet	[leŋukipilet]
airline	lennukompanii	[leŋukompani:]
airport	lennujaam	[leŋuæam]
supersonic (adj)	ülehelikiiruse	[yleheliki:ruse]
captain	lennukikomandör	[leŋukikomandør]
crew	meeskond	[me:skond]
pilot	piloot	[pilo:t]
flight attendant	stjuardess	[styɑrdess]
navigator	tüürimees	[ty:rime:s]
wings	tiivad	[ti:ʋɑd]
tail	saba	[sɑbɑ]
cockpit	kabiin	[kɑbi:n]
engine	mootor	[mo:tor]
undercarriage	telik	[telik]
turbine	turbiin	[turbi:n]
propeller	propeller	[propəller]
black box	must kast	[must kɑstⁱ]
control column	tüür	[ty:r]
fuel	kütus	[kytus]
safety card	instruktsioon	[instrukʦio:n]
oxygen mask	hapnikumask	[hɑpnikumasⁱk]
uniform	vormiriietus	[ʋormiri:etus]
life vest	päästevest	[pæ:steʋest]
parachute	langevari	[lɑŋeʋɑri]
takeoff	õhkutõusmine	[ɪhkutɪusmine]
to take off (vi)	õhku tõusma	[ɪhku tɪusmɑ]
runway	tõusurada	[tɪusurɑdɑ]
visibility	nähtavus	[ɲæhtɑʋus]
flight (act of flying)	lend	[lend]
altitude	kõrgus	[kɪrgus]
air pocket	õhuauk	[ɪhuɑuk]
seat	koht	[koht]
headphones	kõrvaklapid	[kɪrʋɑklɑpid]
folding tray	klapplaud	[klɑpplɑud]

| airplane window | illuminaator | [illumina:tor] |
| aisle | vahekäik | [ʋahekʲæjk] |

170. Train

train	rong	[roŋ]
suburban train	elektrirong	[əlektriroŋ]
express train	kiirrong	[ki:rroŋ]
diesel locomotive	mootorvedur	[mo:torʋedur]
steam engine	auruvedur	[auruʋedur]

| passenger car | vagun | [ʋagun] |
| dining car | restoranvagun | [restoranʋagun] |

rails	rööpad	[rø:pad]
railroad	raudtee	[raudte:]
railway tie	liiper	[li:per]

platform (railway ~)	platvorm	[platʋorm]
track (~ 1, 2, etc.)	tee	[te:]
semaphore	semafor	[semafor]
station	jaam	[æ:m]

engineer	vedurijuht	[ʋeduriyht]
porter (of luggage)	pakikandja	[pakikandʲæ]
train steward	vagunisaatja	[ʋagunisa:tʲæ]
passenger	reisija	[rejsiæ]
conductor	kontrolör	[kontrolør]

| corridor (in train) | koridor | [koridor] |
| emergency break | hädapidur | [hædapidur] |

compartment	kupee	[kupe:]
berth	nari	[nari]
upper berth	ülemine nari	[ylemine nari]
lower berth	alumine nari	[alumine nari]
bed linen	voodipesu	[ʋo:dipesu]

ticket	pilet	[pilet]
schedule	sõiduplaan	[sɪjdupla:n]
information display	tabloo	[tablo:]

to leave, to depart	väljuma	[ʋʲæʎjyma]
departure (of train)	väljumine	[ʋʲæʎjymine]
to arrive (ab. train)	saabuma	[sa:buma]
arrival	saabumine	[sa:bumine]

to arrive by train	rongiga saabuma	[roŋiga sa:buma]
to get on the train	rongile minema	[roŋile minema]
to get off the train	rongilt maha minema	[roŋiʎt maha minema]

train wreck	**rongiõnnetus**	[roŋɪːŋetus]
steam engine	**auruvedur**	[ɑuruʋedur]
stoker, fireman	**kütja**	[kytʲæ]
firebox	**kolle**	[kolle]
coal	**süsi**	[sysi]

171. Ship

| ship | **laev** | [lɑəʋ] |
| vessel | **laev** | [lɑəʋ] |

steamship	**aurik**	[ɑurik]
riverboat	**mootorlaev**	[moːtorlɑəʋ]
ocean liner	**liinilaev**	[liːnilɑəʋ]
cruiser	**ristleja**	[ristleæ]

yacht	**jaht**	[æht]
tugboat	**puksiir**	[puksiːr]
barge	**lodi**	[lodi]
ferry	**parvlaev**	[pɑrʋlɑəʋ]

| sailing ship | **purjelaev** | [purjelɑəʋ] |
| brigantine | **brigantiin** | [brigɑntiːn] |

| ice breaker | **jäälõhkuja** | [æːlɪhkuæ] |
| submarine | **allveelaev** | [ɑʎʋeːlɑəʋ] |

boat (flat-bottomed ~)	**paat**	[pɑːt]
dinghy	**luup**	[luːp]
lifeboat	**päästepaat**	[pæːstepɑːt]
motorboat	**kaater**	[kɑːter]

captain	**kapten**	[kɑpten]
seaman	**madrus**	[mɑdrus]
sailor	**meremees**	[meremeːs]
crew	**meeskond**	[meːskond]

boatswain	**pootsman**	[poːʦmɑn]
ship's boy	**junga**	[yŋɑ]
cook	**kokk**	[kokk]
ship's doctor	**laevaarst**	[lɑəʋɑːrst]

deck	**tekk**	[tekk]
mast	**mast**	[mɑst]
sail	**puri**	[puri]

hold	**trümm**	[trymm]
bow (prow)	**vöör**	[ʋøːr]
stern	**ahter**	[ɑhtər]
oar	**aer**	[ɑər]

screw propeller	kruvi	[kruʋi]
cabin	kajut	[kɑyt]
wardroom	ühiskajut	[yhiskɑyt]
engine room	masinaruum	[mɑsinɑru:m]
bridge	kaptenisild	[kɑptenisiʌd]
radio room	raadiosõlm	[rɑ:diosiʌm]
wave (radio)	raadiolaine	[rɑ:diolɑjne]
logbook	logiraamat	[logirɑ:mɑt]

spyglass	pikksilm	[pikksiʌm]
bell	kirikukell	[kirikukeʌ]
flag	lipp	[lipp]

| rope (mooring ~) | köis | [køjs] |
| knot (bowline, etc.) | sõlm | [siʌm] |

| deckrail | käsipuu | [kʲæsipu:] |
| gangway | trapp | [trɑpp] |

anchor	ankur	[ɑŋkur]
to weigh anchor	ankur sisse	[ɑŋkur sisse]
to drop anchor	ankur välja	[ɑŋkur ʋʲæʌæ]
anchor chain	ankrukett	[ɑŋkrukettʲ]

port (harbor)	sadam	[sɑdɑm]
berth, wharf	sadam	[sɑdɑm]
to berth (moor)	randuma	[rɑndumɑ]
to cast off	kaldast eemalduma	[kɑldɑst eemɑʌdumɑ]

trip, voyage	reis	[rejs]
cruise (sea trip)	kruiis	[krui:s]
course (route)	kurss	[kurss]
route (itinerary)	marsruut	[mɑrsru:t]

fairway	laevasõidutee	[lɑeʋɑsijdute:]
shallows (shoal)	madalik	[mɑdɑlik]
to run aground	madalikule jääma	[mɑdɑlikule æ:mɑ]

storm	torm	[torm]
signal	signaal	[signɑ:l]
to sink (vi)	uppuma	[uppumɑ]
SOS	SOS	[sos]
ring buoy	päästerõngas	[pæ:sterɪŋɑs]

172. Airport

airport	lennujaam	[leŋuæɑm]
airplane	lennuk	[leŋuk]
airline	lennukompanii	[leŋukompɑni:]
air-traffic controller	dispetšer	[dispetʃer]

departure	**väljalend**	[ʋʲæʎælend]
arrival	**saabumine**	[sɑ:bumine]
to arrive (by plane)	**saabuma**	[sɑ:bumɑ]

| departure time | **väljalennuaeg** | [ʋʲæʎæleŋuɑəg] |
| arrival time | **saabumisaeg** | [sɑ:bumisɑəg] |

| to be delayed | **hilinema** | [hilinemɑ] |
| flight delay | **väljalend hilineb** | [ʋʲæʎælend hilineb] |

information board	**teadetetabloo**	[teɑdetetɑblo:]
information	**teave**	[teɑʋe]
to announce (vt)	**teatama**	[teɑtɑmɑ]
flight (e.g., next ~)	**reis**	[rejs]

| customs | **toll** | [toʎ] |
| customs officer | **tolliametnik** | [tolliɑmetnik] |

customs declaration	**deklaratsioon**	[deklɑrɑtsio:n]
to fill out the declaration	**deklaratsiooni täitma**	[deklɑrɑtsio:ni tʲæjtmɑ]
passport control	**passikontroll**	[pɑssikontroʎ]

luggage	**pagas**	[pɑgɑs]
hand luggage	**käsipakid**	[kʲæsipɑkid]
Lost Luggage Desk	**pagasi otsimine**	[pɑgɑsi otsimine]
luggage cart	**pagasikäru**	[pɑgɑsikʲæru]

landing	**maandumine**	[mɑ:ndumine]
landing strip	**maandumisrada**	[mɑ:ndumisrɑdɑ]
to land (vi)	**maanduma**	[mɑ:ndumɑ]
airstairs	**lennukitrepp**	[leŋukitrepp]

check-in	**registreerimine**	[registre:rimine]
check-in desk	**registreerimiselett**	[registre:rimislettʲ]
to check-in (vi)	**registreerima**	[registre:rimɑ]
boarding pass	**lennukissemineku talong**	[leŋukisse mineku tɑloŋ]
departure gate	**lennukisse minek**	[leŋukisse minek]

transit	**transiit**	[trɑnsi:t]
to wait (vt)	**ootama**	[o:tɑmɑ]
departure lounge	**ooteruum**	[o:təru:m]
to see off	**saatma**	[sɑ:tmɑ]
to say goodbye	**hüvasti jätma**	[hyʋɑsti ætmɑ]

173. Bicycle. Motorcycle

bicycle	**jalgratas**	[ælgrɑtɑs]
scooter	**motoroller**	[motoroller]
motorcycle, bike	**mootorratas**	[mo:torrɑtɑs]
to go by bicycle	**jalgrattaga sõitma**	[ælgrɑttɑgɑ sɨjtmɑ]

handlebars	**rool**	[ro:ʎ]
pedal	**pedaal**	[pedɑ:ʎ]
brakes	**pidur**	[pidur]
bicycle seat	**sadul**	[sɑduʎ]

pump	**pump**	[pump]
luggage rack	**pakiruum**	[pɑkiru:m]
front lamp	**lamp**	[lɑmp]
helmet	**kiiver**	[ki:ʋer]

wheel	**ratas**	[rɑtɑs]
fender	**poritiib**	[poriti:b]
rim	**velg**	[ʋeʎg]
spoke	**kodar**	[kodɑr]

Cars

174. Types of cars

automobile, car	auto	[ɑuto]
sports car	spordiauto	[spordiɑuto]
limousine	limusiin	[limusi:n]
off-road vehicle	maastur	[mɑ:stur]
convertible	kabriolett	[kɑbriolet]
minibus	väikebuss	[ʋˈæjkebussʲ]
ambulance	kiirabi	[ki:rɑbi]
snowplow	lumekoristusauto	[luməkoristusɑuto]
truck	veoauto	[ʋeoɑuto]
tank truck	bensiiniauto	[bensi:niɑuto]
van (small truck)	furgoon	[furgo:n]
tractor (big rig)	veduk	[ʋeduk]
trailer	järelkäru	[æreʌkˈæru]
comfortable (adj)	mugav	[mugɑʋ]
second hand (adj)	kasutatud	[kɑsutɑtud]

175. Cars. Bodywork

hood	kapott	[kɑpottʲ]
fender	tiib	[ti:b]
roof	katus	[kɑtus]
windshield	tuuleklaas	[tu:lekIɑ:s]
rear-view mirror	tahavaatepeegel	[tɑhɑʋɑ:tepe:geʌ]
windshield washer	uhtuja	[uhtuæ]
windshield wipers	klaasipuhasti	[klɑ:sipuhɑsti]
side window	küljeklaas	[kyʌjeklɑ:s]
window lift	klaasitõstja	[klɑ:sitıstˈæ]
antenna	antenn	[ɑnteŋ]
sun roof	luuk	[lu:k]
bumper	kaitseraud	[kɑjtserɑud]
trunk	pakiruum	[pɑkiru:m]
door	uksed	[uksed]
door handle	ukselink	[ukseliŋk]

door lock	lukk	[lukk]
license plate	autonumber	[autonumber]
muffler	summutaja	[summutaæ]
gas tank	bensiinipaak	[bensi:nipɑ:k]
tail pipe	heitgaasitoru	[hejtgɑ:sitoru]

gas, accelerator	gaas	[gɑ:s]
pedal	pedaal	[pedɑ:ʎ]
gas pedal	gaasipedaal	[gɑ:sipedɑ:ʎ]
brake	pidur	[pidur]
brake pedal	piduripedaal	[piduripedɑ:ʎ]
to slow down (to brake)	pidurdama	[pidurdama]
parking brake	seisupidur	[sejsupidur]

clutch	sidur	[sidur]
clutch pedal	siduripedaal	[siduripedɑ:ʎ]
clutch plate	siduriketas	[siduriketas]
shock absorber	amortisaator	[amortisɑ:tor]

wheel	ratas	[ratas]
spare tire	tagavararatas	[tagavararatas]
tire	rehv	[rehu]
hubcap	kilp	[kiʎp]

driving wheels	veorattad	[ueorattad]
front-wheel drive (as adj)	eesveoga	[eesueoga]
rear-wheel drive (as adj)	tagaveoga	[tagaueoga]
all-wheel drive (as adj)	täisveoga	[tʲæjsueoga]
gearbox	käigukast	[kʲæjgukastʲ]
automatic (adj)	automaatne	[automa:tne]
mechanical (adj)	mehaaniline	[mehɑ:niline]
gear shift	käigukang	[kʲæjgukaŋ]

headlight	latern	[latern]
headlights	laternad	[laternad]

low beam	lähituled	[ʎæhituled]
high beam	kaugtuled	[kaugtuled]
brake light	stopp-signaal	[stopp signɑ:l]

parking lights	gabariittuled	[gabari:ttuled]
hazard lights	avariituled	[auari:tuled]
fog lights	udulaternad	[udulaternad]
turn signal	pöörmetuled	[pø:rmetuled]
back-up light	tagasikäik	[tagasikʲæjk]

176. Cars. Passenger compartment

car inside	sõitjateruum	[sɪjtʲæteru:m]
leather (as adj)	nahast	[nahast]

| velour (as adj) | veluurist | [ʋelu:rist] |
| upholstery | kattematerjal | [kattəmaterʲæl] |

instrument (gage)	seade	[seade]
dashboard	armatuurlaud	[armatu:rlaud]
speedometer	spidomeeter	[spidome:ter]
needle (pointer)	nool	[no:ʎ]

odometer	taksomeeter	[taksome:ter]
indicator (sensor)	andur	[andur]
level	tase	[tase]
warning light	elektripirn	[əlektripirn]

steering wheel	rool, rooliratas	[ro:ʎ], [ro:liratas]
horn	signaal	[signa:l]
button	nupp	[nupp]
switch	suunatuli	[su:natuli]

seat	iste	[iste]
backrest	seljatugi	[seʎætugi]
headrest	peatugi	[peatugi]
seat belt	turvavöö	[turʋaʋø:]
to fasten the belt	turvavööd kinni panema	[turʋaʋø:d kiŋi panema]
adjustment (of seats)	reguleerimine	[regule:rimine]

| airbag | õhkpadi | [ɪhkpadi] |
| air-conditioner | konditsioneer | [konditsione:r] |

radio	raadio	[ra:dio]
CD player	CD-mängija	[tse:de: mʲæŋiæ]
to turn on	sisse lülitama	[sisse lylitama]
antenna	antenn	[anteŋ]
glove box	kindalaegas	[kindalaegas]
ashtray	tuhatoos	[tuhato:s]

177. Cars. Engine

engine, motor	mootor	[mo:tor]
diesel (as adj)	diisel	[di:seʎ]
gasoline (as adj)	bensiini	[bensi:ni]

engine volume	mootorimaht	[mo:torimaht]
power	võimsus	[ʋɪjmsus]
horsepower	hobujõud	[hobujɪud]
piston	kolb	[kolb]
cylinder	silinder	[silinder]
valve	klapp	[klapp]

| injector | suru-jugapump | [suru ygapump] |
| generator | generaator | [genera:tor] |

| carburetor | karburaator | [karbura:tor] |
| engine oil | mootoriõli | [mo:toriːli] |

radiator	radiaator	[radia:tor]
coolant	jahutusvedelik	[æhutusʋedelik]
cooling fan	ventilaator	[ʋentila:tor]

battery (accumulator)	aku	[aku]
starter	käiviti	[kʲæjʋiti]
ignition	süüde	[sy:de]
spark plug	süüteküünal	[sy:teky:naʎ]

terminal (of battery)	klemm	[klemm]
positive terminal	pluss	[pluss]
negative terminal	miinus	[mi:nus]
fuse	kaitse	[kajtse]

air filter	õhufilter	[ɪhufiʎter]
oil filter	õlifilter	[ɪlifiʎter]
fuel filter	kütusefilter	[kytusefiʎter]

178. Cars. Crash. Repair

car accident	avarii	[aʋari:]
road accident	liiklusõnnetus	[liːklusɪŋetus]
to run into …	sisse sõitma	[sisse sɪjtma]
to have an accident	purunema	[purunema]
damage	vigastus	[ʋigastus]
intact (adj)	terve	[terʋe]

| to break down (vi) | purunema | [purunema] |
| towrope | puksiirtross | [puksi:rtrossʲ] |

puncture	auk	[auk]
to be flat	tühjaks minema	[tyħæks minema]
to pump up	täis pumpama	[tʲæjs pumpama]
pressure	rõhk	[rɪhk]
to check (to examine)	kontrollima	[kontrollima]

repair	remont	[remont]
auto repair shop	autoremonditöökoda	[autoremonditø:koda]
spare part	varuosa	[ʋaruosa]
part	detail	[detajʎ]

bolt (with nut)	polt	[poʎt]
screw bolt (without nut)	vint	[ʋint]
nut	mutter	[mutter]
washer	seib	[sejb]
bearing	kuullaager	[ku:ʎa:ger]
tube	toru	[toru]

| gasket (head ~) | **tihend** | [tihend] |
| cable, wire | **juhe** | [yhe] |

jack	**tungraud**	[tuŋraud]
wrench	**mutrivõti**	[mutriʋɪti]
hammer	**haamer**	[hɑːmer]
pump	**pump**	[pump]
screwdriver	**kruvikeeraja**	[kruʋikeːrɑæ]

| fire extinguisher | **tulekustuti** | [tulekustuti] |
| warning triangle | **avariikolmnurk** | [aʋariːkoʎmnurk] |

to stall (vi)	**välja surema**	[ʋʲæʎæ surema]
stalling	**seisak**	[sejsɑk]
to be broken	**rikkis**	[rikkis]

to overheat (vi)	**üle kuumenema**	[yle kuːmenema]
to be clogged up	**ummistuma**	[ummistuma]
to freeze up (pipes, etc.)	**kinni külmuma**	[kiɲi kyʎmuma]
to burst (vi, ab. tube)	**lõhki minema**	[lɪhki minema]

pressure	**rõhk**	[rɪhk]
level	**tase**	[tɑse]
slack (~ belt)	**nõrk**	[nɪrk]

dent	**muljutis**	[muʎjytis]
abnormal noise (motor)	**koputus**	[koputus]
crack	**pragu**	[prɑgu]
scratch	**kriimustus**	[kriːmustus]

179. Cars. Road

road	**tee**	[teː]
highway	**kiirtee**	[kiːrteː]
freeway	**maantee**	[mɑːnteː]
direction (way)	**suund**	[suːnd]
distance	**vahemaa**	[ʋɑhemɑː]

bridge	**sild**	[siʎd]
parking lot	**parkla**	[pɑrkla]
square	**väljak**	[ʋʲæʎæk]
interchange	**liiklussõlm**	[liːklussɪʎm]
tunnel	**tunnel**	[tuŋeʎ]

gas station	**tankla**	[tɑŋkla]
parking lot	**parkla**	[pɑrkla]
gas pump	**tankla**	[tɑŋkla]
auto repair shop	**garaaž**	[gɑrɑːʒ]
to get gas	**tankima**	[tɑŋkima]
fuel	**kütus**	[kytus]

jerrycan	kanister	[kanister]
asphalt	asfalt	[asfaʌt]
road markings	märgistus	[mʲærgistus]
curb	piire	[piːre]
guardrail	tara	[tara]
ditch	kraav	[kraːʋ]
roadside (shoulder)	teeperv	[teːperʋ]
lamppost	post	[postʲ]

to drive (a car)	juhtima	[yhtima]
to turn (~ to the left)	pöörama	[pøːrama]
to make a U-turn	ümber pöörama	[ymber pøːrama]
reverse (~ gear)	tagasikäik	[tagasikʲæjk]

to honk (vi)	signaali andma	[signaːli andma]
honk (sound)	helisignaal	[helisignaːl]
to get stuck	kinni jääma	[kiɲi æːma]
to spin (in mud)	puksima	[puksima]
to cut, to turn off	seisma jätma	[sejsma ætma]

speed	kiirus	[kiːrus]
to exceed the speed limit	kiirust ületama	[kiːrust yletama]
to give a ticket	trahvima	[trahʋima]
traffic lights	valgusfoor	[ʋalgusfoːr]
driver's license	juhiload	[yhiload]

grade crossing	ülesõit	[ylesɪjt]
intersection	ristmik	[ristmik]
crosswalk	jalakäijate ülekäik	[ælakʲæjate ylekʲæjk]
bend, curve	kurv	[kurʋ]
pedestrian zone	jalakäijate tsoon	[æʌækʲæjate tsoːn]

180. Traffic signs

rules of the road	liikluseeskirjad	[liːkluseeskirʲæd]
traffic sign	liiklusmärk	[liːklus mʲærk]
passing (overtaking)	möödasõit	[møːdasɪjt]
curve	kurv	[kurʋ]
U-turn	tagasipöördekoht	[tagasipøːrdekoht]
traffic circle	ringliiklus	[riɲliːklus]

No entry	sissesõidu keeld	[sissesɪjdu keːld]
No vehicles allowed	sõidu keeld	[sɪjdu keːld]
No passing	möödasõidu keeld	[møːdasɪjdu keːld]
No parking	parkimise keeld	[parkimise keːld]
No stopping	peatumise keeld	[peatumise keːld]

dangerous turn	järsk kurv	[ærsk kurʋ]
steep descent	järsk lang	[ærsk laŋ]
one-way traffic	ühesuunalisele teele	[yhesuːnaline teːle]

crosswalk	**ülekäigurada**	[ylekˈæjgurɑdɑ]
slippery road	**libe tee**	[libe te:]
YIELD	**anna teed**	[ɑŋɑ te:d]

PEOPLE. LIFE EVENTS

Life events

181. Holidays. Event

celebration, holiday	**pidu**	[pidu]
national day	**rahvuspüha**	[rɑhʊuspyhɑ]
public holiday	**pidupäev**	[pidupæːʊ]
to commemorate (vt)	**pidu pidama**	[pidu pidɑmɑ]
event (happening)	**sündmus**	[syndmus]
event (organized activity)	**üritus**	[yritus]
banquet (party)	**bankett**	[bɑŋkett]
reception (formal party)	**vastuvõtt**	[ʊɑstuʊɪtt]
feast	**pidu**	[pidu]
anniversary	**aastapäev**	[ɑːstɑpæːʊ]
jubilee	**juubelipidu**	[yːbelipidu]
to celebrate (vt)	**tähistama**	[tʲæhistɑmɑ]
New Year	**Uusaasta**	[uːsɑːstɑ]
Happy New Year!	**Head uut aastat!**	[heɑd uːt ɑːstɑt]
Santa Claus	**Jõuluvana**	[jɪuluʊɑnɑ]
Christmas	**Jõulud**	[jɪulud]
Merry Christmas!	**Rõõmsaid jõulupühi!**	[rɪːmsɑjd jɪulupyhi]
Christmas tree	**jõulukuusk**	[jɪuluku:sk]
fireworks	**saluut**	[sɑluːt]
wedding	**pulmad**	[puʎmɑd]
groom	**peigmees**	[pejgmeːs]
bride	**pruut**	[pruːt]
to invite (vt)	**kutsuma**	[kuʦumɑ]
invitation card	**kutse**	[kuʦe]
guest	**külaline**	[kylɑline]
to visit	**külla minema**	[kyllɑ minemɑ]
(~ your parents, etc.)		
to greet the guests	**külalisi vastu võtma**	[kylɑlisi ʊɑstu ʊɪtmɑ]
gift, present	**kingitus**	[kiŋitus]
to give (sth as present)	**kinkima**	[kiŋkimɑ]
to receive gifts	**kingitusi saama**	[kiŋitusi sɑːmɑ]

bouquet (of flowers)	**lillekimp**	[lillekimp]
congratulations	**õnnitlus**	[iɲitlus]
to congratulate (vt)	**õnnitlema**	[iɲitlema]
greeting card	**õnnitluskaart**	[iɲitluskɑ:rt]
to send a postcard	**kaarti saatma**	[kɑ:rti sɑ:tmɑ]
to get a postcard	**kaarti saama**	[kɑ:rti sɑ:mɑ]
toast	**toost**	[to:st]
to offer (a drink, etc.)	**kostitama**	[kostitɑmɑ]
champagne	**šampus**	[ʃɑmpus]
to have fun	**lõbutsema**	[lɨbutsemɑ]
fun, merriment	**lust**	[lust]
joy (emotion)	**rõõm**	[rɪ:m]
dance	**tants**	[tɑnts]
to dance (vi, vt)	**tantsima**	[tɑntsimɑ]
waltz	**valss**	[ʋɑʎss]
tango	**tango**	[tɑŋo]

182. Funerals. Burial

cemetery	**kalmistu**	[kɑʎmistu]
grave, tomb	**haud**	[hɑud]
cross	**rist**	[rist]
gravestone	**hauakivi**	[hɑuɑkiʋi]
fence	**piirdeaed**	[pi:rdeɑəd]
chapel	**kabel**	[kɑbeʎ]
death	**surm**	[surm]
to die (vi)	**surema**	[suremɑ]
the deceased	**kadunu**	[kɑdunu]
mourning	**lein**	[lejn]
to bury (vt)	**matma**	[mɑtmɑ]
funeral home	**matusebüroo**	[mɑtusebyro:]
funeral	**matus**	[mɑtus]
wreath	**pärg**	[pʲærg]
casket	**kirst**	[kirst]
hearse	**katafalk**	[kɑtɑfɑlk]
shroud	**surilina**	[surilinɑ]
cremation urn	**urn**	[urn]
crematory	**krematoorium**	[kremɑto:rium]
obituary	**nekroloog**	[nekrolo:g]
to cry (weep)	**nutma**	[nutmɑ]
to sob (vi)	**ulguma**	[uʎgumɑ]

183. War. Soldiers

platoon	jagu	[ægu]
company	rood	[ro:d]
regiment	polk	[polk]
army	kaitsevägi	[kɑjtseuʲægi]
division	divisjon	[diuisʲon]
section, squad	rühm	[ryhm]
host (army)	vägi	[uʲægi]
soldier	sõdur	[sɪdur]
officer	ohvitser	[ohuitsər]
private	reamees	[reɑme:s]
sergeant	seersant	[se:rsɑnt]
lieutenant	leitnant	[lejtnɑnt]
captain	kapten	[kɑpten]
major	major	[mɑør]
colonel	kolonel	[kolonel]
general	kindral	[kindrɑl]
sailor	meremees	[mereme:s]
captain	kapten	[kɑpten]
boatswain	pootsman	[po:tsmɑn]
artilleryman	suurtükiväelane	[su:rtykiuæ:lɑne]
paratrooper	dessantväelane	[dessɑntuæ:lɑne]
pilot	lendur	[lendur]
navigator	tüürimees	[ty:rime:s]
mechanic	mehaanik	[mehɑ:nik]
pioneer (sapper)	sapöör	[sɑpø:r]
parachutist	langevarjur	[lɑŋeuɑrjyr]
reconnaissance scout	luuraja	[lu:rɑæ]
sniper	snaiper	[snɑjper]
patrol (group)	patrull	[pɑtruʎ]
to patrol (vt)	patrullima	[pɑtrullimɑ]
sentry, guard	tunnimees	[tuŋime:s]
warrior	sõjamees	[sɪæme:s]
hero	kangelane	[kɑŋelɑne]
heroine	kangelanna	[kɑŋelɑŋɑ]
patriot	patrioot	[pɑtrio:t]
traitor	äraandja	[ərɑ:ndʲæ]
deserter	desertöör	[desertø:r]
to desert (vi)	deserteerima	[deserte:rimɑ]
mercenary	palgasõdur	[pɑlgɑsɪdur]
recruit	noorsõdur	[no:rsɪdur]

volunteer	**vabatahtlik**	[ʋabatahtlik]
dead (n)	**tapetu**	[tapetu]
wounded (n)	**haavatu**	[haːʋatu]
prisoner of war	**sõjavang**	[sɪæʋaŋ]

184. War. Military actions. Part 1

war	**sõda**	[sɪda]
to be at war	**sõdima**	[sɪdima]
civil war	**kodusõda**	[kodusɪda]

treacherously (adv)	**reetlikult**	[reːtlikuʎt]
declaration of war	**sõjakuulutamine**	[sɪæku:lutamine]
to declare (~ war)	**sõda kuulutama**	[sɪda ku:lutama]
aggression	**agressioon**	[agressio:n]
to attack (invade)	**kallale tungima**	[kallale tuŋima]

to invade (vt)	**anastama**	[anastama]
invader	**anastaja**	[anastaæ]
conqueror	**vallutaja**	[ʋallutaæ]

defense	**kaitse**	[kajtse]
to defend (a country, etc.)	**kaitsma**	[kajtsma]
to defend oneself	**ennast kaitsma**	[əŋast kajtsma]

enemy	**vaenlane**	[ʋaənlane]
foe, adversary	**vastane**	[ʋastane]
enemy (as adj)	**vaenulik**	[ʋaənulik]

| strategy | **strateegia** | [strateːgiæ] |
| tactics | **taktika** | [taktika] |

order	**käsk**	[kʲæsk]
command (order)	**käsk**	[kʲæsk]
to order (vt)	**käskima**	[kʲæskima]
mission	**ülesanne**	[ylesaŋe]
secret (adj)	**salajane**	[salaæne]

| battle | **võitlus** | [ʋɪjtlus] |
| combat | **lahing** | [lahiŋ] |

attack	**rünnak**	[ryŋak]
storming (assault)	**rünnak**	[ryŋak]
to storm (vt)	**ründama**	[ryndama]
siege (to be under ~)	**ümberpiiramine**	[ymberpi:ramine]

offensive (n)	**pealetung**	[pealetuŋ]
to go on the offensive	**peale tungima**	[pealetuŋima]
retreat	**taganemine**	[taganemine]
to retreat (vi)	**taganema**	[taganema]

| encirclement | ümberpiiramine | [ymberpi:ramine] |
| to encircle (vt) | ümber piirama | [ymber pi:rama] |

bombing (by aircraft)	pommitamine	[pommitamine]
to drop a bomb	pommi heitma	[pommi hejtma]
to bomb (vt)	pommitama	[pommitama]
explosion	plahvatus	[plahʋatus]

shot	lask	[lask]
to fire a shot	tulistama	[tulistama]
firing (burst of ~)	tulistamine	[tulistamine]

to take aim (at …)	sihtima	[sihtima]
to point (a gun)	sihikule võtma	[sihikule ʋɪtma]
to hit (the target)	tabama	[tabama]

to sink (~ a ship)	põhja laskma	[pɪhæ laskma]
hole (in a ship)	mürsuauk	[myrsuauk]
to founder, to sink (vi)	põhja minema	[pɪhæ minema]

front (war ~)	rinne	[riɲe]
rear (homefront)	tagala	[tagala]
evacuation	evakuatsioon	[eʋakuatsio:n]
to evacuate (vt)	evakueerima	[eʋakue:rima]

barbwire	okastraat	[okastra:t]
barrier (anti tank ~)	kaitsevall	[kajtseʋaʎ]
watchtower	vaatetorn	[ʋa:tetorn]

hospital	hospital	[hospital]
to wound (vt)	haavama	[ha:ʋama]
wound	haav	[ha:ʋ]
wounded (n)	haavatu	[ha:ʋatu]
to be wounded	haavata saama	[ha:ʋata sa:ma]
serious (wound)	raske	[raske]

185. War. Military actions. Part 2

captivity	vangistus	[ʋaɲistus]
to take captive	vangi võtma	[ʋaɲi ʋɪtma]
to be in captivity	vangis olema	[ʋaɲis olema]
to be taken prisoner	vangi sattuma	[ʋaɲi sattuma]

concentration camp	koonduslaager	[ko:ndusla:ger]
prisoner of war	sõjavang	[sɪæʋaɲ]
to escape (vi)	vangist põgenema	[ʋaɲist pɪgenema]

to betray (vt)	ära andma	[æra andma]
betrayer	äraandja	[əra:ndʲæ]
betrayal	reetmine	[re:tmine]

to execute (shoot)	**maha laskma**	[maha laskma]
execution (by firing squad)	**mahalaskmine**	[mahalaskmine]
equipment (military gear)	**vormiriietus**	[ʋormiriːetus]
shoulder board	**pagun**	[pagun]
gas mask	**gaasimask**	[gaːsimasˈk]
radio transmitter	**raadiosaatja**	[raːdiosaːtʲæ]
cipher, code	**šiffer**	[ʃiffer]
secrecy	**konspiratsioon**	[konspiratsioːn]
password	**parool**	[paroːʎ]
land mine	**miin**	[miːn]
to mine (road, etc.)	**mineerima**	[mineːrima]
minefield	**miiniväli**	[miːniʋˈæli]
air-raid warning	**õhuhäire**	[ɪhuɦæjre]
alarm (warning)	**häire**	[ɦæjre]
signal	**signaal**	[signaːl]
signal flare	**signaalrakett**	[signaːlrakett]
headquarters	**staap**	[staːp]
reconnaissance	**luure**	[luːre]
situation	**olukord**	[olukord]
report	**raport**	[raport]
ambush	**varistus**	[ʋaritsus]
reinforcement (of army)	**lisajõud**	[lisajɪud]
target	**märklaud**	[mˈærklaud]
proving ground	**polügoon**	[polygoːn]
military exercise	**manöövrid**	[manøːʋrid]
panic	**paanika**	[paːnika]
devastation	**häving**	[ɦæʋiŋ]
destruction, ruins	**purustused**	[purustused]
to destroy (vt)	**purustama**	[purustama]
to survive (vi, vt)	**ellu jääma**	[əllu æːma]
to disarm (vt)	**relvituks tegema**	[reʎʋituks tegema]
to handle (~ a gun)	**relva käsitlema**	[reʎʋa kˈæsitlema]
Attention!	**Valvel!**	[ʋalʋeʎ]
At ease!	**Vabalt!**	[ʋabaʎt]
feat (of courage)	**kangelastegu**	[kaŋelastegu]
oath (vow)	**tõotus**	[tɪotus]
to swear (an oath)	**tõotama**	[tɪotama]
decoration (medal, etc.)	**autasu**	[autasu]
to award (give medal to)	**autasustama**	[autasustama]
medal	**medal**	[medaʎ]
order (e.g., ~ of Merit)	**orden**	[orden]

victory	võit	[vɪjt]
defeat	kaotus	[kaotus]
armistice	vaherahu	[vɑherahu]

banner (standard)	lipp	[lipp]
glory (honor, fame)	kuulsus	[ku:lsus]
parade	paraad	[parɑ:d]
to march (on parade)	marssima	[marssima]

186. Weapons

weapons	relv	[reʎʊ]
firearm	tulirelv	[tulireʎʊ]
cold weapons (knives, etc.)	külmrelv	[kyʎmreʎʊ]

chemical weapons	keemiarelv	[ke:miareʎʊ]
nuclear (adj)	tuuma-	[tu:ma]
nuclear weapons	tuumarelv	[tu:mareʎʊ]

| bomb | pomm | [pomm] |
| atomic bomb | aatomipomm | [ɑ:tomipomm] |

pistol (gun)	püstol	[pystoʎ]
rifle	püss	[pyssʲ]
submachine gun	automaat	[automɑ:t]
machine gun	kuulipilduja	[ku:lipiʎduæ]

muzzle	püssitoru	[pyssitoru]
barrel	püssitoru	[pyssitoru]
caliber	kaliiber	[kali:ber]

trigger	vinn	[viɲʲ]
sight (aiming device)	sihik	[sihik]
magazine	padrunisalv	[padrunisaʎʊ]
butt (of rifle)	püssipära	[pyssipʲæra]

| hand grenade | granaat | [granɑ:t] |
| explosive | lõhkeaine | [lɪhkeajne] |

bullet	kuul	[ku:ʎ]
cartridge	padrun	[padrun]
charge	laeng	[laeŋ]
ammunition	lahingumoon	[lahiŋumo:n]

bomber (aircraft)	pommilennuk	[pommileŋuk]
fighter	hävituslennuk	[hæʋitusleŋuk]
helicopter	helikopter	[helikopter]
anti-aircraft gun	õhutõrjekahur	[ɪhutɪrjekahur]
tank	tank	[taŋk]

tank gun	kahur	[kɑhur]
artillery	kahurivägi	[kɑhuriʋæɡi]
cannon	suurtükk	[suːrtykk]
to lay (a gun)	sihikule võtma	[sihikule ʋɪtmɑ]

shell (projectile)	mürsk	[myrsk]
mortar bomb	miin	[miːn]
mortar	miinipilduja	[miːnipiʌduæ]
splinter (shell fragment)	kild	[kiʌd]

submarine	allveelaev	[ɑʌʋeːlɑəʋ]
torpedo	torpeedo	[torpeːdo]
missile	rakett	[rɑket]

to load (gun)	laadima	[lɑːdimɑ]
to shoot (vi)	tulistama	[tulistɑmɑ]
to point at (the cannon)	sihtima	[sihtimɑ]
bayonet	tääk	[tæːk]

epee	mõõk	[mɪːk]
saber (e.g., cavalry ~)	saabel	[sɑːbeʌ]
spear (weapon)	oda	[odɑ]
bow	vibu	[ʋibu]
arrow	nool	[noːʌ]
musket	musket	[musket]
crossbow	arbalett	[ɑrbɑlett]

187. Ancient people

primitive (prehistoric)	ürgne	[yrɡne]
prehistoric (adj)	eelajalooline	[əelɑæloːline]
ancient (~ civilization)	iidne	[iːdnə]

Stone Age	kiviaeg	[kiʋiɑəɡ]
Bronze Age	pronksiaeg	[proŋksiɑəɡ]
Ice Age	jääaeg	[æːɑəɡ]

tribe	suguharu	[suɡuhɑru]
cannibal	inimsööja	[inimsøːæ]
hunter	kütt	[kyttʲ]
to hunt (vi, vt)	jahil käima	[æhiʌ kʲæjmɑ]
mammoth	mammut	[mɑmmut]

cave	koobas	[koːbɑs]
fire	tuli	[tuli]
campfire	lõke	[lɪke]
rock painting	kaljujoonis	[kɑʌjyjoːnis]

| tool (e.g., stone ax) | tööriist | [tøːriːst] |
| spear | oda | [odɑ] |

stone ax	kivikirves	[kiʋikirʋes]
to be at war	sõdima	[sɪdima]
to domesticate (vt)	kodustama	[kodustama]
idol	iidol	[iːdol]
to worship (vt)	kummardama	[kummardama]
superstition	ebausk	[əbausk]
evolution	evolutsioon	[əʋolutsioːn]
development	areng	[arəŋ]
disappearance (extinction)	kadumine	[kadumine]
to adapt oneself	kohanema	[kohanəma]
archeology	arheoloogia	[arheoloːgia]
archeologist	arheoloog	[arheoloːg]
archeological (adj)	arheoloogiline	[arheoloːgiline]
excavation site	väljakaevamised	[ʋʲæʎækaəʋamised]
excavations	väljakaevamised	[ʋʲæʎækaəʋamised]
find (object)	leid	[lejd]
fragment	fragment	[fragment]

188. Middle Ages

people (ethnic group)	rahvas	[rahʋas]
peoples	rahvad	[rahʋad]
tribe	suguharu	[suguharu]
tribes	hõimud	[hɪjmud]
barbarians	barbar	[barbar]
Gauls	gallid	[gallid]
Goths	goodid	[goːdid]
Slavs	slaavlased	[slaːʋlased]
Vikings	viikingid	[ʋiːkiŋid]
Romans	roomlased	[roːmlased]
Roman (adj)	rooma	[roːma]
Byzantines	bütsantslased	[bytsantslased]
Byzantium	Bütsants	[bytsants]
Byzantine (adj)	bütsantsi	[bytsantsi]
emperor	imperaator	[imperaːtor]
leader, chief	pealik	[pealik]
powerful (~ king)	võimas	[ʋɪjmas]
king	kuningas	[kuniŋas]
ruler (sovereign)	valitseja	[ʋalitseæ]
knight	rüütel	[ryːteʎ]
feudal lord	feodaal	[feodaːl]

feudal (adj)	**feodaalne**	[feoda:ʌne]
vassal	**vasall**	[ʋasaʌ]
duke	**hertsog**	[hertsog]
earl	**krahv**	[krahʊ]
baron	**parun**	[parun]
bishop	**piiskop**	[pi:skop]
armor	**lahinguvarustus**	[lahiŋuʋarustus]
shield	**kilp**	[kiʌp]
sword	**mõõk**	[mɪ:k]
visor	**visiir**	[ʋisi:r]
chainmail	**raudrüü**	[raudryu]
crusade	**ristiretk**	[ristiretk]
crusader	**ristirüütel**	[ristiry:teʌ]
territory	**territoorium**	[territo:rium]
to attack (invade)	**kallale tungima**	[kallale tuŋima]
to conquer (vt)	**vallutama**	[ʋallutama]
to occupy (invade)	**anastama**	[anastama]
siege (to be under ~)	**ümberpiiramine**	[ymberpi:ramine]
besieged (adj)	**ümberpiiratud**	[ymberpi:ratud]
to besiege (vt)	**ümber piirama**	[ymber pi:rama]
inquisition	**inkvisitsioon**	[iŋkʋisitsio:n]
inquisitor	**inkvisiitor**	[iŋkʋisi:tor]
torture	**piinamine**	[pi:namine]
cruel (adj)	**julm**	[yʌm]
heretic	**ketser**	[ketser]
heresy	**ketserlus**	[ketserlus]
seafaring	**meresõit**	[meresɪjt]
pirate	**piraat**	[pira:t]
piracy	**piraatlus**	[pira:tlus]
boarding (attack)	**abordaaž**	[aborda:ʒ]
loot, booty	**sõjasaak**	[sɪæsa:k]
treasures	**aarded**	[a:rdəd]
discovery	**maadeavastamine**	[ma:dəaʋastamine]
to discover (new land, etc.)	**avastama**	[aʋastama]
expedition	**ekspeditsioon**	[əkspeditsio:n]
musketeer	**musketär**	[musketər]
cardinal	**kardinal**	[kardinal]
heraldry	**heraldika**	[heraʌdika]
heraldic (adj)	**heraldiline**	[heraʌdiline]

189. Leader. Chief. Authorities

king	kuningas	[kuniŋas]
queen	kuninganna	[kuniŋaŋa]
royal (adj)	kuninglik	[kuniŋlik]
kingdom	kuningriik	[kunigri:k]

| prince | prints | [prinʦ] |
| princess | printsess | [prinʦess] |

president	president	[president]
vice-president	asepresident	[asepresident]
senator	senaator	[sena:tor]

monarch	monarh	[monarh]
ruler (sovereign)	valitseja	[ualitseæ]
dictator	diktaator	[dikta:tor]
tyrant	türann	[tyraŋʲ]
magnate	magnaat	[magna:t]

director	direktor	[direktor]
chief	šeff	[ʃəf]
manager (director)	juhataja	[yhataæ]
boss	boss	[boss]
owner	peremees	[pereme:s]

head (~ of delegation)	juht	[yht]
authorities	võimud	[uıjmud]
superiors	juhtkond	[yhtkond]

governor	kuberner	[kuberner]
consul	konsul	[konsul]
diplomat	diplomaat	[diploma:t]
mayor	linnapea	[liŋapea]
sheriff	šerif	[ʃərif]

emperor	imperaator	[impera:tor]
tsar, czar	tsaar	[ʦa:r]
pharaoh	vaarao	[ua:rao]
khan	khaan	[kha:n]

190. Road. Way. Directions

| road | tee | [te:] |
| way (direction) | tee | [te:] |

freeway	maantee	[ma:nte:]
highway	kiirtee	[ki:rte:]
interstate	üldriiklik tee	[yʎdri:klik te:]

| main road | peatee | [peate:] |
| dirt road | metsavahetee | [metsavahete:] |

| pathway | rada | [rada] |
| footpath (trodder path) | jalgrada | [ælgrada] |

Where?	Kus?	[kus]
Where (to)?	Kuhu?	[kuhu]
Where … from?	Kust?	[kust]

| direction (way) | suund | [su:nd] |
| to point (~ the way) | näitama | [næjtama] |

to the left	vasakule	[ʋasakule]
to the right	paremale	[parəmale]
straight ahead (adv)	otse	[oʦe]
back (e.g., to turn ~)	tagasi	[tagasi]

bend, curve	kurv	[kurʋ]
to turn (~ to the left)	pöörama	[pø:rama]
to make a U-turn	ümber pöörama	[ymber pø:rama]

| to be visible | paistma | [pajstma] |
| to appear (come into view) | paistma | [pajstma] |

stop, halt (in journey)	peatus	[peatus]
to rest, to halt (vi)	puhkama	[puhkama]
rest (pause)	puhkus	[puhkus]

| to lose one's way | ära eksima | [əra eksima] |
| to lead to … (ab. road) | … viima | [ʋi:ma] |

| to arrive at … | … välja jõudma | [ʋʲæʎæ ɪ:udma] |
| stretch (of road) | vahemaa | [ʋahema:] |

asphalt	asfalt	[asfaʎt]
curb	piire	[pi:re]
ditch	kraav	[kra:ʋ]
manhole	luuk	[lu:k]

| roadside (shoulder) | teeperv | [te:perʋ] |
| pit, pothole | auk | [auk] |

| to go (on foot) | minema | [minema] |
| to pass (overtake) | järele jõudma | [ærele jɪudma] |

| step (footstep) | samm | [samm] |
| on foot (adv) | jalgsi | [ælgsi] |

to block (road)	tõkestama	[tɪkestama]
boom barrier	tõkkepuu	[tɪkkepu:]
dead end	umbtänav	[umbtʲænaʋ]

191. Breaking the law. Criminals. Part 1

bandit	**bandiit**	[bɑndiːt]
crime	**kuritegu**	[kuritəgu]
criminal (person)	**kurjategija**	[kurˈætəgiæ]
thief	**varas**	[ʋɑrɑs]
to steal (vi, vt)	**varastama**	[ʋɑrɑstɑmɑ]
stealing, theft	**vargus**	[ʋɑrgus]
to kidnap (vt)	**röövima**	[røːʋimɑ]
kidnapping	**inimrööv**	[inimrøːʋ]
kidnapper	**röövija**	[røːʋiæ]
ransom	**lunaraha**	[lunɑrɑhɑ]
to demand ransom	**lunaraha nõudma**	[lunɑrɑhɑ nɯudmɑ]
to rob (vt)	**röövima**	[røːʋimɑ]
robber	**röövel**	[røːʋəʎ]
to extort (vt)	**välja pressima**	[ʋˈæʎæ pressimɑ]
extortionist	**väljapressija**	[ʋˈæʎæpressiæ]
extortion	**väljapressimine**	[ʋˈæʎæpressimine]
to murder, to kill	**tapma**	[tɑpmɑ]
murder	**mõrv**	[mɪrʋ]
murderer	**mõrvar**	[mɪrʋɑr]
gunshot	**lask**	[lɑsk]
to fire a shot	**tulistama**	[tulistɑmɑ]
to shoot to death	**maha laskma**	[mɑhɑ lɑskmɑ]
to shoot (vi)	**tulistama**	[tulistɑmɑ]
shooting	**laskmine**	[lɑskmine]
incident (fight, etc.)	**juhtum**	[yhtum]
fight, brawl	**kaklus**	[kɑklus]
victim	**ohver**	[ohʋer]
to damage (vt)	**vigastama**	[ʋigɑstɑmɑ]
damage	**vigastus**	[ʋigɑstus]
dead body	**laip**	[lɑjp]
grave (~ crime)	**ränk**	[rˈæŋk]
to attack (vt)	**kallale tungima**	[kɑllɑle tuɲimɑ]
to beat (dog, person)	**lööma**	[løːmɑ]
to beat up	**läbi peksma**	[ʎæbi peksmɑ]
to take (rob of sth)	**ära võtma**	[æra ʋɪtmɑ]
to stab to death	**pussitama**	[pussitɑmɑ]
to maim (vt)	**sandiks peksma**	[sɑndiks peksmɑ]
to wound (vt)	**haavama**	[hɑːʋɑmɑ]
blackmail	**šantaaž**	[ʃɑntɑːʒ]

| to blackmail (vt) | šantažeerima | [ʃantaʒe:rima] |
| blackmailer | šantažeerija | [ʃantaʒe:riæ] |

protection racket	reket	[rəket]
racketeer	väljapressija	[ʋʲæʎæpressiæ]
gangster	gangster	[gaŋster]
mafia, Mob	maffia	[maffia]

pickpocket	taskuvaras	[taskuʋaras]
burglar	murdvaras	[murdʋaras]
smuggling	salakaubandus	[salakaubandus]
smuggler	salakaubavedaja	[salakaubaʋedaæ]

forgery	võltsing	[ʋɪʌtsiŋ]
to forge (counterfeit)	võltsima	[ʋɪʌtsima]
fake (forged)	võltsitud	[ʋɪʌtsitud]

192. Breaking the law. Criminals. Part 2

rape	vägistamine	[ʋʲægistamine]
to rape (vt)	vägistama	[ʋʲægistama]
rapist	vägistaja	[ʋʲægistaæ]
maniac	maniakk	[maniakk]

prostitute (fem.)	prostituut	[prostitu:t]
prostitution	prostitutsioon	[prostitutsio:n]
pimp	sutenöör	[sutenø:r]

| drug addict | narkomaan | [narkoma:n] |
| drug dealer | narkokaupmees | [narkokaupme:s] |

to blow up (bomb)	õhku laskma	[ɪhku laskma]
explosion	plahvatus	[plahʋatus]
to set fire	süütama	[sy:tama]
incendiary (arsonist)	süütaja	[sy:taæ]

terrorism	terrorism	[terrorism]
terrorist	terrorist	[terrorist]
hostage	pantvang	[pantʋaŋ]

to swindle (vt)	petma	[petma]
swindle	pettus	[pettus]
swindler	petis	[petis]

to bribe (vt)	pistist andma	[pistist andma]
bribery	pistise andmine	[pistise andmine]
bribe	altkäemaks	[aʌtkæ:maks]

| poison | mürk | [myrk] |
| to poison (vt) | mürgitama | [myrgitama] |

to poison oneself	ennast mürgitama	[eŋast myrgitama]
suicide (act)	enesetapp	[enesetapp]
suicide (person)	enesetapja	[enesetapⁱæ]
to threaten (vt)	ähvardama	[ehʋardama]
threat	ähvardus	[ehʋardus]
to make an attempt	kallale kippuma	[kallale kippuma]
attempt (attack)	elule kallalekippumine	[elule kallale kippuma]
to steal (a car)	ärandama	[erandama]
to hijack (a plane)	kaaperdama	[kɑːperdama]
revenge	kättemaks	[kⁱættemaks]
to revenge (vt)	kätte maksma	[kⁱætte maksma]
to torture (vt)	piinama	[piːnama]
torture	piinamine	[piːnamine]
to torment (vt)	vaevama	[ʋaeʋama]
pirate	piraat	[pirɑːt]
hooligan	huligaan	[huligɑːn]
armed (adj)	relvastatud	[reʎʋastatud]
violence	vägivald	[ʋⁱægiʋaʎd]
spying (n)	spionaaž	[spionɑːʒ]
to spy (vi)	nuhkima	[nuhkima]

193. Police. Law. Part 1

justice	kohtumõistmine	[kohtumⁱjstmine]
court (court room)	kohus	[kohus]
judge	kohtunik	[kohtunik]
jurors	vandemees	[ʋandemeːs]
jury trial	vandemeeste kohus	[ʋandemeːste kohus]
to judge (vt)	kohut mõistma	[kohut mⁱjstma]
lawyer, attorney	advokaat	[adʋokɑːt]
accused	kohtualune	[kohtualune]
dock	kohtupink	[kohtupiŋk]
charge	süüdistus	[syːdistus]
accused	süüdistatav	[syːdistataʋ]
sentence	kohtuotsus	[kohtuotsus]
to sentence (vt)	süüdi mõistma	[syːdi mⁱjstma]
guilty (culprit)	süüdlane	[syːdlane]
to punish (vt)	karistama	[karistama]
punishment	karistus	[karistus]

fine (penalty)	trahv	[trɑhʊ]
life imprisonment	eluaegne vanglakaristus	[əluɑegne ʊɑŋlɑkɑristus]
death penalty	surmanuhtlus	[surmɑnuhtlus]
electric chair	elektritool	[əlektrito:ʎ]
gallows	võllas	[ʊıllɑs]
to execute (vt)	hukkama	[hukkɑmɑ]
execution	hukkamine	[hukkɑmine]
prison, jail	vangla	[ʊɑŋlɑ]
cell	vangikong	[ʊɑŋikoŋ]
escort	konvoi	[konʊoj]
prison guard	vangivalvur	[ʊɑŋiʊɑʎʊur]
prisoner	vang	[ʊɑŋ]
handcuffs	käerauad	[kæ:rɑuɑd]
to handcuff (vt)	käsi raudu panema	[kʲæsi rɑudu pɑnemɑ]
prison break	põgenemine	[pıgenemine]
to break out (vi)	põgenema	[pıgenemɑ]
to disappear (vi)	kadunuks jääma	[kɑdunuks æ:mɑ]
to release (from prison)	vabastama	[ʊɑbɑstɑmɑ]
amnesty	amnestia	[ɑmnestiɑ]
police	politsei	[politsej]
police officer	politseinik	[politsejnik]
police station	politseijaoskond	[politsejæoskond]
billy club	kumminui	[kumminuj]
bullhorn	ruupor	[ru:por]
patrol car	patrullauto	[pɑtruʎɑuto]
siren	sireen	[sire:n]
to turn on the siren	sireeni sisse lülitama	[sire:ni sisse lylitɑmɑ]
siren call	sireen	[sire:n]
crime scene	sündmuspaik	[syndmuspɑjk]
witness	tunnistaja	[tuŋistɑæ]
freedom	vabadus	[ʊɑbɑdus]
accomplice	kaasosaline	[kɑ:sosɑline]
to flee (vi)	varjuma	[ʊɑrjymɑ]
trace (to leave a ~)	jälg	[æʎg]

194. Police. Law. Part 2

search (investigation)	tagaotsimine	[tɑgɑotsimine]
to look for ...	otsima	[otsimɑ]
suspicion	kahtlustus	[kɑhtlustus]
suspicious (suspect)	kahtlane	[kɑhtlɑne]
to stop (cause to halt)	peatama	[peɑtɑmɑ]

to detain (keep in custody)	kinni pidama	[kiɲi pidama]
case (lawsuit)	kohtuasi	[kohtuasi]
investigation	uurimine	[u:rimine]
detective	detektiiv	[detekti:ʋ]
investigator	uurija	[u:riæ]
hypothesis	versioon	[ʋersio:n]

motive	motiiv	[moti:ʋ]
interrogation	ülekuulamine	[yleku:lamine]
to interrogate (vt)	üle kuulama	[yle ku:lama]
to question (vt)	küsitlema	[kysitlema]
check (identity ~)	kontrollimine	[kontrollimine]

round-up	haarang	[hɑ:raŋ]
search (~ warrant)	läbiotsimine	[ʎæbiotsimine]
chase (pursuit)	tagaajamine	[taga:æmine]
to pursue, to chase	jälitama	[ælitama]
to track (a criminal)	jälgima	[æʎgima]

arrest	arest	[arest]
to arrest (sb)	arreteerima	[arrete:rima]
to catch (thief, etc.)	kinni võtma	[kiɲi ʋɯtma]
capture	kinnivõtmine	[kiɲiʋɯtmine]

document	dokument	[dokument]
proof (evidence)	tõestus	[tɯ:stus]
to prove (vt)	tõestama	[tɯ:stama]
footprint	jälg	[æʎg]
fingerprints	sõrmejäljed	[sɯrmeæʎjed]
piece of evidence	süütõend	[sy:tɯ:nd]

alibi	alibi	[alibi]
innocent (not guilty)	süütu	[sy:tu]
injustice	ebaõiglus	[əbɑijglus]
unjust, unfair (adj)	ebaõiglane	[əbɑijglane]

criminal (adj)	kriminaalne	[krimina:lne]
to confiscate (vt)	konfiskeerima	[konfiske:rima]
drug (illegal substance)	narkootik	[narko:tik]
weapon, gun	relv	[reʎʋ]
to disarm (vt)	relvituks tegema	[reʎʋituks tegema]
to order (command)	käskima	[kʲæskima]
to disappear (vi)	ära kaduma	[əra kaduma]

law	seadus	[seadus]
legal, lawful (adj)	seaduslik	[seaduslik]
illegal, illicit (adj)	ebaseaduslik	[əbaseaduslik]

responsibility (blame)	vastutus	[ʋastutus]
responsible (adj)	vastutama	[ʋastutama]

NATURE

The Earth. Part 1

195. Outer space

cosmos	**kosmos**	[kosmos]
space (as adj)	**kosmiline**	[kosmiline]
outer space	**maailmaruum**	[mɑːiʎmɑruːm]
universe	**universum**	[uniʋersum]
galaxy	**galaktika**	[gɑlɑktikɑ]
star	**täht**	[tʲæht]
constellation	**tähtkuju**	[tʲæhtkuy]
planet	**planeet**	[plɑneːt]
satellite	**satelliit**	[sɑtelliːt]
meteorite	**meteoriit**	[meteoriːt]
comet	**komeet**	[komeːt]
asteroid	**asteroid**	[ɑsterojd]
orbit	**orbiit**	[orbiːt]
to revolve (~ around the Earth)	**keerlema**	[keːrlemɑ]
atmosphere	**atmosfäär**	[ɑtmosfæːr]
the Sun	**Päike**	[pʲæjke]
solar system	**Päikesesüsteem**	[pʲæjkesesysteːm]
solar eclipse	**päiksevarjutus**	[pʲæjkeseʋɑrjytus]
the Earth	**Maa**	[mɑː]
the Moon	**Kuu**	[kuː]
Mars	**Marss**	[mɑrs]
Venus	**Veenus**	[ʋeːnus]
Jupiter	**Jupiter**	[ypiter]
Saturn	**Saturn**	[sɑturn]
Mercury	**Merkuur**	[merkuːr]
Uranus	**Uraan**	[urɑːn]
Neptune	**Neptuun**	[neptuːn]
Pluto	**Pluuto**	[pluːto]
Milky Way	**Linnutee**	[liɲuteː]
Great Bear	**Suur Vanker**	[suːr ʋɑŋker]

North Star	Põhjanael	[pɪhænaeʎ]
Martian	marslane	[marslane]
extraterrestrial (n)	võõra planeedi asukas	[uːra plane:di asukas]
alien	tulnukas	[tulnukas]
flying saucer	lendav taldrik	[lendau taldrik]

spaceship	kosmoselaev	[kosmoselaeu]
space station	orbitaaljaam	[orbitaːʎæam]
blast-off	start	[start]

engine	mootor	[moːtor]
nozzle	düüs	[dyːs]
fuel	kütus	[kytus]

cockpit, flight deck	kabiin	[kabiːn]
antenna	antenn	[anteŋ]
porthole	illuminaator	[illuminaːtor]
solar battery	päikesepatarei	[pʲæjkesepatarej]
spacesuit	skafander	[skafander]

| weightlessness | kaaluta olek | [kaːluta olek] |
| oxygen | hapnik | [hapnik] |

| docking (in space) | põkkumine | [pɪkkumine] |
| to dock (vi, vt) | põkkama | [pɪkkama] |

observatory	observatoorium	[obseruatoːrium]
telescope	teleskoop	[teleskoːp]
to observe (vt)	jälgima	[æʎgima]
to explore (vt)	uurima	[uːrima]

196. The Earth

the Earth	Maa	[maː]
globe (the Earth)	maakera	[maːkera]
planet	planeet	[planeːt]

atmosphere	atmosfäär	[atmosfæːr]
geography	geograafia	[geograːfia]
nature	loodus	[loːdus]

globe (table ~)	gloobus	[gloːbus]
map	kaart	[kaːrt]
atlas	atlas	[atlas]

Europe	Euroopa	[əuroːpa]
Asia	Aasia	[aːsia]
Africa	Aafrika	[aːfrika]
Australia	Austraalia	[austraːlia]
America	Ameerika	[ameːrika]

| North America | **Põhja-Ameerika** | [pɪhæ ame:rika] |
| South America | **Lõuna-Ameerika** | [lɪuna ame:rika] |

| Antarctica | **Antarktis** | [antarktis] |
| the Arctic | **Arktika** | [arktika] |

197. Cardinal directions

north	**põhi**	[pɪhi]
to the north	**põhja**	[pɪhæ]
in the north	**põhjas**	[pɪhæs]
northern (adj)	**põhja-**	[pɪhæ]

south	**lõuna**	[lɪuna]
to the south	**lõunasse**	[lɪunasse]
in the south	**lõunas**	[lɪunas]
southern (adj)	**lõuna-**	[lɪuna]

west	**lääs**	[læ:s]
to the west	**läände**	[læ:nde]
in the west	**läänes**	[læ:nes]
western (adj)	**lääne-**	[læ:ne]

east	**ida**	[ida]
to the east	**itta**	[itta]
in the east	**idas**	[idas]
eastern (adj)	**ida-**	[ida]

198. Sea. Ocean

sea	**meri**	[meri]
ocean	**ookean**	[o:kean]
gulf (bay)	**laht**	[laht]
straits	**väin**	[ʋˈæjn]

solid ground	**maismaa**	[majsma:]
continent (mainland)	**manner**	[maŋer]
island	**saar**	[sa:r]
peninsula	**poolsaar**	[po:ʎsa:r]
archipelago	**arhipelaag**	[arhipela:g]

bay, cove	**laht**	[laht]
harbor	**sadam**	[sadam]
lagoon	**laguun**	[lagu:n]
cape	**neem**	[ne:m]

| atoll | **atoll** | [atoʎ] |
| reef | **riff** | [riff] |

| coral | korall | [koraʎ] |
| coral reef | korallrahu | [koraʎrahu] |

deep (adj)	sügav	[sygɑʊ]
depth (deep water)	sügavus	[sygɑʊus]
abyss	sügavik	[sygɑʊik]
trench (e.g., Mariana ~)	nõgu	[nɪgu]

| current, stream | hoovus | [ho:ʊus] |
| to surround (bathe) | uhtuma | [uhtumɑ] |

| shore | rand | [rɑnd] |
| coast | rannik | [rɑŋik] |

high tide	tõus	[tɪus]
low tide	mõõn	[mɪ:n]
sandbank	madalik	[mɑdɑlik]
bottom	põhi	[pɪhi]

wave	laine	[lɑjne]
crest (~ of a wave)	lainehari	[lɑjnehɑri]
froth (foam)	vaht	[ʊɑht]

storm	torm	[torm]
hurricane	orkaan	[orkɑ:n]
tsunami	tsunami	[ʦunɑmi]
calm (dead ~)	tuulevaikus	[tu:leʊɑjkus]
quiet, calm (adj)	rahulik	[rɑhulik]

| pole | poolus | [po:lus] |
| polar (adj) | polaar- | [polɑ:r] |

latitude	laius	[lɑjus]
longitude	pikkus	[pikkus]
parallel	paralleel	[pɑralle:ʎ]
equator	ekvaator	[ekʊɑ:tor]

sky	taevas	[tɑeʊɑs]
horizon	silmapiir	[siʎmɑpi:r]
air	õhk	[ɪhk]

lighthouse	majakas	[mɑækɑs]
to dive (vi)	sukelduma	[sukeʎdumɑ]
to sink (ab. boat)	uppuma	[uppumɑ]
treasures	aarded	[ɑ:rdəd]

199. Seas' and Oceans' names

| Atlantic Ocean | **Atlandi ookean** | [ɑtlɑndi o:keɑn] |
| Indian Ocean | **India ookean** | [indiɑ o:keɑn] |

Pacific Ocean	**Vaikne ookean**	[ʋɑjkne oːkeɑn]
Arctic Ocean	**Põhja-Jäämeri**	[pɪhæ æːmeri]
Black Sea	**Must meri**	[must meri]
Red Sea	**Punane meri**	[punɑne meri]
Yellow Sea	**Kollane meri**	[kollɑne meri]
White Sea	**Valge meri**	[ʋɑlge meri]
Caspian Sea	**Kaspia meri**	[kɑspiɑ meri]
Dead Sea	**Surnumeri**	[surnumeri]
Mediterranean Sea	**Vahemeri**	[ʋɑhemeri]
Aegean Sea	**Egeuse meri**	[əgeuse meri]
Adriatic Sea	**Aadria meri**	[ɑːdriɑ meri]
Arabian Sea	**Araabia meri**	[ɑrɑːbiɑ meri]
Sea of Japan	**Jaapani meri**	[æːpɑni meri]
Bering Sea	**Beringi meri**	[beriŋi meri]
South China Sea	**Lõuna-Hiina meri**	[lɪunɑ hiːnɑ meri]
Coral Sea	**Korallide meri**	[korɑllide meri]
Tasman Sea	**Tasmaania meri**	[tɑsmɑːniɑ meri]
Caribbean Sea	**Kariibi meri**	[kɑriːbi meri]
Barents Sea	**Barentsi meri**	[bɑrentsi meri]
Kara Sea	**Kara meri**	[kɑrɑ meri]
North Sea	**Põhjameri**	[pɪhæmeri]
Baltic Sea	**Läänemeri**	[læːnemeri]
Norwegian Sea	**Norra meri**	[norrɑ meri]

200. Mountains

mountain	**mägi**	[mˈægi]
mountain range	**mäeahelik**	[mæːɑhelik]
mountain ridge	**mäeahelik**	[mæːɑhelik]
summit, top	**tipp**	[tipp]
peak	**mäetipp**	[mæːtipp]
foot (of mountain)	**jalam**	[ælɑm]
slope (mountainside)	**nõlv**	[nɪʌʋ]
volcano	**vulkaan**	[ʋulkɑːn]
active volcano	**tegutsev vulkaan**	[tegutseʋ ʋulkɑːn]
dormant volcano	**kustunud vulkaan**	[kustunud ʋulkɑːn]
eruption	**vulkaanipurse**	[ʋulkɑːnipurse]
crater	**kraater**	[krɑːter]
magma	**magma**	[mɑgmɑ]
lava	**laava**	[lɑːʋɑ]

molten (~ lava)	hõõguv	[hɪːguʊ]
canyon	kanjon	[kɑɲon]
gorge	kuristik	[kuristik]
crevice	kaljulõhe	[kaʎjylɪhe]

pass, col	kuru	[kuru]
plateau	platoo	[plɑtoː]
cliff	kalju	[kaʎjy]
hill	küngas	[kyŋɑs]

glacier	liustik	[liustik]
waterfall	juga	[ygɑ]
geyser	geiser	[gejser]
lake	järv	[æruʊ]

plain	lausmaa	[lausmɑː]
landscape	maastik	[mɑːstik]
echo	kaja	[kɑæ]

alpinist	alpinist	[ɑʎpinist]
rock climber	kaljuronija	[kaʎjyroniæ]
to conquer (in climbing)	vallutama	[ʊallutɑmɑ]
climb (an easy ~)	mäkketõus	[mʲækketɪus]

201. Mountains names

Alps	Alpid	[ɑʎpid]
Mont Blanc	Mont Blanc	[monblɑn]
Pyrenees	Püreneed	[pyreneːd]

Carpathians	Karpaadid	[karpɑːdid]
Ural Mountains	Uurali mäed	[uːrɑli mæːd]
Caucasus	Kaukasus	[kaukɑsus]
Elbrus	Elbrus	[əʎbrus]

Altai	Altai	[ɑltɑj]
Tien Shan	Tjan-Šan	[tʲæn ʃɑn]
Pamir Mountains	Pamiir	[pɑmiːr]
Himalayas	Himaalaja	[himɑːlɑæ]
Everest	Everest	[əʊerest]

| Andes | Andid | [ɑndid] |
| Kilimanjaro | Kilimandžaaro | [kilimɑndʒɑːro] |

202. Rivers

| river | jõgi | [jɪgi] |
| spring (natural source) | allikas | [ɑllikɑs] |

riverbed	**säng**	[sʲæŋ]
basin	**bassein**	[bɑssejn]
to flow into …	**suubuma**	[su:bumɑ]
tributary	**lisajõgi**	[lisɑjɪgi]
bank (of river)	**kallas**	[kɑllɑs]
current, stream	**vool**	[ʋo:ʎ]
downstream (adv)	**allavoolu**	[ɑllɑʋo:lu]
upstream (adv)	**ülesvoolu**	[ylesʋo:lu]
inundation	**üleujutus**	[yleuytus]
flooding	**suurvesi**	[su:rʋesi]
to overflow (vi)	**üle ujutama**	[yle uytɑmɑ]
to flood (vt)	**uputama**	[uputɑmɑ]
shallows (shoal)	**madalik**	[mɑdɑlik]
rapids	**lävi**	[ʎæʋi]
dam	**pais**	[pɑjs]
canal	**kanal**	[kɑnɑl]
artificial lake	**veehoidla**	[ʋe:hojdlɑ]
sluice, lock	**lüüs**	[ly:s]
water body (pond, ǝtc.)	**veekogu**	[ʋe:kogu]
swamp, bog	**soo**	[so:]
marsh	**õõtssoo**	[ɪːʦso:]
whirlpool	**veekeeris**	[ʋe:ke:ris]
stream (brook)	**oja**	[oæ]
drinking (ab. water)	**joogi-**	[jo:gi]
fresh (~ water)	**mage-**	[mɑge]
ice	**jää**	[æ:]
to freeze (ab. river, ǝtc.)	**külmuma**	[kyʎmumɑ]

203. Rivers' names

Seine	**Seine**	[senɑ]
Loire	**Loire**	[luɑ:r]
Thames	**Thames**	[tems]
Rhine	**Rein**	[rejn]
Danube	**Doonau**	[do:nɑu]
Volga	**Volga**	[ʋolgɑ]
Don	**Don**	[don]
Lena	**Leena**	[le:nɑ]
Yellow River	**Huang He**	[huɑnhe]
Yangtze	**Jangtse**	[æŋʦe]

| Mekong | **Mekong** | [mekoŋ] |
| Ganges | **Ganges** | [gɑŋes] |

Nile River	**Niilus**	[niːlus]
Congo	**Kongo**	[koŋo]
Okavango	**Okavango**	[okɑʋɑŋo]
Zambezi	**Zambezi**	[sɑmbesi]
Limpopo	**Limpopo**	[limpopo]
Mississippi River	**Mississippi**	[mississipi]

204. Forest

| forest | **mets** | [mets] |
| forest (as adj) | **metsa-** | [metsɑ] |

thick forest	**tihnik**	[tihnik]
grove	**salu**	[sɑlu]
forest clearing	**lagendik**	[lɑgendik]

| thicket | **padrik** | [pɑdrik] |
| scrubland | **põõsastik** | [pɪːsɑstik] |

| footpath (troddenpath) | **jalgrada** | [ælgrɑdɑ] |
| gully | **jäärak** | [æːrɑk] |

tree	**puu**	[puː]
leaf	**leht**	[leht]
leaves	**lehestik**	[lehestik]

fall of leaves	**lehtede langemine**	[lehtede lɑŋemine]
to fall (ab. leaves)	**langema**	[lɑŋemɑ]
top (of the tree)	**latv**	[lɑtʊ]

branch	**oks**	[oks]
bough	**oks**	[oks]
bud (on shrub, tree)	**pung**	[puŋ]
needle (of pine tree)	**okas**	[okɑs]
pine cone	**käbi**	[kⁱæbi]

hollow (in a tree)	**puuõõs**	[puːɪːs]
nest	**pesa**	[pesɑ]
burrow (animal hole)	**urg**	[urg]

trunk	**tüvi**	[tyʋi]
root	**juur**	[yːr]
bark	**koor**	[koːr]
moss	**sammal**	[sɑmmɑʎ]

| to uproot (vt) | **juurima** | [yːrimɑ] |
| to chop down | **raiuma** | [rɑjumɑ] |

| to deforest (vt) | maha raiuma | [mɑhɑ rɑjumɑ] |
| tree stump | känd | [kʲænd] |

campfire	lõke	[lıke]
forest fire	tulekahju	[tulekɑɦjy]
to extinguish (vt)	kustutama	[kustutɑmɑ]

forest ranger	metsavaht	[metsɑʊɑht]
protection	taimekaitse	[tɑjmekɑjtse]
to protect (~ nature)	looduskaitse	[loːduskɑjtse]
poacher	salakütt	[sɑlɑkyttʲ]
trap (e.g., bear ~)	püünis	[pyːnis]

| to gather, to pick (vt) | korjama | [korʲæmɑ] |
| to lose one's way | ära eksima | [ərɑ əksimɑ] |

205. Natural resources

natural resources	loodusvarad	[loːdusʋɑrɑd]
minerals	maavarad	[mɑːʋɑrɑd]
deposits	lademed	[lɑdemed]
field (e.g., oilfield)	leiukoht	[lejukoht]

to mine (extract)	kaevandama	[kɑəʋɑndɑmɑ]
mining (extraction)	kaevandamine	[kɑəʋɑndɑmine]
ore	maak	[mɑːk]
mine (e.g., for coal)	kaevandus	[kɑəʋɑndus]
mine shaft, pit	šaht	[ʃɑht]
miner	kaevur	[kɑəʋur]

| gas | gaas | [gɑːs] |
| gas pipeline | gaasijuhe | [gɑːsiyhe] |

oil (petroleum)	nafta	[nɑftɑ]
oil pipeline	naftajuhe	[nɑftɑyhe]
oil well	nafta puurtorn	[nɑftɑ puːrtorn]
derrick	puurtorn	[puːrtorn]
tanker	tanker	[tɑŋker]

sand	liiv	[liːʋ]
limestone	paekivi	[pɑəkiʋi]
gravel	kruus	[kruːs]
peat	turvas	[turʋɑs]
clay	savi	[sɑʋi]
coal	süsi	[sysi]

iron	raud	[rɑud]
gold	kuld	[kuʎd]
silver	hõbe	[hıbe]
nickel	nikkel	[nikkeʎ]

copper	vask	[vasʲk]
zinc	tsink	[ʦiŋk]
manganese	mangaan	[maŋɑːn]
mercury	elavhõbe	[əlɑʊhɪbe]
lead	seatina	[seɑtinɑ]

mineral	mineraal	[minerɑːʎ]
crystal	kristall	[kristɑʎ]
marble	marmor	[mɑrmor]
uranium	uraan	[urɑːn]

The Earth. Part 2

206. Weather

weather	**ilm**	[iʌm]
weather forecast	**ilmaennustus**	[iʌmaəŋustus]
temperature	**temperatuur**	[temperɑtuːr]
thermometer	**kraadiklaas**	[krɑːdiklɑːs]
barometer	**baromeeter**	[bɑromeːter]
humidity	**niiskus**	[niːskus]
heat (extreme ~)	**kuumus**	[kuːmus]
hot (torrid)	**kuum**	[kuːm]
it's hot	**on kuum**	[on kuːm]
it's warm	**soojus**	[soːys]
warm (moderately ʜot)	**soe**	[soə]
it's cold	**on külm**	[on kyʌm]
cold (adj)	**külm**	[kyʌm]
sun	**päike**	[pʲæjke]
to shine (vi)	**paistma**	[pɑjstmɑ]
sunny (day)	**päikseline**	[pʲæjkseline]
to come up (vi)	**tõusma**	[tɪusmɑ]
to set (vi)	**loojuma**	[loːymɑ]
cloud	**pilv**	[piʌʊ]
cloudy (adj)	**pilves**	[piʌʊes]
rain cloud	**pilv**	[piʌʊ]
somber (gloomy)	**sompus**	[sompus]
rain	**vihm**	[ʊihm]
it's raining	**vihma sajab**	[ʊihmɑ sɑæb]
rainy (day)	**vihmane**	[ʊihmɑne]
to drizzle (vi)	**tibutama**	[tibutɑmɑ]
pouring rain	**paduvihm**	[pɑduʊihm]
downpour	**hoovihm**	[hoːʊihm]
heavy (e.g., ~ rain)	**tugev**	[tugeʊ]
puddle	**lomp**	[lomp]
to get wet (in rain)	**märjaks saama**	[mʲærʲæks sɑːmɑ]
fog (mist)	**udu**	[udu]
foggy	**udune**	[udune]
snow	**lumi**	[lumi]
it's snowing	**lund sajab**	[lund sɑæb]

207. Severe weather. Natural disasters

thunderstorm	äike	[əjke]
lightning (~ strike)	välk	[ʊˈæʎk]
to flash (vi)	välku lööma	[ʊˈæʎku løːma]
thunder	kõu	[kɪu]
to thunder (vi)	müristama	[myristama]
it's thundering	müristab	[myristab]
hail	rahe	[rahe]
it's hailing	rahet sajab	[raheɪt saæb]
to flood (vt)	üle ujutama	[yle uytama]
flood, inundation	üleujutus	[yleuytus]
earthquake	maavärin	[maːʊˈærin]
tremor, quake	tõuge	[tɪuge]
epicenter	epitsenter	[əpɪtsenter]
eruption	vulkaanipurse	[ʊulkaːnipurse]
lava	laava	[laːʊa]
twister	tromb	[tromb]
tornado	tornaado	[tornaːdo]
typhoon	taifuun	[tajfuːn]
hurricane	orkaan	[orkaːn]
storm	torm	[torm]
tsunami	tsunami	[ʦunami]
cyclone	tsüklon	[ʦyklon]
bad weather	halb ilm	[haʎb iʎm]
fire (accident)	tulekahju	[tulekaɦjy]
disaster	katastroof	[katastroːf]
meteorite	meteoriit	[meteoriːt]
avalanche	laviin	[laʊiːn]
snowslide	varing	[ʊariŋ]
blizzard	lumetorm	[lumetorm]
snowstorm	tuisk	[tujsk]

208. Noises. Sounds

silence (quiet)	vaikus	[ʊajkus]
sound	heli	[heli]
noise	lärm	[ʎærm]
to make noise	lärmama	[ʎærmama]
noisy (adj)	lärmakas	[ʎærmakas]

loudly (to speak, etc.)	**valjusti**	[vaʎjysti]
loud (voice, etc.)	**vali**	[vali]
constant (continuous)	**pidev**	[pidev]
shout (n)	**karje**	[karje]
to shout (vi)	**karjuma**	[karjyma]
whisper	**sosin**	[sosin]
to whisper (vi, vt)	**sosistama**	[sosistama]
barking (of dog)	**haukumine**	[haukumine]
to bark (vi)	**haukuma**	[haukuma]
groan (of pain)	**oie**	[oje]
to groan (vi)	**oigama**	[ojgama]
cough	**köha**	[køha]
to cough (vi)	**köhima**	[køhima]
whistle	**vile**	[vile]
to whistle (vi)	**vilistama**	[vilistama]
knock (at the door)	**koputus**	[koputus]
to knock (at the dcor)	**koputama**	[koputama]
to crack (vi)	**ragisema**	[ragisema]
crack (plank, etc.)	**ragin**	[ragin]
siren	**sireen**	[sire:n]
whistle (factory ~)	**vile**	[vile]
to whistle (ship, train)	**undama**	[undama]
honk (signal)	**signaal**	[signa:l]
to honk (vi)	**signaali andma**	[signa:li andma]

209. Winter

winter (n)	**talv**	[taʎv]
winter (as adj)	**talvine**	[taʎvine]
in winter	**talvel**	[taʎveʎ]
snow	**lumi**	[lumi]
it's snowing	**lund sajab**	[lund saæb]
snowfall	**lumesadu**	[lumesadu]
snowdrift	**hang**	[haŋ]
snowflake	**lumehelbeke**	[lumeheʎbeke]
snowball	**lumepall**	[lumepaʎ]
snowman	**lumememm**	[lumememm]
icicle	**purikas**	[purikas]
December	**detsember**	[detsember]
January	**jaanuar**	[æ:nuar]
February	**veebruar**	[ve:bruar]

severe frost	**pakane**	[pɑkɑne]
frosty (weather, air)	**pakasene**	[pɑkɑsene]
below zero (adv)	**alla nulli**	[ɑllɑ nulli]
first frost	**öökülmad**	[ø:kyʌmɑd]
hoarfrost	**härmatis**	[hærmɑtis]
cold (cold weather)	**külm**	[kyʌm]
it's cold	**külmalt**	[kyʌmɑʌt]
fur coat	**kasukas**	[kɑsukɑs]
mittens	**labakindad**	[lɑbɑkindɑd]
to get sick	**haigeks jääma**	[hɑjgeks æ:mɑ]
cold (illness)	**külmetus**	[kyʌmetus]
to catch a cold	**külmetuma**	[kyʌmetumɑ]
ice	**jää**	[æ:]
black ice	**kiilasjää**	[ki:lɑsæ:]
to freeze (ab. river, etc.)	**külmuma**	[kyʌmumɑ]
ice floe	**jääpank**	[æ:pɑŋk]
skis	**suusad**	[su:sɑd]
skier	**suusataja**	[su:sɑtɑæ]
to ski (vi)	**suusatama**	[su:sɑtɑmɑ]
to skate (vi)	**uisutama**	[ujsutɑmɑ]

Fauna

210. Mammals. Predators

predator	**kiskja**	[kiskʲæ]
tiger	**tiiger**	[tiːger]
lion	**lõvi**	[lɪʋi]
wolf	**hunt**	[huɲt]
fox	**rebane**	[rebɑne]
jaguar	**jaaguar**	[æːguɑr]
leopard	**leopard**	[leopɑrd]
cheetah	**gepard**	[gepɑrd]
black panther	**panter**	[pɑnter]
puma	**puuma**	[puːmɑ]
snow leopard	**lumeleopard**	[lumeleopɑrd]
lynx	**ilves**	[iʌʋes]
coyote	**koiott**	[koøt]
jackal	**šaakal**	[ʃɑːkɑl]
hyena	**hüään**	[hyæːn]

211. Wild animals

animal	**loom**	[loːm]
beast (animal)	**metsloom**	[metsloːm]
squirrel	**orav**	[orɑʋ]
hedgehog	**siil**	[siːʎ]
hare	**jänes**	[ænes]
rabbit	**küülik**	[kyːlik]
badger	**mäger**	[mʲæger]
raccoon	**pesukaru**	[pesukɑru]
hamster	**hamster**	[hɑmstər]
marmot	**koopaorav**	[koːpɑorɑʋ]
mole	**mutt**	[muttʲ]
mouse	**hiir**	[hiːr]
rat	**rott**	[rottʲ]
bat	**nahkhiir**	[nɑhkhiːr]
ermine	**kärp**	[kʲærp]
sable	**soobel**	[soːbeʌ]

marten	nugis	[nugis]
weasel	nirk	[nirk]
mink	naarits	[nɑ:rits]

beaver	kobras	[kobrɑs]
otter	saarmas	[sɑ:rmɑs]

horse	hobune	[hobune]
moose	põder	[pɪder]
deer	põhjapõder	[pɪhæpɪder]
camel	kaamel	[kɑ:meʎ]

bison	piison	[pi:son]
aurochs	euroopa piison	[əuro:pɑ pi:son]
buffalo	pühvel	[pyhʊeʎ]

zebra	sebra	[sebrɑ]
antelope	antiloop	[antilo:p]
roe deer	metskits	[metskits]
fallow deer	kabehirv	[kabehirʊ]
chamois	mägikits	[mʲægikits]
wild boar	metssiga	[metssigɑ]

whale	vaal	[ʊɑ:l]
seal	hüljes	[hyʎjes]
walrus	merihobu	[merihobu]
fur seal	kotik	[kotik]
dolphin	delfiin	[deʎfi:n]

bear	karu	[kɑru]
polar bear	jääkaru	[æ:kɑru]
panda	panda	[pɑndɑ]

monkey	ahv	[ɑhʊ]
chimpanzee	šimpans	[ʃimpɑns]
orangutan	orangutang	[orɑɲutɑŋ]
gorilla	gorilla	[gorillɑ]
macaque	makaak	[mɑkɑ:k]
gibbon	gibon	[gibon]

elephant	elevant	[eleʊɑnt]
rhinoceros	ninasarvik	[ninɑsɑrʊik]
giraffe	kaelkirjak	[kɑeʎkirʲæk]
hippopotamus	jõehobu	[jɪ:hobu]

kangaroo	känguru	[kʲæɲuru]
koala (bear)	koaala	[koɑ:lɑ]

mongoose	mangust	[mɑɲust]
chinchilla	tšintšilja	[ʧinʧiʎæ]
skunk	skunk	[skuŋk]
porcupine	okassiga	[okɑssigɑ]

212. Domestic animals

cat	kass	[kassʲ]
tomcat	kass	[kassʲ]
dog	koer	[koər]
horse	hobune	[hobune]
stallion	täkk	[tʲækk]
mare	mära	[mʲæra]
cow	lehm	[lehm]
bull	pull	[puʎ]
ox	härg	[ɦærg]
sheep	lammas	[lammɑs]
ram	oinas	[ojnɑs]
goat	kits	[kiʦ]
billy goat, he-goat	sokk	[sokk]
donkey	eesel	[əeseʎ]
mule	muul	[muːʎ]
pig	siga	[sigɑ]
piglet	põrsas	[pɪrsɑs]
rabbit	küülik	[kyːlik]
hen (chicken)	kana	[kɑnɑ]
rooster	kukk	[kukk]
duck	part	[pɑrt]
drake	sinikaelpart	[sinikɑəʎpɑrt]
goose	hani	[hɑni]
tom turkey	kalkun	[kɑlkun]
turkey (hen)	kalkun	[kɑlkun]
domestic animals	koduloomad	[koduloːmɑd]
tame (e.g., ~ hamster)	kodustatud	[kodustɑtud]
to tame (vt)	taltsutama	[tɑʎʦutɑmɑ]
to breed (vt)	üles kasvatama	[yles kɑsʋɑtɑmɑ]
farm	farm	[fɑrm]
poultry	kodulinnud	[koduliŋud]
cattle	kariloomad	[kɑriloːmɑd]
herd (cattle)	kari	[kɑri]
stable	hobusetall	[hobusetɑʎ]
pigsty	sigala	[sigɑlɑ]
cowshed	lehmalaut	[lehmɑlɑut]
rabbit hutch	küülikukasvandus	[kyːlikukɑsʋɑtus]
hen house	kanala	[kɑnɑlɑ]

213. Dogs. Dog breeds

dog	koer	[koər]
sheepdog	lambakoer	[lambakoər]
poodle	puudel	[pu:dəʎ]
dachshund	taksikoer	[taksikoər]
bulldog	buldog	[buʎdog]
boxer	bokser	[bokser]
mastiff	Mastif	[mastif]
rottweiler	Rotveiler	[rotʋejler]
Doberman	dobermann	[doberman]
basset	basset	[basset]
bobtail	vana-inglise lambakoer	[ʋana iŋlise lambakoər]
Dalmatian	Dalmaatsia koer	[dalmaːtsia koər]
cocker spaniel	kokkerspanjel	[kokker spaŋjeʎ]
Newfoundland	Newfoundlandi koer	[ɲjyfaundlandi koər]
Saint Bernard	bernhardiin	[bernhardiːn]
husky	siberi husky	[siberi haski]
Chow Chow	Tšau-tšau	[tʃau tʃau]
spitz	spits	[spits]
pug	mops	[mops]

214. Sounds made by animals

barking (n)	haukumine	[haukumine]
to bark (vi)	haukuma	[haukuma]
to meow (vi)	näuguma	[næuguma]
to purr (vi)	nurru lööma	[nurru løːma]
to moo (vi)	ammuma	[ammuma]
to bellow (bull)	möirgama	[møjrgama]
to growl (vi)	urisema	[urisema]
howl (n)	ulg	[uʎg]
to howl (vi)	ulguma	[uʎguma]
to whine (vi)	niutsuma	[niutsuma]
to bleat (sheep)	määgima	[mæːgima]
to oink, to grunt (pig)	röhkima	[røhkima]
to squeal (vi)	vinguma	[ʋiŋuma]
to croak (vi)	krooksuma	[kroːksuma]
to buzz (insect)	vinguma	[ʋiŋuma]
to stridulate (vi)	siristama	[siristama]

215. Young animals

cub	**loomalaps**	[loːmalaps]
kitten	**kassipoeg**	[kassipoeg]
baby mouse	**hiirepoeg**	[hiːrepoeg]
pup, puppy	**kutsikas**	[kutsikas]
leveret	**jänesepoeg**	[ænesepoeg]
baby rabbit	**küülikupoeg**	[kyːlikupoeg]
wolf cub	**hundikutsikas**	[hundikutsikas]
fox cub	**rebasekutsikas**	[rebasekutsikas]
bear cub	**karupoeg**	[karupoeg]
lion cub	**lõvikutsikas**	[lɹuikutsikas]
tiger cub	**tiigrikutsikas**	[tiːgrikutsikas]
elephant calf	**elevandipoeg**	[eleuandipoeg]
piglet	**põrsas**	[pɪrsas]
calf (young cow, bull)	**vasikas**	[uasikas]
kid (young goat)	**kitsetall**	[kitsetaʎ]
lamb	**lambatall**	[lambataʎ]
fawn (young deer)	**põdravasikas**	[pɪdrauasikas]
young camel	**kaamelipoeg**	[kaːmelipoeg]
baby snake	**ussipoeg**	[ussipoeg]
baby frog	**konnapoeg**	[konŋapoeg]
nestling	**linnupoeg**	[liɲupoeg]
chick (of chicken)	**kanapoeg**	[kanapoeg]
duckling	**pardipoeg**	[pardipoeg]

216. Birds

bird	**lind**	[lind]
pigeon	**tuvi**	[tuui]
sparrow	**varblane**	[uarblane]
tit	**tihane**	[tihane]
magpie	**harakas**	[harakas]
raven	**ronk**	[ronk]
crow	**vares**	[uares]
jackdaw	**hakk**	[hakk]
rook	**künnivares**	[kyɲiuares]
duck	**part**	[part]
goose	**hani**	[hani]
pheasant	**faasan**	[faːsan]
eagle	**kotkas**	[kotkas]
hawk	**kull**	[kuʎ]

falcon	kotkas	[kotkɑs]
vulture	raisakull	[rɑjsɑkuʎ]
condor (Andean ~)	kondor	[kondor]

swan	luik	[lujk]
crane	kurg	[kurg]
stork	toonekurg	[toːnekurg]

parrot	papagoi	[pɑpɑgoj]
hummingbird	koolibri	[koːlibri]
peacock	paabulind	[pɑːbulind]

ostrich	jaanalind	[æːnɑlind]
heron	haigur	[hɑjgur]
flamingo	flamingo	[flɑmiŋo]
pelican	pelikan	[pelikɑn]

| nightingale | ööbik | [øːbik] |
| swallow | suitsupääsuke | [sujtsupæːsuke] |

thrush	rästas	[rʲæstɑs]
song thrush	laulurästas	[lɑulurʲæstɑs]
blackbird	musträstas	[mustrʲæstɑs]

swift	piiripääsuke	[piːripæːsuke]
lark	lõoke	[lɪoke]
quail	vutt	[ʊuttʲ]

woodpecker	rähn	[rʲæhn]
cuckoo	kägu	[kʲægu]
owl	öökull	[øːkuʎ]
eagle owl	kakk	[kɑkk]
wood grouse	metsis	[metsis]
black grouse	teder	[teder]
partridge	põldpüü	[pɪʎdpyː]

starling	kuldnokk	[kuʎdnokk]
canary	kanaarilind	[kɑnɑːrilind]
hazel grouse	laanepüü	[lɑːnepyu]
chaffinch	metsvint	[metsʊint]
bullfinch	leevike	[leːʊike]

seagull	kajakas	[kɑækɑs]
albatross	albatross	[ɑʎbatross]
penguin	pingviin	[piŋʊiːn]

217. Birds. Singing and sounds

| to sing (vi) | laulma | [lɑuʎmɑ] |
| to call (animal, bird) | karjuma | [kɑrjymɑ] |

to crow (rooster)	**kirema**	[kirema]
cock-a-doodle-dco	**kikerikii**	[kikeriki:]

to cluck (hen)	**kaagutama**	[ka:gutama]
to caw (vi)	**kraaksuma**	[kra:ksuma]
to quack (duck)	**prääksuma**	[præ:ksuma]
to cheep (vi)	**piiksuma**	[pi:ksuma]
to chirp, to twitter	**siristama**	[siristama]

218. Fish. Marine animals

bream	**latikas**	[latikas]
carp	**karpkala**	[karpkala]
perch	**ahven**	[ahʋen]
catfish	**säga**	[sʲæga]
pike	**haug**	[haug]

salmon	**lõhe**	[lɪhe]
sturgeon	**tuurakala**	[tu:rakala]

herring	**heeringas**	[he:riŋas]
Atlantic salmon	**väärislõhe**	[ʋæ:rislɪhe]
mackerel	**skumbria**	[skumbriæ]
flatfish	**lest**	[lest]

zander, pike perch	**kohakala**	[kohakala]
cod	**tursk**	[tursk]
tuna	**tuunikala**	[tu:nikala]
trout	**forell**	[foreʌ]
eel	**angerjas**	[aŋerʲæs]
electric ray	**elektrirai**	[əlektriraj]
moray eel	**mureen**	[mure:n]
piranha	**piraaja**	[pira:æ]

shark	**haikala**	[hajkala]
dolphin	**delfiin**	[deʌfi:n]
whale	**vaal**	[ʋɑ:l]

crab	**krabi**	[krabi]
jellyfish	**meduus**	[medu:s]
octopus	**kaheksajalg**	[kaheksaælg]

starfish	**meritäht**	[meritʲæht]
sea urchin	**merisiil**	[merisi:ʌ]
seahorse	**merihobuke**	[merihobuke]

oyster	**auster**	[auster]
shrimp	**krevett**	[kreʋett]
lobster	**homaar**	[homa:r]
spiny lobster	**langust**	[laŋust]

219. Amphibians. Reptiles

snake	**uss**	[ussʲ]
venomous (snake)	**mürgine**	[myrgine]
viper	**rästik**	[rʲæstik]
cobra	**kobra**	[kobrɑ]
python	**püüton**	[py:ton]
boa	**boamadu**	[boɑmɑdu]
grass snake	**nastik**	[nɑstik]
rattle snake	**lõgismadu**	[lɪgismɑdu]
anaconda	**anakonda**	[ɑnɑkondɑ]
lizard	**sisalik**	[sisɑlik]
iguana	**iguaan**	[iguɑ:n]
monitor lizard	**varaan**	[ʋɑrɑ:n]
salamander	**salamander**	[sɑlɑmɑnder]
chameleon	**kameeleon**	[kɑme:leon]
scorpion	**skorpion**	[skorpion]
turtle	**kilpkonn**	[kiʎpkoŋʲ]
frog	**konn**	[koŋʲ]
toad	**kärnkonn**	[kʲærŋkoŋʲ]
crocodile	**krokodill**	[krokodiʎ]

220. Insects

insect, bug	**putukas**	[putukɑs]
butterfly	**liblikas**	[liblikɑs]
ant	**sipelgas**	[sipeʎgɑs]
fly	**kärbes**	[kʲærbes]
mosquito	**sääsk**	[sæ:sk]
beetle	**sitikas**	[sitikɑs]
wasp	**herilane**	[herilɑne]
bee	**mesilane**	[mesilɑne]
bumblebee	**metsmesilane**	[metsmesilɑne]
gadfly	**kiin**	[ki:n]
spider	**ämblik**	[əmblik]
spider's web	**ämblikuvõrk**	[əmblikuʊirk]
dragonfly	**kiil**	[ki:ʎ]
grasshopper	**rohutirts**	[rohutirʦ]
moth (night butterfly)	**liblikas**	[liblikɑs]
cockroach	**tarakan**	[tɑrɑkɑn]
tick	**puuk**	[pu:k]

| flea | **kirp** | [kirp] |
| midge | **kihulane** | [kihulɑne] |

locust	**rändtirts**	[rʲændtirts]
snail	**tigu**	[tigu]
cricket	**ritsikas**	[ritsikɑs]
lightning bug	**jaaniuss**	[æːniuss]
ladybug	**lepatriinu**	[lepɑtriːnu]
cockchafer	**maipõrnikas**	[mɑjpɪrnikɑs]

leech	**kaan**	[kɑːn]
caterpillar	**tõuk**	[tɪuk]
earthworm	**vagel**	[ʋɑgeʎ]
larva	**tõuk**	[tɪuk]

221. Animals. Body parts

beak	**nokk**	[nokk]
wings	**tiivad**	[tiːʋɑd]
foot (of bird)	**jalg**	[ælg]

feathering	**sulestik**	[sulestik]
feather	**sulg**	[suʎg]
crest	**pappus**	[pɑppus]

gill	**lõpused**	[lɪpused]
spawn	**kalamari**	[kɑlɑmɑri]
larva	**vastne**	[ʋɑstne]

| fin | **uim** | [ujm] |
| scales (of fish, reptile) | **soomus** | [soːmus] |

fang (canine)	**kihv**	[kihʊ]
paw (e.g., cat's ~)	**käpp**	[kʲæpp]
muzzle (snout)	**nägu**	[nægu]
mouth (of cat, dog)	**koon**	[koːn]

| tail | **saba** | [sɑbɑ] |
| whiskers | **vurrud** | [ʋurrud] |

| hoof | **kabi** | [kɑbi] |
| horn | **sarv** | [sɑrʊ] |

carapace	**soomuskate**	[soːmuskɑte]
shell (of mollusk)	**koda**	[kodɑ]
eggshell	**munakoor**	[munɑkoːr]

| animal's hair (pelage) | **karvad** | [kɑrʊɑd] |

| pelt (hide) | **nahk** | [nɑhk] |

222. Actions of animals

to fly (vi)	**lendama**	[lendɑmɑ]
to make circles	**keerlema**	[keːrlemɑ]
to fly away	**ära lendama**	[ərɑ lendɑmɑ]
to flap (~ the wings)	**lehvitama**	[lehʋitɑmɑ]
to peck (vi)	**nokkima**	[nokkimɑ]
to sit on eggs	**poegi välja hauduma**	[poegi ʋʲæʎæ hɑudumɑ]
to hatch out (vi)	**munast välja tulema**	[munɑst ʋʲæʎæ tulemɑ]
to build the nest	**pesa punuma**	[pesɑ punumɑ]
to slither, to crawl	**roomama**	[roːmɑmɑ]
to sting, to bite (insect)	**nõelama**	[nɪːlɑmɑ]
to bite (ab. animal)	**hammustama**	[hɑmmustɑmɑ]
to sniff (vt)	**nuusutama**	[nuːsutɑmɑ]
to bark (vi)	**haukuma**	[hɑukumɑ]
to hiss (snake)	**susisema**	[susisemɑ]
to scare (vt)	**ehmatama**	[əhmɑtɑmɑ]
to attack (vt)	**kallale tungima**	[kɑllɑle tuŋimɑ]
to gnaw (bone, etc.)	**närima**	[ɲærimɑ]
to scratch (with claws)	**kriimustama**	[kriːmustɑmɑ]
to hide (vi)	**ennast ära peitma**	[əŋɑst ərɑ pejtmɑ]
to play (kittens, etc.)	**mängima**	[mʲæŋimɑ]
to hunt (vi, vt)	**jahil käima**	[æhiʎ kʲæjmɑ]
to hibernate (vi)	**talveunes olema**	[tɑʎʋeunəs olemɑ]
to become extinct	**välja surema**	[ʋʲæʎæ suremɑ]

223. Animals. Habitats

habitat	**elukeskkond**	[əlukeskkond]
migration	**migratsioon**	[migrɑtsioːn]
mountain	**mägi**	[mʲægi]
reef	**riff**	[riff]
cliff	**kalju**	[kɑʎjy]
forest	**mets**	[mets]
jungle	**džungel**	[dʒuŋeʎ]
savanna	**savann**	[sɑʋɑŋ]
tundra	**tundra**	[tundrɑ]
steppe	**stepp**	[stepp]
desert	**kõrb**	[kɪrb]
oasis	**oaas**	[oɑːs]
sea	**meri**	[meri]

lake	**järv**	[ærʊ]
ocean	**ookean**	[oːkeɑn]

swamp	**soo**	[soː]
freshwater (adj)	**mageveeline**	[mageʋeːline]
pond	**tiik**	[tiːk]
river	**jõgi**	[jɪgi]

den	**karukoobas**	[karukoːbɑs]
nest	**pesa**	[pesɑ]
hollow (in a tree)	**õõs**	[ɪːs]
burrow (animal hole)	**urg**	[urg]
anthill	**sipelgapesa**	[sipeʎgapesɑ]

224. Animal care

zoo	**loomaaed**	[loːmaːəd]
nature preserve	**looduskaitseala**	[loːduskɑjtseɑlɑ]

breeder, breed club	**kasvandus**	[kasʋandus]
open-air cage	**jooksuaed**	[joːksuɑəd]
cage	**puur**	[puːr]
kennel	**kuut**	[kuːt]

dovecot	**tuvila**	[tuʋilɑ]
aquarium	**akvaarium**	[akʋɑːrium]
dolphinarium	**delfinaarium**	[deʎfinɑːrium]

to breed (animals)	**loomi pidama**	[loːmi pidamɑ]
brood, litter	**järglased**	[ærglased]
to tame (vt)	**taltsutama**	[taʎtsutamɑ]
feed (fodder, etc.)	**sööt**	[søːt]
to feed (vt)	**söötma**	[søːtmɑ]
to train (animals)	**dresseerima**	[dresseːrimɑ]

pet store	**zookauplus**	[zoːkauplus]
muzzle (for dog)	**suukorv**	[suːkorʋ]
collar	**kaelarihm**	[kaəlarihm]
name (of animal)	**nimi**	[nimi]
pedigree (of dog)	**sugupuu**	[sugupuː]

225. Animals. Miscellaneous

pack (wolves)	**hundikari**	[hundikari]
flock (birds)	**linnuparv**	[liɲuparʊ]
shoal (fish)	**kalaparv**	[kalaparʊ]
herd of horses	**hobusekari**	[hobusekari]
male (n)	**isasloom**	[isasloːm]

female	emasloom	[əmɑslo:m]
hungry (adj)	näljane	[ɲæʌæne]
wild (adj)	metsik	[metsik]
dangerous (adj)	ohtlik	[ohtlik]

226. Horses

| horse | hobune | [hobune] |
| breed (race) | tõug | [tɪug] |

| foal, colt | varss | [ʊɑrs] |
| mare | mära | [mʲæra] |

mustang	mustang	[mustaŋ]
pony	poni	[poni]
draft horse	raskeveohobune	[rɑskeʊeohobune]

| mane | lakk | [lɑkk] |
| tail | saba | [sɑba] |

hoof	kabi	[kɑbi]
horseshoe	hobuseraud	[hobuserɑud]
to shoe (vt)	hobust rautama	[hobust rɑutɑma]
blacksmith	sepp	[sepp]

saddle	sadul	[sɑduʌ]
stirrup	jalus	[ælus]
bridle	valjad	[ʊɑʌæd]
reins	ohjad	[ohæd]
whip (for riding)	piits	[pi:ts]

rider	ratsutaja	[rɑtsutɑæ]
to break in (horse)	välja õpetama	[ʊʲæʌæ ɪpetɑma]
to saddle (vt)	saduldama	[sɑduʌdɑma]
to mount a horse	sadulasse istuma	[sɑdulɑsse istuma]

gallop	galopp	[gɑlopp]
to gallop (vi)	galoppi sõitma	[gɑloppi sɪjtma]
trot (n)	traav	[trɑ:ʊ]
at a trot (adv)	traavima	[trɑ:ʊima]

| racehorse | ratsahobune | [rɑtsahobune] |
| horse racing | ratsavõistlused | [rɑtsaʊɪjstlused] |

stable	hobusetall	[hobusetɑʌ]
to feed (vt)	söötma	[sø:tma]
hay	hein	[hejn]
to water (animals)	jootma	[jo:tma]
to wash (horse)	puhastama	[puhɑstɑma]
to hobble (tether)	kammitsema	[kɑmmitsema]

to graze (vi)	**karjamaal olema**	[karˈæmɑːʎ olema]
to neigh (vi)	**hirnuma**	[hirnumɑ]
to kick (horse)	**jalaga lööma**	[ælɑgɑ løːmɑ]

Flora

227. Trees

tree	puu	[pu:]
deciduous (adj)	lehtpuu	[lehtpu:]
coniferous (adj)	okaspuu	[okaspu:]
evergreen (adj)	igihaljas	[igihaʎæs]
apple tree	õunapuu	[ɪunɑpu:]
pear tree	pirnipuu	[pirnipu:]
sweet cherry tree	murelipuu	[murelipu:]
sour cherry tree	kirsipuu	[kirsipu:]
plum tree	ploomipuu	[plo:mipu:]
birch	kask	[kɑsk]
oak	tamm	[tɑmm]
linden tree	pärn	[pʲærn]
aspen	haav	[hɑ:ʋ]
maple	vaher	[ʋɑher]
spruce	kuusk	[ku:sk]
pine	mänd	[mʲænd]
larch	lehis	[lehis]
fir tree	nulg	[nuʎg]
cedar	seeder	[se:dər]
poplar	pappel	[pɑppeʎ]
rowan	pihlakas	[pihlɑkɑs]
willow	paju	[pɑy]
alder	lepp	[lepp]
beech	pöök	[pø:k]
elm	jalakas	[ælɑkɑs]
ash (tree)	saar	[sɑ:r]
chestnut	kastan	[kɑstɑn]
magnolia	magnoolia	[mɑgno:liɑ]
palm tree	palm	[pɑʎm]
cypress	küpress	[kypressʲ]
mangrove	mangroovipuu	[mɑŋro:ʋipu:]
baobab	ahvileivapuu	[ɑhʋilejʋɑpu:]
eucalyptus	eukalüpt	[əukɑlypt]
sequoia	sekvoia	[sekʋojɑ]

228. Shrubs

bush	**põõsas**	[pɪːsɑs]
shrub	**põõsastik**	[pɪːsɑstik]
grapevine	**viinamarjad**	[ʋiːnɑmɑrˈæd]
vineyard	**viinamarjaistandus**	[ʋiːnɑmɑrˈæistɑndus]
raspberry bush	**vaarikas**	[ʋɑːrikɑs]
redcurrant bush	**punane sõstar**	[punɑne sɪstɑr]
gooseberry bush	**karusmari**	[kɑrusmɑri]
acacia	**akaatsia**	[ɑkɑːtsiæ]
barberry	**kukerpuu**	[kukerpuː]
jasmine	**jasmiin**	[æsmiːn]
juniper	**kadakas**	[kɑdɑkɑs]
rosebush	**roosipõõsas**	[roːsipɪesɑs]
dog rose	**kibuvits**	[kibuʋits]

229. Mushrooms

mushroom	**seen**	[seːn]
edible mushroom	**söödav seen**	[søːdɑu seːn]
toadstool	**mürgine seen**	[myrgine seːn]
cap (of mushroom)	**seenekübar**	[seːnekybɑr]
stipe (of mushroom)	**seenejalg**	[seːneælg]
cep (Boletus edulis)	**kivipuravik**	[kiʋipurɑʋik]
orange-cap boletus	**haavapuravik**	[hɑːʋɑpurɑʋik]
birch bolete	**kasepuravik**	[kɑsepurɑʋik]
chanterelle	**kukeseen**	[kukeseːn]
russula	**pilvik**	[piʎʋik]
morel	**mürkel**	[myrkeʎ]
fly agaric	**kärbseseen**	[kˈærpseseːn]
death cap	**sitaseen**	[sitɑseːn]

230. Fruits. Berries

apple	**õun**	[ɪun]
pear	**pirn**	[pirn]
plum	**ploom**	[ploːm]
strawberry	**aedmaasikas**	[ɑedmɑːsikɑs]
sour cherry	**kirss**	[kirss]
sweet cherry	**murel**	[mureʎ]

grape	viinamarjad	[ʋi:namarʲæd]
raspberry	vaarikas	[ʋɑ:rikɑs]
blackcurrant	must sõstar	[must sɪstɑr]
redcurrant	punane sõstar	[punɑne sɪstɑr]
gooseberry	karusmari	[kɑrusmɑri]
cranberry	jõhvikas	[jɪhʋikɑs]

orange	apelsin	[apeʎsin]
mandarin	mandariin	[mɑndɑri:n]
pineapple	ananass	[ɑnɑnɑs]
banana	banaan	[bɑnɑ:n]
date	dattel	[dɑtteʎ]

lemon	sidrun	[sidrun]
apricot	aprikoos	[ɑpriko:s]
peach	virsik	[ʋirsik]
kiwi	kiivi	[ki:ʋi]
grapefruit	greip	[grejp]

berry	mari	[mɑri]
berries	marjad	[mɑrʲæd]
cowberry	pohlad	[pohlad]
field strawberry	maasikas	[mɑ:sikɑs]
bilberry	mustikas	[mustikɑs]

231. Flowers. Plants

flower	lill	[liʎ]
bouquet (of flowers)	lillekimp	[lillekimp]

rose (flower)	roos	[ro:s]
tulip	tulp	[tuʎp]
carnation	nelk	[neʎk]
gladiolus	gladiool	[glɑdio:l]

cornflower	rukkilill	[rukkiliʎ]
bluebell	kellukas	[kellukɑs]
dandelion	võilill	[ʋɪjliʎ]
camomile	karikakar	[kɑrikɑkɑr]

aloe	aaloe	[ɑ:loə]
cactus	kaktus	[kɑktus]
rubber plant, ficus	kummipuu	[kummipu:]

lily	liilia	[li:liɑ]
geranium	geraanium	[gerɑ:nium]
hyacinth	hüatsint	[hyɑtsint]

mimosa	mimoos	[mimo:s]
narcissus	nartsiss	[nɑrtsiss]

nasturtium	**kress**	[kress]
orchid	**orhidee**	[orhide:]
peony	**pojeng**	[pojeŋ]
violet	**kannike**	[kaŋike]

pansy	**võõrasemad**	[ʋɪ:rasəmad]
forget-me-not	**meelespea**	[me:lespea]
daisy	**margareeta**	[margare:ta]

poppy	**moon**	[mo:n]
hemp	**kanep**	[kanep]
mint	**piparmünt**	[piparmynt]

| lily of the valley | **maikelluke** | [majkelluke] |
| snowdrop | **lumikelluke** | [lymikelluke] |

nettle	**nõges**	[nɪges]
sorrel	**hapuoblikas**	[hapuoblikas]
water lily	**vesiroos**	[ʋesiro:s]
fern	**sõnajalg**	[sɪnaælg]
lichen	**samblik**	[samblik]

tropical greenhouse	**kasvuhoone**	[kasʋuho:ne]
grass lawn	**muru**	[muru]
flowerbed	**lillepeenar**	[lillepe:nar]

plant	**taim**	[tajm]
grass, herb	**rohi**	[rohi]
blade of grass	**rohulible**	[rohulible]

leaf	**leht**	[leht]
petal	**õieleht**	[ɪjəleht]
stem	**vars**	[ʋars]
tuber	**sibul**	[sibuʎ]

| young plant (shoot) | **idu** | [idu] |
| thorn | **okas** | [okas] |

to blossom (vi)	**õitsema**	[ɪjtsema]
to fade, to wither	**närtsima**	[nærtsima]
smell (odor)	**lõhn**	[lɪhn]
to cut (flowers)	**lõikama**	[lɪjkama]
to pick (a flower)	**murdma**	[murdma]

232. Cereals, grains

grain	**vili**	[ʋili]
cereal crops	**teraviljad**	[teraʋiʎæd]
ear (of barley, etc.)	**kõrs**	[kɪrs]
wheat	**nisu**	[nisu]

rye	rukis	[rukis]
oats	kaer	[kɑər]
millet	hirss	[hirs]
barley	oder	[odər]

corn	mais	[mɑjs]
rice	riis	[ri:s]
buckwheat	tatar	[tɑtɑr]

pea plant	hernes	[hernes]
kidney bean	aedoad	[ɑədoɑd]
soy	soja	[soæ]
lentil	lääts	[læ:ts]
beans (pulse crops)	põldoad	[pɪʎdoɑd]

233. Vegetables. Greens

| vegetables | juurviljad | [y:rʊiʎæd] |
| greens | maitseroheline | [mɑjtseroheline] |

tomato	tomat	[tomɑt]
cucumber	kurk	[kurk]
carrot	porgand	[porgɑnd]
potato	kartul	[kɑrtuʎ]
onion	sibul	[sibuʎ]
garlic	küüslauk	[ky:slɑuk]

cabbage	kapsas	[kɑpsɑs]
cauliflower	lillkapsas	[liʎkɑpsɑs]
Brussels sprouts	brüsseli kapsas	[brysseli kɑpsɑs]
beetroot	peet	[pe:t]
eggplant	baklažaan	[bɑklɑʒɑ:n]
zucchini	kabatšokk	[kɑbɑtʃokk]
pumpkin	kõrvits	[kɪrʊits]
turnip	naeris	[nɑəris]

parsley	petersell	[peterseʎ]
dill	till	[tiʎ]
lettuce	salat	[sɑlɑt]
celery	seller	[seller]
asparagus	aspar	[ɑspɑr]
spinach	spinat	[spinɑt]

pea	hernes	[hernes]
beans	põldoad	[pɪʎdoɑd]
corn (maize)	mais	[mɑjs]
kidney bean	aedoad	[ɑədoɑd]
pepper	pipar	[pipɑr]
radish	redis	[redis]
artichoke	artišokk	[ɑrtiʃok]

REGIONAL GEOGRAPHY

Countries. Nationalities

234. Western Europe

Europe	**Euroopa**	[əuro:pa]
European Union	**Euroopa Liit**	[əuro:pa li:t]
European (n)	**eurooplane**	[əuro:plane]
European (adj)	**euroopa**	[əuro:pa]

Austria	**Austria**	[austria]
Austrian (masc.)	**austerlane**	[austerlane]
Austrian (fem.)	**austerlanna**	[austerlaŋa]
Austrian (adj)	**austria**	[austria]

Great Britain	**Suurbritannia**	[su:r britaŋia]
England	**Inglismaa**	[iŋlisma:]
British (masc.)	**inglane**	[iŋlane]
British (fem.)	**inglanna**	[iŋlaŋa]
English, British (adj)	**inglise**	[iŋlise]

Belgium	**Belgia**	[beʌgiæ]
Belgian (masc.)	**belglane**	[beʌglane]
Belgian (fem.)	**belglanna**	[beʌglaŋa]
Belgian (adj)	**belgia**	[beʌgiæ]

Germany	**Saksamaa**	[saksama:]
German (masc.)	**sakslane**	[sakslane]
German (fem.)	**sakslanna**	[sakslaŋa]
German (adj)	**saksa**	[saksa]

Netherlands	**Madalmaad**	[madaʌma:d]
Holland	**Holland**	[holland]
Dutchman	**hollandlane**	[hollandlane]
Dutchwoman	**hollandlanna**	[hollandlaŋa]
Dutch (adj)	**hollandi**	[hollandi]

Greece	**Kreeka**	[kre:ka]
Greek (masc.)	**kreeklane**	[kre:klane]
Greek (fem.)	**kreeklanna**	[kre:klaŋa]
Greek (adj)	**kreeka**	[kre:ka]

| Denmark | **Taani** | [ta:ni] |
| Dane (masc.) | **taanlane** | [ta:nlane] |

| Dane (fem.) | **taanlanna** | [tɑ:nlɑŋɑ] |
| Danish (adj) | **taani** | [tɑ:ni] |

Ireland	**Iirimaa**	[i:rimɑ:]
Irishman	**iirlane**	[i:rlɑne]
Irishwoman	**iirlanna**	[i:rlɑŋɑ]
Irish (adj)	**iiri**	[i:ri]

Iceland	**Island**	[islɑnd]
Icelander (masc.)	**islandlane**	[islɑndlɑne]
Icelander (fem.)	**islandlanna**	[islɑndlɑŋɑ]
Icelandic (adj)	**islandi**	[islɑndi]

Spain	**Hispaania**	[hispɑ:niɑ]
Spaniard (masc.)	**hispaanlane**	[hispɑ:nlɑne]
Spaniard (fem.)	**hispaanlanna**	[hispɑ:nlɑŋɑ]
Spanish (adj)	**hispaania**	[hispɑ:niɑ]

Italy	**Itaalia**	[itɑ:liɑ]
Italian (masc.)	**itaallane**	[itɑ:llɑne]
Italian (fem.)	**itaallanna**	[itɑ:llɑŋɑ]
Italian (adj)	**itaalia**	[itɑ:liɑ]

Cyprus	**Küpros**	[kypros]
Cypriot (masc.)	**küproslane**	[kyproslɑne]
Cypriot (fem.)	**küproslanna**	[kyproslɑŋɑ]
Cypriot (adj)	**küprose**	[kyprose]

Malta	**Malta**	[mɑʎtɑ]
Maltese (masc.)	**maltalane**	[mɑʎtalɑne]
Maltese (fem.)	**maltalanna**	[mɑʎtalɑŋɑ]
Maltese (adj)	**malta**	[mɑʎtɑ]

Norway	**Norra**	[norrɑ]
Norwegian (masc.)	**norralane**	[norralɑne]
Norwegian (fem.)	**norralanna**	[norralɑŋɑ]
Norwegian (adj)	**norra**	[norrɑ]

Portugal	**Portugal**	[portugɑʎ]
Portuguese (masc.)	**portugallane**	[portugallɑne]
Portuguese (fem.)	**portugallanna**	[portugallɑŋɑ]
Portuguese (adj)	**portugali**	[portugɑli]

Finland	**Soome**	[so:me]
Finn (masc.)	**soomlane**	[so:mlɑne]
Finn (fem.)	**soomlanna**	[so:mlɑŋɑ]
Finnish (adj)	**soome**	[so:me]

France	**Prantsusmaa**	[prɑntsusmɑ:]
Frenchman	**prantslane**	[prɑntslɑne]
Frenchwoman	**prantslanna**	[prɑntslɑŋɑ]
French (adj)	**prantsuse**	[prɑntsuse]

Sweden	**Rootsi**	[ro:tsi]
Swede (masc.)	**rootslane**	[ro:tslane]
Swede (fem.)	**rootslanna**	[ro:tslaŋa]
Swedish (adj)	**rootsi**	[ro:tsi]

Switzerland	**Šveits**	[ʃʋejts]
Swiss (masc.)	**šveitslane**	[ʃʋejtslane]
Swiss (fem.)	**šveitslanna**	[ʃʋejtslaŋa]
Swiss (adj)	**šveitsi**	[ʃʋejtsi]

Scotland	**Šotimaa**	[ʃotima:]
Scottish (masc.)	**šotlane**	[ʃotlane]
Scottish (fem.)	**šotlanna**	[ʃotlaŋa]
Scottish (adj)	**šoti**	[ʃoti]

Vatican	**Vatikan**	[ʋatikan]
Liechtenstein	**Liechtenstein**	[lihtenʃtejn]
Luxembourg	**Luxembourg**	[lyksemburg]
Monaco	**Monaco**	[monako]

235. Central and Eastern Europe

Albania	**Albaania**	[alba:nia]
Albanian (masc.)	**albaanlane**	[alba:nlane]
Albanian (fem.)	**albaanlanna**	[alba:nlaŋa]
Albanian (adj)	**albaania**	[alba:nia]

Bulgaria	**Bulgaaria**	[bulga:ria]
Bulgarian (masc.)	**bulgaarlane**	[bulga:rlane]
Bulgarian (fem.)	**bulgaarlanna**	[bulga:rlaŋa]
Bulgarian (adj)	**bulgaaria**	[bulga:ria]

Hungary	**Ungari**	[uŋari]
Hungarian (masc.)	**ungarlane**	[uŋarlane]
Hungarian (fem.)	**ungarlanna**	[uŋarlaŋa]
Hungarian (adj)	**ungari**	[uŋari]

Latvia	**Läti**	[ʎæti]
Latvian (masc.)	**lätlane**	[ʎætlane]
Latvian (fem.)	**lätlanna**	[ʎætlaŋa]
Latvian (adj)	**läti**	[ʎæti]

Lithuania	**Leedu**	[le:du]
Lithuanian (masc.)	**leedulane**	[le:dulane]
Lithuanian (fem.)	**leedulanna**	[le:dulaŋa]
Lithuanian (adj)	**leedu**	[le:du]

Poland	**Poola**	[po:la]
Pole (masc.)	**poolakas**	[po:lakas]
Pole (fem.)	**poolatar**	[po:latar]

Polish (adj)	poola	[po:lɑ]
Romania	Rumeenia	[rume:niɑ]
Romanian (masc.)	rumeenlane	[rume:nlɑne]
Romanian (fem.)	rumeenlanna	[rume:nlɑŋɑ]
Romanian (adj)	rumeenia	[rume:niɑ]

Serbia	Serbia	[serbiæ]
Serbian (masc.)	serblane	[serblɑne]
Serbian (fem.)	serblanna	[serblɑŋɑ]
Serbian (adj)	serbia	[serbiæ]

Slovakia	Slovakkia	[slouɑkkiɑ]
Slovak (masc.)	slovakk	[slouɑkk]
Slovak (fem.)	slovakitar	[slouɑkitɑr]
Slovak (adj)	slovaki	[slouɑki]

Croatia	Kroaatia	[kroɑ:tiɑ]
Croatian (masc.)	kroaat	[kroɑ:t]
Croatian (fem.)	horvaaditar	[horuɑ:ditɑr]
Croatian (adj)	kroaadi	[kroɑ:di]

Czech Republic	Tšehhia	[tʲehiɑ]
Czech (masc.)	tšehh	[tʲeh]
Czech (fem.)	tšehhitar	[tʲehitɑr]
Czech (adj)	tšehhi	[tʲehi]

Estonia	Eesti	[əesti]
Estonian (masc.)	eestlane	[əestlɑne]
Estonian (fem.)	eestlanna	[əestlɑŋɑ]
Estonian (adj)	eesti	[əesti]

Bosnia-Herzegovina	Bosnia ja Hertsegoviina	[bosniæ æ hertsegoui:nɑ]
Macedonia	Makedoonia	[mɑkedo:niæ]
Slovenia	Sloveenia	[sloue:niæ]
Montenegro	Montenegro	[montənegro]

236. Former USSR countries

Azerbaijan	Aserbaidžaan	[ɑzerbɑjdʒɑ:n]
Azerbaijani (masc.)	aserbaidžaanlane	[ɑzerbɑjdʒɑ:nlɑne]
Azerbaijani (fem.)	aserbaidžaanlanna	[ɑzerbɑjdʒɑ:nlɑŋɑ]
Azerbaijani (adj)	aserbaidžaani	[ɑzerbɑjdʒɑ:ni]

Armenia	Armeenia	[ɑrme:niɑ]
Armenian (masc.)	armeenlane	[ɑrme:nlɑne]
Armenian (fem.)	armeenlanna	[ɑrme:nlɑŋɑ]
Armenian (adj)	armeenia	[ɑrme:niɑ]

| Belarus | Valgevenemaa | [uɑlgeuenemɑ:] |
| Belarusian (masc.) | valgevenelane | [uɑlgeuenelɑne] |

Belarusian (fem.)	**valgevenelanna**	[ʋɑlgeʋenelɑŋɑ]
Belarusian (adj)	**valgevene**	[ʋɑlgeʋene]
Georgia	**Gruusia**	[gruːsiɑ]
Georgian (masc.)	**grusiin**	[grusiːn]
Georgian (fem.)	**grusiinlanna**	[grusiːnlɑŋɑ]
Georgian (adj)	**gruusia**	[gruːsiɑ]
Kazakhstan	**Kasahstan**	[kɑsɑhstɑn]
Kazakh (masc.)	**kasahh**	[kɑsɑh]
Kazakh (fem.)	**kasahhitar**	[kɑsɑhitɑr]
Kazakh (adj)	**kasahhi**	[kɑsɑhi]
Kirghizia	**Kõrgõzstan**	[kɪrgɪstɑn]
Kirghiz (masc.)	**kirgiis**	[kirgiːs]
Kirghiz (fem.)	**kirgiisitar**	[kirgiːsitɑr]
Kirghiz (adj)	**kirgiisi**	[kirgiːsi]
Moldavia	**Moldova**	[moldoʋɑ]
Moldavian (masc.)	**moldaavlane**	[moldaːʋlɑne]
Moldavian (fem.)	**moldaavlanna**	[moldaːʋlɑŋɑ]
Moldavian (adj)	**moldaavia**	[moldaːʋiɑ]
Russia	**Venemaa**	[ʋenemɑː]
Russian (masc.)	**venelane**	[ʋenelɑne]
Russian (fem.)	**venelanna**	[ʋenelɑŋɑ]
Russian (adj)	**vene**	[ʋene]
Tajikistan	**Tadžikistan**	[tɑʤikistɑn]
Tajik (masc.)	**tadžikk**	[tɑʤikk]
Tajik (fem.)	**tadžikitar**	[tɑʤikitɑr]
Tajik (adj)	**tadžiki**	[tɑʤiki]
Turkmenistan	**Türkmenistan**	[tyrkmenistɑn]
Turkmen (masc.)	**turkmeen**	[turkmeːn]
Turkmen (fem.)	**turkmeenlanna**	[turkmeːnlɑŋɑ]
Turkmenian (adj)	**turkmeeni**	[turkmeːni]
Uzbekistan	**Usbekistan**	[usbekistɑn]
Uzbek (masc.)	**usbekk**	[usbekk]
Uzbek (fem.)	**usbekitar**	[usbekitɑr]
Uzbek (adj)	**usbeki**	[usbeki]
Ukraine	**Ukraina**	[ukrɑjnɑ]
Ukrainian (masc.)	**ukrainlane**	[ukrɑjnlɑne]
Ukrainian (fem.)	**ukrainlanna**	[ukrɑjnlɑŋɑ]
Ukrainian (adj)	**ukraina**	[ukrɑjnɑ]

237. Asia

Asia	**Aasia**	[ɑːsiɑ]
Asian (adj)	**aasialik**	[ɑːsiɑlik]

Vietnam	**Vietnam**	[ʋietnam]
Vietnamese (masc.)	**vietnamlane**	[ʋietnamlane]
Vietnamese (fem.)	**vietnamlanna**	[ʋietnamlaŋa]
Vietnamese (adj)	**vietnami**	[ʋietnami]

India	**India**	[india]
Indian (masc.)	**hindu**	[hindu]
Indian (fem.)	**hindulanna**	[hindulaŋa]
Indian (adj)	**india**	[india]

Israel	**Iisrael**	[i:sraeʎ]
Israeli (masc.)	**iisraellane**	[i:sraeʎane]
Israeli (fem.)	**iisraellanna**	[i:sraeʎaŋa]
Israeli (adj)	**iisraeli**	[i:sraeli]

Jew (n)	**juut**	[y:t]
Jewess (n)	**juuditar**	[y:ditar]
Jewish (adj)	**juudi**	[y:di]

China	**Hiina**	[hi:na]
Chinese (masc.)	**hiinlane**	[hi:nlane]
Chinese (fem.)	**hiinlanna**	[hi:nlaŋa]
Chinese (adj)	**hiina**	[hi:na]

Korean (masc.)	**korealane**	[korealane]
Korean (fem.)	**korealanna**	[korealaŋa]
Korean (adj)	**korea**	[korea]

Lebanon	**Liibanon**	[li:banon]
Lebanese (masc.)	**liibanonlane**	[li:banonlane]
Lebanese (fem.)	**liibanonlanna**	[li:banonlaŋa]
Lebanese (adj)	**liibanoni**	[li:banoni]

Mongolia	**Mongoolia**	[moŋo:liæ]
Mongolian (masc.)	**mongol**	[moŋol]
Mongolian (fem.)	**mongolitar**	[moŋolitar]
Mongolian (adj)	**mongoli**	[moŋoli]

Malaysia	**Malaisia**	[malajsia]
Malaysian (masc.)	**malailane**	[malajlane]
Malaysian (fem.)	**malailanna**	[malajlaŋa]
Malaysian (adj)	**malai**	[malaj]

Pakistan	**Pakistan**	[pakistan]
Pakistani (masc.)	**pakistanlane**	[pakistanlane]
Pakistani (fem.)	**pakistanlanna**	[pakistanlaŋa]
Pakistani (adj)	**pakistani**	[pakistani]

Saudi Arabia	**Saudi Araabia**	[saudi ara:bia]
Arab (masc.)	**araablane**	[ara:blane]
Arab (fem.)	**araablanna**	[ara:blaŋa]
Arabian (adj)	**araabia**	[ara:bia]

Thailand	**Tai**	[taj]
Thai (masc.)	**tailane**	[tajlane]
Thai (fem.)	**tailanna**	[tajlaŋa]
Thai (adj)	**tai**	[taj]

Taiwan	**Taivan**	[tajʋan]
Taiwanese (masc.)	**taivanlane**	[tajʋanlane]
Taiwanese (fem.)	**taivanlanna**	[tajʋanlaŋa]
Taiwanese (adj)	**taivani**	[tajʋani]

Turkey	**Türgi**	[tyrgi]
Turk (masc.)	**türklane**	[tyrklane]
Turk (fem.)	**türklanna**	[tyrklaŋa]
Turkish (adj)	**türgi**	[tyrgi]

Japan	**Jaapan**	[æ:pan]
Japanese (masc.)	**jaapanlane**	[æ:panlane]
Japanese (fem.)	**jaapanlanna**	[æ:panlaŋa]
Japanese (adj)	**jaapani**	[æ:pani]

Afghanistan	**Afganistan**	[afganistan]
Bangladesh	**Bangladesh**	[baŋladeʃ]
Indonesia	**Indoneesia**	[indone:siæ]
Jordan	**Jordaania**	[ørda:niæ]

Iraq	**Iraak**	[ira:k]
Iran	**Iraan**	[ira:n]
Cambodia	**Kambodža**	[kambodʒa]
Kuwait	**Kuveit**	[kuʋejt]

Laos	**Laos**	[laos]
Myanmar	**Mjanma**	[mʲænma]
Nepal	**Nepal**	[nepal]
United Arab Emirates	**Araabia Ühendemiraadid**	[ara:biæ yhendemira:did]

| Syria | **Süüria** | [sy:ria] |
| Palestine | **Palestiina autonoomia** | [palesti:na autono:miæ] |

| South Korea | **Lõuna-Korea** | [lɪuna korea] |
| North Korea | **Põhja-Korea** | [pɪhæ korea] |

238. North America

United States of America	**Ameerika Ühendriigid**	[ame:rika yhendri:gid]
American (masc.)	**ameeriklane**	[ame:riklane]
American (fem.)	**ameeriklanna**	[ame:riklaŋa]
American (adj)	**ameerika**	[ame:rika]

| Canada | **Kanada** | [kanada] |
| Canadian (masc.) | **kanadalane** | [kanadalane] |

Canadian (fem.)	kanadalanna	[kanadalaŋa]
Canadian (adj)	kanada	[kanada]
Mexico	Mehhiko	[mehiko]
Mexican (masc.)	mehhiklane	[mehiklane]
Mexican (fem.)	mehhiklanna	[mehiklaŋa]
Mexican (adj)	mehhiko	[mehiko]

239. Central and South America

Argentina	Argentiina	[argenti:na]
Argentinian (masc.)	argentiinlane	[argenti:nlane]
Argentinian (fem.)	argentiinlanna	[argenti:nlaŋa]
Argentinian (adj)	argentiina	[argenti:na]

Brazil	Brasiilia	[brasi:lia]
Brazilian (masc.)	brasiillane	[brasi:llane]
Brazilian (fem.)	brasiillanna	[brasi:llaŋa]
Brazilian (adj)	brasiilia	[brasi:lia]

Colombia	Kolumbia	[kolumbia]
Colombian (masc.)	kolumbialane	[kolumbialane]
Colombian (fem.)	kolumbialanna	[kolumbialaŋa]
Colombian (adj)	kolumbia	[kolumbia]

Cuba	Kuuba	[ku:ba]
Cuban (masc.)	kuubalane	[ku:balane]
Cuban (fem.)	kuubalanna	[ku:balaŋa]
Cuban (adj)	kuuba	[ku:ba]

Chile	Tšiili	[tʃi:li]
Chilean (masc.)	tšiilane	[tʃi:llane]
Chilean (fem.)	tšiilitar	[tʃi:litar]
Chilean (adj)	tšiili	[tʃi:li]

| Bolivia | Boliivia | [boli:via] |
| Venezuela | Venetsueela | [venetsue:la] |

| Paraguay | Paraguai | [paraguaj] |
| Peru | Peruu | [peru:] |

Suriname	Suriname	[suriname]
Uruguay	Uruguai	[uruguaj]
Ecuador	Ecuador	[ekuador]

The Bahamas	Bahama saared	[bahama sa:red]
Haiti	Haiiti	[hai:ti]
Dominican Republic	Dominikaani Vabariik	[dominika:ni vabari:k]

| Panama | Panama | [panama] |
| Jamaica | Jamaika | [æmajka] |

240. Africa

Egypt	**Egiptus**	[əgiptus]
Egyptian (masc.)	**egiptlane**	[əgiptlane]
Egyptian (fem.)	**egiptlanna**	[əgiptlaŋa]
Egyptian (adj)	**egiptuse**	[əgiptuse]

Morocco	**Maroko**	[maroko]
Moroccan (masc.)	**marokolane**	[marokolane]
Moroccan (fem.)	**marokolanna**	[marokolaŋa]
Moroccan (adj)	**maroko**	[maroko]

Tunisia	**Tuneesia**	[tune:sia]
Tunisian (masc.)	**tuneeslane**	[tune:slane]
Tunisian (fem.)	**tuneeslanna**	[tune:slaŋa]
Tunisian (adj)	**tuneesia**	[tune:sia]

Ghana	**Gaana**	[ga:na]
Zanzibar	**Sansibar**	[sansibar]
Kenya	**Keenia**	[ke:nia]
Libya	**Liibüa**	[li:bya]
Madagascar	**Madagaskar**	[madagaskar]

Namibia	**Namiibia**	[nami:bia]
Senegal	**Senegal**	[senegal]
Tanzania	**Tansaania**	[tansa:nia]
South Africa	**Lõuna-Aafrika Vabariik**	[lıuna a:frika ʋabari:k]

African (masc.)	**aafriklane**	[a:friklane]
African (fem.)	**aafriklanna**	[a:friklaŋa]
African (adj)	**aafrika**	[a:frika]

241. Australia. Oceania

| Australia | **Australia** | [austra:lia] |
| Australian (masc.) | **austraallane** | [austra:llane] |

| Australian (fem.) | **austraallanna** | [austra:llaŋa] |
| Australian (adj) | **austraalia** | [austra:lia] |

| New Zealand | **Uus Meremaa** | [u:s merema:] |
| New Zealander (masc.) | **uusmeremaalane** | [u:smerema:lane] |

| New Zealander (fem.) | **uusmeremaalanna** | [u:smerema:laŋa] |
| New Zealand (as adj) | **uusmeremaa** | [u:smerema:] |

| Tasmania | **Tasmaania** | [tasma:nia] |
| French Polynesia | **Prantsuse Polüneesia** | [prantsuse polyne:sia] |

242. Cities

Amsterdam	**Amsterdam**	[amsterdam]
Ankara	**Ankara**	[aŋkara]
Athens	**Ateena**	[ate:na]
Baghdad	**Bagdad**	[bagdad]
Bangkok	**Bangkok**	[baŋkok]
Barcelona	**Barcelona**	[barselona]
Beijing	**Peking**	[pekiŋ]
Beirut	**Beirut**	[bejrut]
Berlin	**Berliin**	[berli:n]
Bombay, Mumbai	**Bombay**	[bombej]
Bonn	**Bonn**	[boŋ]
Bordeaux	**Bordeaux**	[bordo:]
Bratislava	**Bratislava**	[bratislaʋa]
Brussels	**Brüssel**	[brysseʌ]
Bucharest	**Bukarest**	[bukarest]
Budapest	**Budapest**	[budapest]
Cairo	**Kairo**	[kajro]
Calcutta	**Kalkuta**	[kalkuta]
Chicago	**Chicago**	[ʧikago]
Copenhagen	**Kopenhaagen**	[kopenha:gen]
Dar-es-Salaam	**Dar Es Salaam**	[dar əs salam]
Delhi	**Delhi**	[deli]
Dubai	**Dubai**	[dubai]
Dublin	**Dublin**	[dublin]
Düsseldorf	**Düsseldorf**	[dysseʌdorf]
Florence	**Firenze**	[firenze]
Frankfurt	**Frankfurt**	[fraŋkfurt]
Geneva	**Genf**	[genf]
The Hague	**Haag**	[ha:g]
Hamburg	**Hamburg**	[hamburg]
Hanoi	**Hanoi**	[hanoj]
Havana	**Havanna**	[haʋaŋa]
Helsinki	**Helsingi**	[heʌsiŋi]
Hiroshima	**Hiroshima**	[hiroʃima]
Hong Kong	**Hongkong**	[hoŋkoŋ]
Istanbul	**Istanbul**	[istanbul]
Jerusalem	**Jeruusalemm**	[ieru:salemm]
Kiev	**Kiiev**	[ki:əu]
Kuala Lumpur	**Kuala Lumpur**	[kuala lumpur]
Lisbon	**Lissabon**	[lissabon]
London	**London**	[london]
Los Angeles	**Los Angeles**	[los anʤeles]

Lyons	**Lyon**	[lion]
Madrid	**Madrid**	[mɑdriːd]
Marseille	**Marseille**	[mɑrseʎ]
Mexico City	**Mexico**	[mehiko]
Miami	**Miami**	[mɑjæmi]
Montreal	**Montreal**	[monreɑːʎ]
Moscow	**Moskva**	[moskʋɑ]
Munich	**München**	[mynhen]

Nairobi	**Nairobi**	[nɑjrobi]
Naples	**Napoli**	[nɑpoli]
New York	**New York**	[njy ørk]
Nice	**Nice**	[nitse]
Oslo	**Oslo**	[oslo]
Ottawa	**Ottawa**	[ottɑʋɑ]

Paris	**Pariis**	[pɑriːs]
Prague	**Praha**	[prɑhɑ]
Rio de Janeiro	**Rio de Janeiro**	[rio de ʒɑnejro]
Rome	**Rooma**	[roːmɑ]

Saint Petersburg	**Peterburi**	[peterburi]
Seoul	**Sõul**	[soul]
Shanghai	**Shanghai**	[ʃɑnhɑj]
Singapore	**Singapur**	[siŋɑpur]
Stockholm	**Stockholm**	[stokhoʎm]
Sydney	**Sidney**	[sidni]

Taipei	**Taibei**	[tɑjbej]
Tokyo	**Tokio**	[tokio]
Toronto	**Toronto**	[toronto]

Venice	**Veneetsia**	[ʋeneːtsiæ]
Vienna	**Viin**	[ʋiːn]
Warsaw	**Varssavi**	[ʋɑrssɑʋi]
Washington	**Washington**	[uoʃiŋton]

243. Politics. Government. Part 1

politics	**poliitika**	[poliːtikɑ]
political (adj)	**poliitiline**	[poliːtiline]
politician	**poliitik**	[poliːtik]

state (country)	**riik**	[riːk]
citizen	**kodanik**	[kodɑnik]
citizenship	**kodakondsus**	[kodɑkondsus]

national emblem	**riigivapp**	[riːgiʋɑpp]
national anthem	**riigihümn**	[riːgihymn]
government	**valitsus**	[ʋɑlitsus]

head of state	**riigijuht**	[ri:giyht]
parliament	**riigikogu**	[ri:gikogu]
party	**erakond**	[ərakond]
capitalism	**kapitalism**	[kapitalism]
capitalist (adj)	**kapitalistlik**	[kapitalistlik]
socialism	**sotsialism**	[sotsialism]
socialist (adj)	**sotsialistlik**	[sotsialistlik]
communism	**kommunism**	[kommunism]
communist (adj)	**kommunistlik**	[kommunistlik]
communist (n)	**kommunist**	[kommunist]
democracy	**demokraatia**	[demokra:tia]
democrat	**demokraat**	[demokra:t]
democratic (adj)	**demokraatlik**	[demokra:tlik]
Democratic party	**demokraatlik erakond**	[demokra:tlik ərakond]
liberal (n)	**liberaal**	[libera:l]
liberal (adj)	**liberaalne**	[libera:lne]
conservative (n)	**konservaator**	[konserʋa:tor]
conservative (adj)	**konservatiivne**	[konserʋati:ʋne]
republic (n)	**vabariik**	[ʋabari:k]
republican (n)	**vabariiklane**	[ʋabari:klane]
Republican party	**vabariiklik erakond**	[ʋabari:klik ərakond]
poll, elections	**valimised**	[ʋalimised]
to elect (vt)	**valima**	[ʋalima]
elector, voter	**valija**	[ʋaliæ]
election campaign	**valimiskampaania**	[ʋalimiskampa:nia]
voting (n)	**hääletamine**	[hæ:letamine]
to vote (vi)	**hääletama**	[hæ:letama]
suffrage, right to vote	**hääleõigus**	[hæ:leijgus]
candidate	**kandidaat**	[kandida:t]
to be a candidate	**kandideerima**	[kandide:rima]
campaign	**kampaania**	[kampa:nia]
opposition (as adj)	**opositsiooniline**	[opositsio:niline]
opposition (n)	**opositsioon**	[opositsio:n]
visit	**visiit**	[ʋisi:t]
official visit	**ametlik visiit**	[ametlik ʋisi:t]
international (adj)	**rahvusvaheline**	[rahʋusʋaheline]
negotiations	**läbirääkimised**	[ʎæbiræ:kimised]
to negotiate (vi)	**läbirääkimisi pidama**	[ʎæbiræ:kimisi pidama]

244. Politics. Government. Part 2

society	ühiskond	[yhiskond]
constitution	konstitutsioon	[konstitutsio:n]
power (political control)	võim	[vijm]
corruption	korruptsioon	[korruptsio:n]

| law (justice) | seadus | [seadus] |
| legal (legitimate) | seaduslik | [seaduslik] |

| justice (fairness) | õiglus | [ijglus] |
| just (fair) | õiglane | [ijglane] |

committee	komitee	[komite:]
bill (draft law)	seaduseelnõu	[seaduseeʌnıu]
budget	eelarve	[eeʌærʋe]
policy	poliitika	[poli:tika]
reform	reform	[reform]
radical (adj)	radikaalne	[radika:ʌne]

power (strength, force)	jõud	[jıud]
powerful (adj)	tugev	[tugeʋ]
supporter	pooldaja	[po:ʌdaæ]
influence	mõju	[mıy]

regime (e.g., military ~)	režiim	[reʒi:m]
conflict	konflikt	[konflikt]
conspiracy (plot)	vandenõu	[ʋandənıu]
provocation	provokatsioon	[proʋokatsio:n]

to overthrow (regime, etc.)	kukutama	[kukutama]
overthrow (of government)	kukutamine	[kukutamine]
revolution	revolutsioon	[reʋolutsio:n]

| coup d'état | riigipööre | [ri:gipø:re] |
| military coup | sõjaväeline riigipööre | [sıæʋæ:line ri:gipø:re] |

crisis	kriis	[kri:s]
economic recession	majanduslangus	[maænduslaŋus]
demonstrator (protester)	demonstrant	[demonstrant]
demonstration	demonstratsioon	[demonstratsio:n]
martial law	sõjaseisukord	[sıæsejsukord]
military base	sõjaväebaas	[sıæʋæ:ba:s]

| stability | stabiilsus | [stabi:ʌsus] |
| stable (adj) | stabiilne | [stabi:ʌne] |

exploitation	ekspluateerimine	[əkspluate:rimine]
to exploit (workers)	ekspluateerima	[əkspluate:rima]
racism	rassism	[rassism]
racist	rassist	[rassist]

fascism	fašism	[faʃism]
fascist	fašist	[faʃist]

245. Countries. Miscellaneous

foreigner	välismaalane	[ʋⁱælismaːlɑne]
foreign (adj)	välismaine	[ʋⁱælismɑjne]
abroad (adv)	välismaal	[ʋⁱælismaːʌ]

emigrant	emigrant	[əmigrɑnt]
emigration	emigratsioon	[əmigrɑtsioːn]
to emigrate (vi)	emigreerima	[əmigreːrimɑ]

the West	Lääs	[læːs]
the East	Ida	[idɑ]
the Far East	Kaug-Ida	[kɑug idɑ]

civilization	tsivilisatsioon	[tsiʋilisɑtsioːn]
humanity (mankind)	inimkond	[inimkond]

world (earth)	maailm	[maːiʌm]
peace	rahu	[rɑhu]
worldwide (adj)	ülemaailmne	[ylemaːiʌmne]

homeland	kodumaa	[kodumɑː]
people (population)	rahvas	[rɑhʋɑs]
population	elanikkond	[əlɑnikkond]
people (a lot of ~)	inimesed	[inimesed]

nation (people)	rahvus	[rɑhʋus]
generation	põlvkond	[pɪʌʊkond]

territory (area)	territoorium	[territoːrium]
region	regioon	[regioːn]
state (part of a country)	osariik	[osɑriːk]

tradition	traditsioon	[trɑditsioːn]
custom (tradition)	komme	[komme]
ecology	ökoloogia	[økoloːgiæ]

Indian (Native American)	indiaanlane	[indiaːnlɑne]
Gipsy (masc.)	mustlane	[mustlɑne]
Gipsy (fem.)	mustlasnaine	[mustlɑsnɑjne]
Gipsy (adj)	mustlaslik	[mustlɑslik]

empire	impeerium	[impeːrium]
colony	koloonia	[koloːniɑ]
slavery	orjus	[orjys]
invasion	kallaletung	[kɑllɑletuŋ]
famine	näljahäda	[ɲæʌæɦædɑ]

246. Major religious groups. Confessions

religion	**religioon**	[religio:n]
religious (adj)	**religioosne**	[religio:sne]
faith, belief	**usk**	[usk]
to believe (in God)	**jumalat uskuma**	[ymalat uskuma]
believer	**usklik**	[usklik]
atheism	**ateism**	[atəism]
atheist	**ateist**	[atəist]
Christianity	**kristlus**	[kristlus]
Christian (n)	**kristlane**	[kristlane]
Christian (adj)	**kristlik**	[kristlik]
Catholicism	**katoliiklus**	[katoli:klus]
Catholic (n)	**katoliiklane**	[katoli:klane]
Catholic (adj)	**katoliiklik**	[katoli:klik]
Protestantism	**protestantism**	[protestantism]
Protestant Church	**protestantlik kirik**	[protestantlik kirik]
Protestant	**protestant**	[protestant]
Orthodoxy	**õigeusk**	[ijgeusk]
Orthodox Church	**õigeusukirik**	[ijgeusukirik]
Orthodox	**õigeusklik**	[ijgeusklik]
Presbyterianism	**presbüterlus**	[presbyterlus]
Presbyterian Church	**presbüterlaste kirik**	[presbyterlaste kirik]
Presbyterian (n)	**presbüterlane**	[presbytelane]
Lutheranism	**luteri kirik**	[luteri kirik]
Lutheran (n)	**luterlane**	[luterlane]
Baptist Church	**baptism**	[baptism]
Baptist (n)	**baptist**	[baptist]
Anglican Church	**anglikaani kirik**	[aŋlika:ni kirik]
Anglican (n)	**anglikaan**	[aŋlika:n]
Mormonism	**mormoonlus**	[mormo:nlus]
Mormon (n)	**mormoon**	[mormo:n]
Judaism	**judaism**	[ydaism]
Jew (n)	**juudalane**	[y:dalane]
Buddhism	**budism**	[budism]
Buddhist (n)	**budist**	[budist]
Hinduism	**hinduism**	[induism]
Hindu (n)	**hinduist**	[induist]

Islam	islam	[islam]
Muslim (n)	moslem	[moslem]
Muslim (adj)	moslemi	[moslemi]

Shiah Islam	šiiitlus	[ʃiːjtlus]
Shiite (n)	šiiit	[ʃiːt]
Sunni Islam	sunnism	[suɲism]
Sunnite (n)	sunniit	[suɲiːt]

247. Religions. Priests

priest	vaimulik	[ʋɑjmulik]
the Pope	Rooma paavst	[roːmɑ pɑːʊst]

monk, friar	munk	[muŋk]
nun	nunn	[nuŋ]
pastor	pastor	[pɑstor]

abbot	abee	[ɑbeː]
vicar (parish priest)	vikaar	[ʋikɑːr]
bishop	piiskop	[piːskop]
cardinal	kardinal	[kɑrdinɑl]

preacher	jutlustaja	[ytlustɑæ]
preaching	jutlus	[ytlus]
parishioners	koguduse liikmed	[koguduse liːkmed]

believer	usklikud	[usklikud]
atheist	ateist	[ɑtəist]

248. Faith. Christianity. Islam

Adam	Aadam	[ɑːdɑm]
Eve	Eeva	[əeʋɑ]

God	Jumal	[ymɑʎ]
the Lord	Issand	[issɑnd]
the Almighty	Kõigevägevam	[kɪjgeʊˈægeʊɑm]

sin	patt	[pɑtt]
to sin (vi)	pattu tegema	[pɑttu tegemɑ]
sinner (masc.)	patustaja	[pɑtustɑæ]
sinner (fem.)	patustaja	[pɑtustɑæ]

hell	põrgu	[pɪrgu]
paradise	paradiis	[pɑrɑdiːs]
Jesus	Jeesus	[jeːsus]
Jesus Christ	Jeesus Kristus	[jeːsus kristus]

the Holy Spirit	Püha Vaim	[pyha ʋajm]
the Savior	Päästja	[pæːstʲæ]
the Virgin Mary	Jumalaema	[ymalaəma]

the Devil	kurat	[kurɑt]
devil's (adj)	kuratlik	[kuratlik]
Satan	saatan	[sɑːtɑn]
satanic (adj)	saatanlik	[sɑːtɑnlik]

angel	ingel	[iŋeʎ]
guardian angel	päästeingel	[pæːsteiŋeʎ]
angelic (adj)	ingellik	[iŋellik]

| apostle | apostel | [aposteʎ] |
| archangel | peaingel | [peaiŋeʎ] |

Church	kirik	[kirik]
Bible	piibel	[piːbeʎ]
biblical (adj)	piibli-	[piːbli]

Old Testament	Vana Testament	[ʋɑnɑ testament]
New Testament	Uus Testament	[uːs testament]
Gospel	Evangeelium	[əʋɑŋeːlium]
Holy Scripture	Pühakiri	[pyhakiri]
heaven	Taevas, Taevariik	[taəʋas], [taəʋariːk]

Commandment	käsk	[kʲæsk]
prophet	prohvet	[prohʋet]
prophecy	ettekuulutus	[əttekuːlutus]

Allah	Allah	[allah]
Mohammed	Muhamed	[muhamed]
the Koran	Koraan	[korɑːn]

mosque	mošee	[moʃeː]
mullah	mulla	[mulla]
prayer	palve	[palʋe]
to pray (vi, vt)	palvetama	[palʋetama]

pilgrimage	palverändamine	[palʋerʲændamine]
pilgrim	palverändur	[palʋerʲændur]
Mecca	Meka	[meka]

church	kirik	[kirik]
temple	pühakoda	[pyhakoda]
cathedral	katedraal	[katedrɑːl]
Gothic (adj)	gooti	[goːti]
synagogue	sünagoog	[synagoːg]
mosque	mošee	[moʃeː]

| chapel | kabel | [kabeʎ] |
| abbey | abtkond | [abtkond] |

convent	**nunnaklooster**	[nuŋaklo:ster]
monastery	**mungaklooster**	[muŋaklo:ster]
bell (in church)	**kirikukell**	[kirikukeʎ]
bell tower	**kellatorn**	[kellatorn]
to ring (ab. bells)	**kella lööma**	[kella lø:ma]
cross	**rist**	[rist]
cupola (roof)	**kuppel**	[kuppeʎ]
icon	**ikoon**	[iko:n]
soul	**hing**	[hiŋ]
fate (destiny)	**saatus**	[sɑ:tus]
evil (n)	**kurjus**	[kurjys]
good (n)	**headus**	[headus]
vampire	**vampiir**	[ʋampi:r]
witch (sorceress)	**nõid**	[nɪjd]
demon	**deemon**	[de:mon]
devil	**kurat**	[kurat]
spirit	**vaim**	[ʋɑjm]
redemption (giving us ~)	**lunastamine**	[lunɑstamine]
to redeem (vt)	**lunastama**	[lunɑstama]
church service, mass	**jumalateenistus**	[ymalate:nistus]
to say mass	**teenima**	[te:nima]
confession	**pihtimus**	[pihtimus]
to confess (vi)	**pihtima**	[pihtima]
saint (n)	**püha**	[pyha]
sacred (holy)	**püha**	[pyha]
holy water	**püha vesi**	[pyha ʋesi]
ritual (n)	**kombetalitus**	[kombetalitus]
ritual (adj)	**rituaalne**	[ritua:ʎne]
sacrifice	**ohverdamine**	[ohʋerdamine]
superstition	**ebausk**	[əbausk]
superstitious (adj)	**ebausklik**	[əbausklik]
afterlife	**hauatagune elu**	[hauatagune əlu]

MISCELLANEOUS

249. Various useful words

background (green ~)	**foon**	[fo:n]
balance (of situat on)	**bilanss**	[bilɑns]
barrier (obstacle)	**tõke**	[tɪke]
base (basis)	**baas**	[bɑ:s]
beginning	**algus**	[ɑlgus]
category	**kategooria**	[kɑtego:riɑ]
cause (reason)	**põhjus**	[pɪhjys]
choice	**valik**	[ʋɑlik]
coincidence	**kokkulangevus**	[kokkulɑŋeʋus]
comfortable (~ chair)	**mugav**	[mugɑʋ]
comparison	**võrdlus**	[ʋɪrdlus]
compensation	**kompensatsioon**	[kompensɑtsio:n]
degree (extent, amount)	**aste**	[ɑste]
development	**areng**	[ɑrəŋ]
difference	**erinevus**	[ərineʋus]
effect (e.g., of drugs)	**efekt**	[əffekt]
effort (exertion)	**jõupingutus**	[jɪupiŋutus]
element	**element**	[əlement]
end (finish)	**lõpp**	[lɪpp]
example (illustration)	**näide**	[næjde]
fact	**tõsiasi**	[tɪsiɑsi]
frequent (adj)	**sagedane**	[sɑgedɑne]
growth (development)	**kasv**	[kɑsʋ]
help	**abi**	[ɑbi]
ideal	**ideaal**	[idea:l]
kind (sort, type)	**ala**	[ɑlɑ]
labyrinth	**labürint**	[lɑbyrint]
mistake, error	**viga**	[ʋigɑ]
moment	**moment**	[moment]
object (thing)	**ese**	[əse]
obstacle	**takistus**	[tɑkistus]
original (original copy)	**originaal**	[originɑ:ʎ]
part (~ of sth)	**osa**	[osɑ]
particle, small part	**osake**	[osɑke]
pause (break)	**paus**	[pɑus]

position	positsioon	[positsio:n]
principle	põhimõte	[pɪhimɪte]
problem	probleem	[proble:m]

process	protsess	[protsess]
progress	progress	[progress]
property (quality)	omadus	[omɑdus]
reaction	reaktsioon	[reɑktsio:n]
risk	risk	[risk]

secret	saladus	[sɑlɑdus]
section (sector)	sektsioon	[sektsio:n]
series	seeria	[se:riɑ]
shape (outer form)	vorm	[ʋorm]
situation	situatsioon	[situɑtsio:n]

solution	lahendamine	[lɑhendɑmine]
standard (adj)	standardne	[stɑndɑrdne]
standard (level of quality)	standard	[stɑndɑrd]
stop (pause)	seisak	[sejsɑk]
style	stiil	[sti:ʎ]
system	süsteem	[syste:m]

table (chart)	tabel	[tɑbeʎ]
tempo, rate	tempo	[tempo]
term (word, expression)	mõiste	[mɪjste]
thing (object, item)	asi	[ɑsi]
truth	tõde	[tɪde]
turn (please wait your ~)	järjekord	[ærjekord]
type (sort, kind)	tüüp	[ty:p]

urgent (adj)	kiire	[ki:re]
urgently (adv)	kiiresti	[ki:resti]
utility (usefulness)	kasu	[kɑsu]

variant (alternative)	variant	[ʋɑriɑnt]
way (means, method)	viis	[ʋi:s]
zone	tsoon	[tso:n]

250. Modifiers. Adjectives. Part 1

additional (adj)	täiendav	[tʲæjendɑʋ]
ancient (~ civilization)	iidne	[i:dne]
artificial (adj)	kunstlik	[kunstlik]
back, rear (adj)	tagumine	[tɑgumine]
bad (adj)	halb	[hɑʎb]

beautiful (~ palace)	imeilus	[imeilus]
beautiful (person)	ilus	[ilus]
big (in size)	suur	[su:r]

bitter (taste)	**mõru**	[mɪru]
blind (sightless)	**pime**	[pime]
calm, quiet (adj)	**rahulik**	[rɑhulik]
careless (negligent)	**hooletu**	[hoːletu]
caring (~ father)	**hoolitsev**	[hoːlitseʊ]
central (adj)	**kesk-**	[kesk]
cheap (adj)	**odav**	[odɑʊ]
cheerful (adj)	**lõbus**	[lɪbus]
children's (adj)	**laste-**	[lɑste]
civil (~ law)	**tsiviil-**	[ʦiʊiːʎ]
clandestine (secret)	**põrandaalune**	[pɪrɑndɑːlune]
clean (free from dirt)	**puhas**	[puhɑs]
clear (explanation etc.)	**arusaadav**	[ɑrusɑːdɑʊ]
clever (smart)	**tark**	[tɑrk]
close (near in space)	**lähedane**	[ʎæhedɑne]
closed (adj)	**kinnine**	[kiɲine]
cloudless (sky)	**pilvitu**	[piʎʊitu]
cold (drink, weather)	**külm**	[kyʎm]
compatible (adj)	**ühtesobiv**	[yhtesobiʊ]
contented (adj)	**rahulolev**	[rɑhuloleʊ]
continuous (adj)	**kauakestev**	[kɑuɑkesteʊ]
continuous (incessant)	**katkematu**	[kɑtkemɑtu]
convenient (adj)	**kõlblik**	[kɪʎblik]
cool (weather)	**jahe**	[æhe]
dangerous (adj)	**ohtlik**	[ohtlik]
dark (room)	**pime**	[pime]
dead (not alive)	**surnud**	[surnud]
dense (fog, smoke)	**tihe**	[tihe]
different (adj)	**mitmesugune**	[mitmesugune]
difficult (decision)	**raske**	[rɑske]
difficult (problem, task)	**keeruline**	[keːruline]
dim, faint (light)	**ähmane**	[əhmɑne]
dirty (not clean)	**määrdunud**	[mæːrdunud]
distant (faraway)	**kauge**	[kɑuge]
distant (in space)	**kauge**	[kɑuge]
dry (clothes, etc.)	**kuiv**	[kujʊ]
easy (not difficult)	**lihtne**	[lihtne]
empty (glass, room)	**tühi**	[tyhi]
exact (amount)	**täpne**	[tʲæpne]
excellent (adj)	**eeskujulik**	[əeskuylik]
excessive (adj)	**ülearune**	[ylearune]
expensive (adj)	**kallis**	[kɑllis]
exterior (adj)	**väline**	[ʊʲæline]
fast (quick)	**kiire**	[kiːre]

fatty (food)	rasvane	[rɑsʋɑne]
fertile (land, soil)	viljakas	[ʋiʌækɑs]
flat (~ panel display)	lame	[lɑme]
even (e.g., ~ surface)	tasane	[tɑsɑne]
foreign (adj)	välismaine	[ʋʲælismɑjne]
fragile (china, glass)	habras	[hɑbrɑs]
free (at no cost)	tasuta	[tɑsutɑ]
free (unrestricted)	vaba	[ʋɑbɑ]
fresh (~ water)	mage	[mɑge]
fresh (e.g., ~ bread)	värske	[ʋʲærske]
frozen (food)	külmutatud	[kyʌmutɑtud]
full (completely filled)	täis	[tʲæjs]
good (book, etc.)	hea	[heɑ]
good (kindhearted)	hea	[heɑ]
grateful (adj)	tänulik	[tʲænulik]
happy (adj)	õnnelik	[ɪŋelik]
hard (not soft)	kõva	[kiʋɑ]
heavy (in weight)	raske	[rɑske]
hostile (adj)	vaenulik	[ʋɑenulik]
hot (adj)	kuum	[ku:m]
huge (adj)	tohutu	[tohutu]
humid (adj)	niiske	[ni:ske]
hungry (adj)	näljane	[næʌæne]
ill (sick, unwell)	haige	[hɑjge]
immobile (adj)	liikumatu	[li:kumɑtu]
important (adj)	tähtis	[tʲæhtis]
impossible (adj)	võimatu	[ʋɪjmɑtu]
incomprehensible	arusaamatu	[ɑrusɑ:mɑtu]
indispensable (adj)	vajalik	[ʋɑɑælik]
inexperienced (adj)	kogenematu	[kogenemɑtu]
insignificant (adj)	tühine	[tyhine]
interior (adj)	sisemine	[sisemine]
joint (~ decision)	ühine	[yhine]
last (e.g., ~ week)	möödunud	[mø:dunud]
last (final)	viimane	[ʋi:mɑne]
left (e.g., ~ side)	vasak	[ʋɑsɑk]
legal (legitimate)	seaduslik	[seɑduslik]
light (in weight)	kerge	[kerge]
light (pale color)	hele	[hele]
limited (adj)	piiratud	[pi:rɑtud]
liquid (fluid)	vedel	[ʋedəʌ]
long (e.g., ~ way)	pikk	[pikk]
loud (voice, etc.)	vali	[ʋɑli]
low (voice)	vaikne	[ʋɑjkne]

251. Modifiers. Adjectives. Part 2

main (principal)	**peamine**	[peamine]
matt (paint)	**matt**	[mattʲ]
meticulous (job)	**korralik**	[korralik]
mysterious (adj)	**salapärane**	[salapʲærane]
narrow (street, etc.)	**kitsas**	[kitsas]
native (of country)	**kodu-**	[kodu]
nearby (adj)	**lähedane**	[ʎæhedane]
near-sighted (adj)	**lühinägelik**	[lyhiɲægelik]
necessary (adj)	**vajalik**	[ʋaælik]
negative (~ response)	**negatiivne**	[negatiːune]
neighboring (adj)	**naabri-**	[naːbri]
nervous (adj)	**närviline**	[ɲærʋiline]
new (adj)	**uus**	[uːs]
next (e.g., ~ week)	**järgmine**	[ærgmine]
nice (kind)	**armas**	[armas]
nice (voice)	**meeldiv**	[meːʎdiu]
normal (adj)	**normaalne**	[normaːʎne]
not big (adj)	**väheldane**	[uʲæheʎdane]
unclear (adj)	**arusaamatu**	[arusaːmatu]
not difficult (adj)	**üsna lihtne**	[ysna lihtne]
obligatory (adj)	**kohustuslik**	[kohustuslik]
old (house)	**vana**	[ʋana]
open (adj)	**avatud**	[aʋatud]
opposite (adj)	**vastandlik**	[ʋastandlik]
ordinary (usual)	**tavaline**	[taʋaline]
original (unusual)	**algupärane**	[algupʲærane]
past (recent)	**möödunud**	[møːdunud]
permanent (adj)	**alaline**	[alaline]
personal (adj)	**isiklik**	[isiklik]
polite (adj)	**viisakas**	[ʋiːsakas]
poor (not rich)	**vaene**	[ʋaene]
possible (adj)	**võimalik**	[ʋijmalik]
destitute (extremely poor)	**kerjuslik**	[kerjyslik]
present (current)	**tõeline**	[tɪːline]
principal (main)	**peamine**	[peamine]
private (~ jet)	**era-**	[əra]
probable (adj)	**tõenäoline**	[tɪːɲæoline]
public (open to all)	**ühiskondlik**	[yhiskondlik]
punctual (person)	**täpne**	[tʲæpne]
quiet (tranquil)	**vaikne**	[ʋajkne]
rare (adj)	**haruldane**	[haruʎdane]

raw (uncooked)	**toores**	[to:res]
right (not left)	**parem**	[parem]
right, correct (adj)	**õige**	[ɪjge]
ripe (fruit)	**küps**	[kyps]
risky (adj)	**riskantne**	[riskɑntne]
sad (~ look)	**kurb**	[kurb]
sad (depressing)	**kurb**	[kurb]
safe (not dangerous)	**ohutu**	[ohutu]
salty (food)	**soolane**	[so:lɑne]
satisfied (customer)	**rahuldav**	[rɑhuʎdɑʊ]
second hand (adj)	**kasutatud**	[kɑsutatud]
shallow (water)	**madal**	[mɑdɑʎ]
sharp (blade, etc.)	**terav**	[terɑʊ]
short (in length)	**lühike**	[lyhike]
short, short-lived (adj)	**lühiajaline**	[lyhiɑæline]
significant (notable)	**märkimisväärne**	[mʲærkimisʊæ:rne]
similar (adj)	**sarnane**	[sɑrnɑne]
simple (easy)	**lihtne**	[lihtne]
skinny	**kõhetu**	[kɪhetu]
thin (person)	**kõhn**	[kɪhn]
smooth (surface)	**sile**	[sile]
soft (to touch)	**pehme**	[pehme]
solid (~ wall)	**vastupidav**	[ʊɑstupidɑʊ]
somber, gloomy (adj)	**sünge**	[syŋe]
sour (flavor, taste)	**hapu**	[hɑpu]
spacious (house, etc.)	**avar**	[ɑʊar]
special (adj)	**spetsiaalne**	[spetsiɑ:ʎne]
straight (line, road)	**sirge**	[sirge]
strong (person)	**tugev**	[tugeʊ]
stupid (foolish)	**rumal**	[rumɑʎ]
sunny (day)	**päiksepaisteline**	[pʲæjksepɑjsteline]
superb, perfect (adj)	**suurepärane**	[su:repʲærɑne]
swarthy (adj)	**tõmmu**	[tɪmmu]
sweet (sugary)	**magus**	[mɑgus]
tan (adj)	**päevitunud**	[pæ:ʊitunud]
tasty (adj)	**maitsev**	[mɑjtseʊ]
tender (affectionate)	**hell**	[heʎ]
the highest (adj)	**kõrgem**	[kɪrgem]
the most important	**kõige tähtsam**	[kɪjge tʲæhtsɑm]
the nearest	**lähim**	[ʎæhim]
the same, equal (adj)	**ühesugune**	[yhesugune]
thick (e.g., ~ fog)	**tihe**	[tihe]
thick (wall, slice)	**paks**	[pɑks]

tired (exhausted)	**väsinud**	[ʋʲæsinud]
tiring (adj)	**väsitav**	[ʋʲæsitɑʋ]
transparent (adj)	**läbipaistev**	[ʎæbipɑjsteʋ]

unique (exceptional)	**ainulaadne**	[ɑjnulɑːdne]
various (adj)	**erinev**	[erineʋ]
warm (moderately hot)	**soe**	[soe]
wet (e.g., ~ clothes)	**märg**	[mʲærg]
whole (entire, complete)	**terve**	[terʋe]
wide (e.g., ~ road)	**lai**	[lɑj]
young (adj)	**noor**	[noːr]

MAIN 500 VERBS

252. Verbs A-C

to accompany (vt)	saatma	[sɑːtma]
to accuse (vt)	süüdistama	[syːdistama]
to acknowledge (admit)	tunnistama	[tuɲistama]
to act (take action)	tegutsema	[tegutsema]

to add (supplement)	lisama	[lisama]
to address (speak to)	pöörduma	[pøːrduma]
to admire (vi)	vaimustuma	[vɑjmustuma]
to advertise (vt)	reklaamima	[reklɑːmima]

to advise (vt)	soovitama	[soːvitama]
to affirm (insist)	kinnitama	[kiɲitama]
to agree (say yes)	nõustuma	[nɪustuma]
to allow (sb to do sth)	lubama	[lubama]

to allude (vi)	vihjama	[viɦæma]
to amputate (vt)	amputeerima	[ɑmputeːrima]
to answer (vi, vt)	vastama	[vɑstama]
to apologize (vi)	vabandama	[vɑbandama]

to appear (come into view)	ilmuma	[iʎmuma]
to applaud (vi, vt)	aplodeerima	[aplodeːrima]
to appoint (assign)	määrama	[mæːrama]
to approach (come closer)	ligi tulema	[ligi tulema]

to arrive (ab. train)	saabuma	[sɑːbuma]
to ask (~ sb to do sth)	paluma	[paluma]
to aspire to ...	püüdma	[pyːdma]
to assist (help)	assisteerima	[ɑssisteːrima]

to attack (mil.)	ründama	[ryndama]
to attain (objectives)	saavutama	[sɑːvutama]
to revenge (vt)	kätte maksma	[kʲætte maksma]
to avoid (danger, task)	vältima	[vʲæʎtima]

to award (give medal to)	autasustama	[autasustama]
to battle (vi)	võitlema	[vɪjtlema]

to be (~ on the table)	lamama	[lamama]
to be (vi)	olema	[olema]
to be afraid	kartma	[kartma]
to be angry (with ...)	vihastama	[vihastama]

to be at war	**sõdima**	[sɪdima]
to be based (on …)	**paiknema**	[pajknema]
to be bored	**igavlema**	[igavlema]
to be convinced	**veenduma**	[ve:nduma]
to be enough	**piisama**	[pi:sama]
to be envious	**kadestama**	[kadestama]
to be indignant	**pahane olema**	[pahane olema]
to be interested in …	**huvi tundma**	[huvi tundma]
to be lying down	**lesima**	[lesima]
to be needed	**tarvis olema**	[tarvis olema]
to be perplexed	**nõutu olema**	[nɪutu olema]
to be preserved	**säilima**	[sʲæjlima]
to be required	**vajalik olema**	[vɑæɛlik olema]
to be surprised	**imestama**	[imestama]
to be worried	**muretsema**	[muretsema]
to beat (dog, person)	**lööma**	[lø:ma]
to become (e.g., ~ old)	**saama**	[sɑ:ma]
to become pensive	**mõttesse jääma**	[mɪttesse æ:ma]
to behave (vi)	**käituma**	[kʲæjtuma]
to believe (think)	**uskuma**	[uskuma]
to belong to …	**kuuluma**	[ku:luma]
to berth (moor)	**randuma**	[randuma]
to blind (other drivers)	**pimestama**	[pimestama]
to blow (wind)	**puhuma**	[puhuma]
to blush (vi)	**punastama**	[runastama]
to boast (vi)	**kiitlema**	[ki:tlema]
to borrow (money)	**laenama**	[laənama]
to break (branch, toy, etc.)	**murdma**	[murdma]
to breathe (vi)	**hingama**	[hiŋama]
to bring (sth)	**kohale vedama**	[kohale vedama]
to burn (paper, logs)	**ära põletama**	[əra pɪletama]
to buy (purchase)	**ostma**	[ostma]
to call (for help)	**kutsuma**	[kutsuma]
to call (with one's voice)	**kutsuma**	[kutsuma]
to calm down (vt)	**rahustama**	[rahustama]
can (v aux)	**võima**	[vɪjma]
to cancel (call off)	**ära jätma**	[əra ætma]
to cast off	**kaldast eemalduma**	[kaldast eemaʎduma]
to catch (e.g., ~ a ball)	**püüdma**	[py:dma]
to catch sight (of . .)	**märkama**	[mʲærkama]
to cause …	**põhjustama**	[pɪhjystama]
to change (~ one's opinion)	**muutma**	[mu:tma]
to change (exchange)	**vahetama**	[vahetama]
to charm (vt)	**võluma**	[vɪluma]

to choose (select)	**valima**	[ʋɑlimɑ]
to chop off (with an ax)	**ära raiuma**	[ərɑ rɑjumɑ]
to clean (from dirt)	**puhastama**	[puhɑstɑmɑ]
to clean (shoes, etc.)	**puhastama**	[puhɑstɑmɑ]
to clean (tidy)	**korda tegema**	[kordɑ tegemɑ]
to close (vt)	**kinni panema**	[kiɳi panemɑ]
to comb one's hair	**kammima**	[kɑmmimɑ]
to come down (the stairs)	**laskuma**	[lɑskumɑ]
to come in (enter)	**sisse tulema**	[sisse tulemɑ]
to come out (book)	**ilmuma**	[iʎmumɑ]
to compare (vt)	**võrdlema**	[ʋɪrdlemɑ]
to compensate (vt)	**hüvitama**	[hyʋitɑmɑ]
to compete (vi)	**konkureerima**	[koɳkureːrimɑ]
to compile (~ a list)	**koostama**	[koːstɑmɑ]
to complain (vi, vt)	**kaebama**	[kɑebɑmɑ]
to complicate (vt)	**keeruliseks tegema**	[keːruliseks tegemɑ]
to compose (music, etc.)	**looma**	[loːmɑ]
to compromise (reputation)	**head nime kahjustama**	[head nime kɑɧjystɑmɑ]
to concentrate (vi)	**kontsentreeruma**	[kontsentreːrumɑ]
to confess (criminal)	**üles tunnistama**	[yles tuɳistɑmɑ]
to confuse (mix up)	**segi ajama**	[segi ɑæmɑ]
to congratulate (vt)	**õnnitlema**	[ɪɳitlemɑ]
to consult (doctor, expert)	**konsulteerima**	[konsuʎteːrimɑ]
to continue (~ to do sth)	**jätkama**	[ætkɑmɑ]
to control (vt)	**kontrollima**	[kontrollimɑ]
to convince (vt)	**veenma**	[ʋeːnmɑ]
to cooperate (vi)	**koostööd tegema**	[koːstɪːd tegemɑ]
to coordinate (vt)	**koordineerima**	[koːrdineːrimɑ]
to correct (an error)	**parandama**	[pɑrɑndɑmɑ]
to cost (vt)	**maksma**	[mɑksmɑ]
to count (money, etc.)	**lugema**	[lugemɑ]
to count on ...	**arvestama**	[ɑrʋestɑmɑ]
to crack (ceiling, wall)	**pragunema**	[prɑgunemɑ]
to create (vt)	**looma**	[loːmɑ]
to cry (weep)	**nutma**	[nutmɑ]
to cut off (with a knife)	**ära lõikama**	[ərɑ lɪjkɑmɑ]

253. Verbs D-G

to dare (~ to do sth)	**julgema**	[yʎgemɑ]
to date from ...	**kuupäevastatud**	[kuːpæːʋɑstɑtud]
to deceive (vi, vt)	**petma**	[petmɑ]

to decide (~ to do sth)	otsustama	[otsustama]
to decorate (tree, street)	ehtima	[əhtima]
to dedicate (book, etc.)	pühendama	[pyhendama]
to defend (a country, etc.)	kaitsma	[kajtsma]
to defend oneself	ennast kaitsma	[əŋast kajtsma]
to demand (request firmly)	nõudma	[nɪudma]

to denounce (vt)	peale kaebama	[peale kaəbama]
to deny (vt)	eitama	[ejtama]
to depend on ...	sõltuma	[sɪʎtuma]
to deprive (vt)	ilma jätma	[iʎma ætma]

to deserve (vt)	väärt olema	[ʊæːrt olema]
to design (machine, etc.)	projekteerima	[proekteːrima]
to desire (want, wish)	soovima	[soːʊima]
to despise (vt)	põlgama	[pɪʎgama]
to destroy (documents, etc.)	hävitama	[hæʊitama]

to differ (from sth)	silma paistma	[siʎma pajstma]
to dig (tunnel, etc.)	kaevama	[kaəʊama]
to direct (point the way)	suunama	[suːnama]
to disappear (vi)	ära kaduma	[əra kaduma]

to discover (new land, etc.)	avastama	[aʊastama]
to discuss (vt)	arutama	[arutama]
to distribute (leaflets, etc.)	levitama	[leʊitama]
to disturb (vt)	segama	[segama]
to dive (vi)	sukelduma	[sukeʎduma]

to divide (math)	jagama	[ægama]
to do (vt)	tegema	[tegema]
to do the laundry	pesu pesema	[pesu pesema]
to double (increase)	kahekordistama	[kahekordistama]

to doubt (have doubts)	kahtlema	[kahtlema]
to draw a conclusion	kokkuvõtet tegema	[kokkuʊɪtet tegema]
to dream (daydream)	unistama	[unistama]
to dream (in sleep)	und nägema	[und ɲægema]
to drink (vi, vt)	jooma	[joːma]

to drive a car	autot juhtima	[autot yhtima]
to drive away (scare away)	ära ajama	[əra aæma]
to drop (let fall)	pillama	[pillama]
to drown (ab. person)	uppuma	[uppuma]

to dry (clothes, hair)	kuivatama	[kujʊatama]
to eat (vi, vt)	sööma	[søːma]
to eavesdrop (vi)	pealt kuulama	[peaʎt kuːlama]
to emit (give out - odor, etc.)	levitama	[leʊitama]
to enter (on the list)	sisse kirjutama	[sisse kirjytama]

to entertain (amuse)	lõbustama	[lɪbustama]
to equip (fit out)	seadmetega varustama	[seadmetega ʋarustama]
to examine (proposal)	läbi vaatama	[ʎæbi ʋɑːtama]
to exchange (sth)	vahetama	[ʋɑhetama]

to exclude, to expel	välja heitma	[ʋʲæʎæ hejtma]
to excuse (forgive)	vabandama	[ʋabandama]
to exist (vi)	olemas olema	[olemas olema]
to expect (anticipate)	ootama	[oːtama]
to expect (foresee)	ette nägema	[ette ɲægema]

to explain (vt)	seletama	[seletama]
to express (vt)	väljendama	[ʋʲæʎjendama]
to extinguish (a fire)	kustutama	[kustutama]
to fall in love (with …)	armuma	[armuma]

to feed (provide food)	toitma	[tojtma]
to fight (against the enemy)	võitlema	[ʋɪjtlema]
to fight (vi)	kaklema	[kaklema]
to fill (glass, bottle)	täitma	[tʲæjtma]
to find (~ lost items)	leidma	[lejdma]

to finish (vt)	lõpetama	[lɪpetama]
to fish (angle)	kala püüdma	[kala pyːdma]
to fit (ab. dress, etc.)	paras olema	[paras olema]
to flatter (vt)	pugema	[pugema]

to fly (bird, plane)	lendama	[lendama]
to follow … (come after)	järgnema	[ærgnema]
to forbid (vt)	keelama	[keːlama]
to force (compel)	sundima	[sundima]
to forget (vi, vt)	unustama	[unustama]

to forgive (pardon)	andeks andma	[andeks andma]
to form (constitute)	haridust andma	[haridust andma]
to get dirty (vi)	ära määrima	[æra mæːrima]
to get infected (with …)	nakatuma	[nakatuma]

to get irritated	ärrituma	[ærrituma]
to get married	naist võtma	[najst ʋɪtma]
to get rid of …	vabanema	[ʋabanema]
to get tired	väsima	[ʋʲæsima]
to get up (arise from bed)	üles tõusma	[yles tɪusma]

to give a bath	vannitama	[ʋaɲitama]
to give a hug, to hug (vt)	embama	[embama]
to give in (yield to)	alla jääma	[alla æːma]

to go (by car, etc.)	sõitma	[sɪjtma]
to go (on foot)	minema	[minema]
to go for a swim	suplema	[suplema]

to go out (for dinner, etc.)	**välja minema**	[ʋælʲæ minema]
to go to bed	**magama heitma**	[magama hejtma]
to greet (vt)	**tervitama**	[terʋitama]
to grow (plants)	**kasvatama**	[kasʋatama]
to guarantee (vt)	**tagama**	[tagama]
to guess right	**ära arvama**	[æra arʋama]

254. Verbs H-M

to hand out (distribute)	**laiali jagama**	[lajali ægama]
to hang (curtains, etc.)	**riputama**	[riputama]
to have (vt)	**omama**	[omama]
to have a try	**püüdma**	[py:dma]
to have breakfast	**hommikust sööma**	[hommikust sø:ma]
to have dinner	**õhtust sööma**	[ɪhtust sø:ma]
to have fun	**lõbutsema**	[lɪbutsema]
to have lunch	**lõunat sööma**	[lɪunat sø:ma]
to head (group, etc.)	**etteotsa asuma**	[etteotsa asuma]
to hear (vt)	**kuulma**	[ku:ʎma]
to heat (vt)	**soojendama**	[so:endama]
to help (vt)	**aitama**	[ajtama]
to hide (vt)	**peitma**	[pejtma]
to hire (e.g., ~ a boat)	**võtma**	[ʋɪtma]
to hire (staff)	**palkama**	[palkama]
to hope (vi, vt)	**lootma**	[lo:tma]
to hunt (for food, sport)	**jahil käima**	[æhiʎ kʲæjma]
to hurry (sb)	**kiirustama**	[ki:rustama]
to hurry (vi)	**kiirustama**	[ki:rustama]
to imagine (to picture)	**endale ette kujutama**	[endale ette kuytama]
to imitate (vt)	**imiteerima**	[imite:rima]
to implore (vt)	**anuma**	[anuma]
to import (vt)	**sisse vedama**	[sisse ʋedama]
to increase (v)	**suurenema**	[su:renema]
to increase (vt)	**suurendama**	[su:rendama]
to infect (vt)	**nakatama**	[nakatama]
to influence (vt)	**mõjuma**	[mɪyma]
to inform (~ sb about ...)	**teatama**	[teatama]
to inform (vt)	**teavitama**	[teaʋitama]
to inherit (vt)	**pärima**	[pʲærima]
to inquire (about ...)	**teada saama**	[teada sa:ma]
to insist (vi, vt)	**nõudma**	[nɪudma]
to inspire (vt)	**innustama**	[iŋustama]
to instruct (teach)	**instrueerima**	[instrue:rima]

to insult (offend)	solvama	[soʌʋɑmɑ]
to interest (vt)	huvitama	[huʋitɑmɑ]

to intervene (vi)	vahele segama	[ʋɑhele segɑmɑ]
to introduce (present)	tutvustama	[tutʋustɑmɑ]
to invent (machine, etc.)	leiutama	[lejutɑmɑ]
to invite (vt)	kutsuma	[kutsumɑ]
to iron (laundry)	triikima	[triːkimɑ]

to irritate (annoy)	ärritama	[ərritɑmɑ]
to isolate (vt)	isoleerima	[isoleːrimɑ]
to join (political party, etc.)	ühinema	[yhinemɑ]
to joke (be kidding)	nalja tegema	[nɑʌæ tegemɑ]

to keep (old letters, etc.)	alles hoidma	[ɑlles hojdmɑ]
to keep silent	vaikima	[ʋɑjkimɑ]
to kill (vt)	tapma	[tɑpmɑ]
to knock (at the door)	koputama	[koputɑmɑ]
to know (sb)	tundma	[tundmɑ]

to know (sth)	teadma	[teɑdmɑ]
to laugh (vi)	naerma	[nɑermɑ]
to launch (start up)	käiku laskma	[kⁱæjku lɑskmɑ]

to leave (spouse)	maha jätma	[mɑhɑ ætmɑ]
to leave behind (forget)	jätma	[ætmɑ]
to liberate (city, etc.)	vabastama	[ʋɑbɑstɑmɑ]
to lie (tell untruth)	valetama	[ʋɑletɑmɑ]
to light (campfire, etc.)	süütama	[syːtɑmɑ]

to light up (illuminate)	valgustama	[ʋɑlgustɑmɑ]
to love (e.g., ~ dancing)	armastama	[ɑrmɑstɑmɑ]
to like (I like ...)	meeldima	[meːʌdimɑ]
to limit (vt)	piirama	[piːrɑmɑ]

to listen (vi)	kuulama	[kuːlɑmɑ]
to live (~ in France)	elama	[əlɑmɑ]
to live (exist)	elama	[əlɑmɑ]
to load (gun)	laadima	[lɑːdimɑ]
to load (vehicle, etc.)	laadima	[lɑːdimɑ]

to look (I'm just ~ing)	vaatama	[ʋɑːtɑmɑ]
to look for ... (search)	otsima	[otsimɑ]
to look like (resemble)	sarnanema	[sɑrnɑnemɑ]
to lose (umbrella, etc.)	kaotama	[kɑotɑmɑ]

to love (sb)	armastama	[ɑrmɑstɑmɑ]
to lower (blind, head)	alla laskma	[ɑllɑ lɑskmɑ]
to make (~ dinner)	süüa tegema	[syːɑ tegemɑ]
to make a mistake	eksima	[əksimɑ]
to make angry	ärritama	[ərritɑmɑ]
to make copies	paljundama	[pɑʌjyndɑmɑ]

to make easier	kergendama	[kergendama]
to make the acquaintance	tutvuma	[tutuuma]
to make use (of ...)	kasutama	[kasutama]

to manage, to run	juhtima	[yhtima]
to mark (make a mark)	ära märkima	[əra mʲærkima]
to mean (signify)	tähendama	[tʲæhendama]
to memorize (vt)	meelde jätma	[meːʎde ætma]
to mention (talk about)	meelde tuletama	[meːʎde tuletama]

to miss (school, etc.)	puuduma	[puːduma]
to mix (combine, blend)	vahele segama	[uahele segama]
to mock (make fun of)	pilkama	[piʎkama]
to move (to shift)	ümber paigutama	[ymber pajgutama]
to multiply (math)	korrutama	[korrutama]
must (v aux)	pidama	[pidama]

255. Verbs N-S

to name, to call (vt)	nimetama	[nimetama]
to negotiate (vi)	läbirääkimisi pidama	[ʎæbiræːkimisi pidama]
to note (write down)	üles kirjutama	[yles kirjytama]
to notice (see)	märkama	[mʲærkama]

to obey (vi, vt)	alluma	[alluma]
to object (vi, vt)	vastu vaidlema	[uastu uajdlema]
to observe (see)	jälgima	[æʎgima]
to offend (vt)	solvama	[soʎuama]
to omit (word, phrase)	vahele jätma	[uahele ætma]

to open (vt)	lahti tegema	[lahti tegema]
to order (in restaurant)	tellima	[tellima]
to order (mil.)	käskima	[kʲæskima]
to organize (concert, party)	korraldama	[korraʎdama]

to overestimate (vt)	ümber hindama	[ymber hindama]
to own (possess)	valdama	[uaʎdama]
to participate (vi)	osa võtma	[osa uitma]
to pass (go beyond)	mööda sõitma	[møːda sijtma]
to pay (vi, vt)	maksma	[maksma]

to peep, spy on	piiluma	[piːluma]
to penetrate (vt)	sisse tungima	[sisse tuŋima]
to permit (vt)	lubama	[lubama]
to pick (flowers)	noppima	[noppima]

to place (put, set)	paigutama	[pajgutama]
to plan (~ to do sth)	planeerima	[planeːrima]
to play (actor)	mängima	[mʲæŋima]
to play (children)	mängima	[mʲæŋima]

to point (~ the way)	näitama	[ɲæjtɑmɑ]
to pour (liquid)	valama	[ʋɑlɑmɑ]
to pray (vi, vt)	palvetama	[pɑlʋetɑmɑ]
to predominate (vi)	ülekaalus olema	[yleka:lus olemɑ]
to prefer (vt)	eelistama	[əelistɑmɑ]

to prepare (~ a plan)	ette valmistama	[ette ʋɑʎmistɑmɑ]
to present (sb to sb)	esindama	[əsindɑmɑ]
to preserve (peace, life)	säilitama	[sʲæjlitɑmɑ]
to progress (move forward)	karjääri tegema	[karʲæəri tegemɑ]
to promise (vt)	lubama	[lubɑmɑ]

to pronounce (vt)	hääldama	[hæ:ʎdɑmɑ]
to propose (vt)	pakkuma	[pɑkkumɑ]
to protect (e.g., ~ nature)	valvama	[ʋɑʎʋɑmɑ]
to protest (vi)	protesteerima	[proteste:rimɑ]

to prove (vt)	tõestama	[tɪ:stɑmɑ]
to provoke (vt)	provotseerima	[proʋotseerimɑ]
to pull (~ the rope)	tõmbama	[tɪmbɑmɑ]
to punish (vt)	karistama	[kɑristɑmɑ]
to push (~ the door)	tõukama	[tɪukɑmɑ]

to put away (vt)	ära koristama	[ərɑ koristɑmɑ]
to put in (insert)	vahele panema	[ʋɑhele pɑnemɑ]
to put in order	korda tegema	[kordɑ tegemɑ]
to put, to place	panema	[pɑnemɑ]

to quote (cite)	tsiteerima	[tsite:rimɑ]
to reach (arrive at)	jõudma	[jɪudmɑ]
to read (vi, vt)	lugema	[lugemɑ]
to realize (a dream)	teostama	[teostɑmɑ]
to recall (~ one's name)	meenutama	[me:nutɑmɑ]

to recognize (identify sb)	ära tundma	[ərɑ tundmɑ]
to recommend (vt)	soovitama	[so:ʋitɑmɑ]
to recover (~ from flu)	terveks saama	[terʋeks sɑ:mɑ]
to redo (do again)	ümber tegema	[ymber tegemɑ]

to reduce (speed, etc.)	vähendama	[ʋʲæhendɑmɑ]
to refuse (~ sb)	ära ütlema	[ərɑ ytlemɑ]
to regret (be sorry)	kahetsema	[kɑhetsemɑ]
to reinforce (vt)	kindlustama	[kindlustɑmɑ]
to remember (vt)	mäletama	[mʲæletɑmɑ]

to remind of ...	meelde tuletama	[me:ʎde tuletɑmɑ]
to remove (~ a stain)	eemaldama	[əemɑʎdɑmɑ]
to remove (~ an obstacle)	kõrvaldama	[kɪrʋɑʎdɑmɑ]
to rent (sth from sb)	üürima	[y:rimɑ]
to repair (mend)	parandama	[pɑrɑndɑmɑ]
to repeat (say again)	kordama	[kordɑmɑ]

to report (make a report)	**ette kandma**	[ətte kɑndmɑ]
to reproach (vt)	**ette heitma**	[ətte hejtmɑ]
to reserve, to book	**broneerima**	[brone:rimɑ]
to restrain (hold back)	**tagasi hoidma**	[tɑgɑsi hojdmɑ]
to return (come back)	**tagasi tulema**	[tɑgɑsi tulemɑ]
to risk, to take a risk	**riskima**	[riskimɑ]
to rub off (erase)	**maha kustutama**	[mɑhɑ kustutɑmɑ]
to run (move fast)	**jooksma**	[jo:ksmɑ]
to satisfy (please)	**rahuldama**	[rɑhuʎdɑmɑ]
to save (rescue)	**päästma**	[pæː stmɑ]
to say (~ thank you)	**ütlema**	[ytlemɑ]
to scold (vt)	**sõimama**	[sɪjmɑmɑ]
to scratch (with claws)	**kriimustama**	[kri:mustɑmɑ]
to select (to pick)	**välja valima**	[ʊʲæʎæ ʊɑlimɑ]
to sell (goods)	**müüma**	[my:mɑ]
to send (a letter)	**saatma**	[sɑ:tmɑ]
to send back (vt)	**tagasi saatma**	[tɑgɑsi sɑ:tmɑ]
to sense (danger)	**tundma**	[tundmɑ]
to sentence (vt)	**süüdi mõistma**	[sy:di mɪjstmɑ]
to serve (in restaurant)	**teenindama**	[te:nindɑmɑ]
to settle (a conflict)	**korda ajama**	[kordɑ ɑæmɑ]
to shake (vt)	**raputama**	[rɑputɑmɑ]
to shave (vi)	**habet ajama**	[hɑbet ɑæmɑ]
to shine (gleam)	**helendama**	[helendɑmɑ]
to shiver (with cold)	**värisema**	[ʊʲæɾisemɑ]
to shoot (vi)	**tulistama**	[tulistɑmɑ]
to shout (vi)	**karjuma**	[kɑrjymɑ]
to show (to display)	**näitama**	[ɲæjtɑmɑ]
to shudder (vi)	**võpatama**	[ʊɪpɑtɑmɑ]
to sigh (vi)	**ohkama**	[ohkɑmɑ]
to sign (document)	**allkirjastama**	[ɑʎkirʲæstɑmɑ]
to signify (mean)	**tähendama**	[tʲæhendɑmɑ]
to simplify (vt)	**lihtsustama**	[lihtsustɑmɑ]
to sin (vi)	**pattu tegema**	[pɑttu tegemɑ]
to sit (be sitting)	**istuma**	[istumɑ]
to sit down (vi)	**istuma**	[istumɑ]
to smash (~ a bug)	**puruks litsuma**	[puruks litsumɑ]
to smell (scent)	**lõhnama**	[lɪhnɑmɑ]
to smell (sniff at)	**nuusutama**	[nu:sutɑmɑ]
to smile (vi)	**naeratama**	[nɑerɑtɑmɑ]
to snap (vi, ab. rope)	**katki minema**	[kɑtʲki minemɑ]
to solve (problem)	**lahendama**	[lɑhendɑmɑ]
to sow (seed, crop)	**külvama**	[kyʎʊɑmɑ]

to spill (liquid)	maha valama	[mɑhɑ ʋɑlɑmɑ]
to spit (vi)	sülitama	[sylitɑmɑ]
to stand (toothache, cold)	välja kannatama	[ʋʲæʎæ kɑŋɑtɑmɑ]
to start (begin)	alustama	[ɑlustɑmɑ]

to steal (money, etc.)	varastama	[ʋɑrɑstɑmɑ]
to stop (please ~ calling me)	katkestama	[kɑtkestɑmɑ]
to stop (for pause, etc.)	peatuma	[peɑtumɑ]
to stop talking	vait jääma	[ʋɑjt æ:mɑ]

to stroke (caress)	silitama	[silitɑmɑ]
to study (vt)	uurima	[u:rimɑ]
to suffer (feel pain)	kannatama	[kɑŋɑtɑmɑ]
to support (cause, idea)	toetama	[toetɑmɑ]
to suppose (assume)	eeldama	[ee↗dɑmɑ]

to surface (ab. submarine)	pinnale tõusma	[piŋɑle tɪusmɑ]
to surprise (amaze)	üllatama	[yllɑtɑmɑ]
to suspect (vt)	kahtlustama	[kɑhtlustɑmɑ]
to swim (vi)	ujuma	[uymɑ]
to turn on (computer, etc.)	sisse lülitama	[sisse lylitɑmɑ]

256. Verbs T-W

to take (get hold of)	võtma	[ʋɪtmɑ]
to take a bath	pesema	[pesemɑ]
to take a rest	puhkama	[puhkɑmɑ]

to take aim (at ...)	sihtima	[sihtimɑ]
to take away	ära viima	[ərɑ ʋi:mɑ]
to take off (airplane)	õhku tõusma	[ɪhku tɪusmɑ]
to take off (remove)	maha võtma	[mɑhɑ ʋɪtmɑ]

to take pictures	pildistama	[piʎdistɑmɑ]
to talk to ...	rääkima	[ræ:kimɑ]
to teach (give lessons)	koolitama	[ko:litɑmɑ]

to tear off (vt)	ära rebima	[ərɑ rebimɑ]
to tell (story, joke)	jutustama	[ytustɑmɑ]
to thank (vt)	tänama	[tʲænɑmɑ]
to think (believe)	arvama	[ɑrʋɑmɑ]

to think (vi, vt)	mõtlema	[mɪtlemɑ]
to threaten (vt)	ähvardama	[əhʋɑrdɑmɑ]
to throw (stone)	viskama	[ʋiskɑmɑ]

to tie to ...	kinni siduma	[kiŋi sidumɑ]
to tie up (prisoner)	siduma	[sidumɑ]
to tire (make tired)	väsitama	[ʋʲæsitɑmɑ]

to touch (one's arm, etc.)	**puutuma**	[pu:tuma]
to tower (over ...)	**esile kerkima**	[əsile kerkima]
to train (animals)	**dresseerima**	[dresse:rima]
to train (sb)	**treenima**	[tre:nima]
to train (vi)	**treenima**	[tre:nima]
to transform (vt)	**transformeerima**	[transforme:rima]
to translate (vt)	**tõlkima**	[tiʎkima]
to treat (patient, illness)	**ravima**	[rauima]
to trust (vt)	**usaldama**	[usaʎdama]
to try (attempt)	**püüdma**	[py:dma]
to turn (~ to the left)	**pöörama**	[pø:rama]
to turn away (vi)	**nägu ära pöörama**	[ɲægu əra pø:rama]
to turn off (the light)	**välja lülitama**	[uʲæʎæ lylitama]
to turn over (stone, etc.)	**ümber pöörama**	[ymber pø:rama]
to underestimate (vt)	**alahindama**	[alahindama]
to underline (vt)	**alla kriipsutama**	[alla kri:psutama]
to understand (vt)	**aru saama**	[aru sa:ma]
to undertake (vt)	**ette võtma**	[ətte uitma]
to unite (vt)	**ühendama**	[yhendama]
to untie (vt)	**lahti laskma**	[lahti laskma]
to use (phrase, word)	**tarvitama**	[taruitama]
to vaccinate (vt)	**vaktsineerima**	[uaktsine:rima]
to vote (vi)	**hääletama**	[hæ:letama]
to wait (vt)	**ootama**	[o:tama]
to wake (sb)	**äratama**	[əratama]
to want (wish, desire)	**tahtma**	[tahtma]
to warn (of the danger)	**hoiatama**	[hojatama]
to wash (clean)	**pesema**	[pesema]
to water (plants)	**kastma**	[kastma]
to wave (the hand)	**lehvitama**	[lehuitama]
to weigh (have weight)	**kaaluma**	[ka:luma]
to work (vi)	**töötama**	[tø:tama]
to worry (make anxious)	**muret tegema**	[muret tegema]
to worry (vi)	**muretsema**	[muretsema]
to wrap (parcel, etc.)	**sisse pakkima**	[sisse pakkima]
to wrestle (sport)	**võistlema**	[uijstlema]
to write (vt)	**kirjutama**	[kirjytama]
to write down	**üles kirjutama**	[yles kirjytama]

Printed in Great Britain
by Amazon.co.uk, Ltd.,
Marston Gate.